Library of
Davidson College

Race
and Rapprochement

Also by Stuart Anderson:

*Horse to Helicopter: The First Century of
the Atlanta Police Department* (coauthor)

Race and Rapprochement

Anglo-Saxonism and Anglo-American Relations, 1895–1904

Stuart Anderson

Rutherford • Madison • Teaneck
Fairleigh Dickinson University Press
London and Toronto: Associated University Presses

© 1981 by Associated University Presses, Inc.

Associated University Presses, Inc.
4 Cornwall Drive
East Brunswick, New Jersey 08816

Associated University Presses Ltd.
69 Fleet Street
London EC4Y 1EU, England

Associated University Presses
Toronto, Ontario, Canada M5E 1A7

Library of Congress Cataloging in Publication Data

Anderson, Stuart.
  Race and rapprochement.

  Bibliography: p.
  Includes index.
  1. United States—Relations (general) with Great Britain. 2. Great Britain—Relations (general) with the United States. 3. United States—Foreign relations—1865-1921. 4. Great Britain—Foreign relations—1837-1901. 5. Great Britain—Foreign relations—1901-1910. 6. Nationalism—United States—History. 7. Nationalism—Great Britain—History. 8. Anglo-Saxon race. I. Title.
E183.8.G7A55   301.29′73′041   79-24185
ISBN 0-8386-3001-4

Printed in the United States of America

to my Mother and Father

Contents

Acknowledgments	9
Introduction	11
1 The Cult of Anglo-Saxonism	17
2 Historical and Intellectual Antecedents	26
3 International Rivalry and the Struggle for Existence	62
4 Anglo-Saxonism and the Shapers of Foreign Policy	73
5 The Venezuela Boundary Dispute and the Olney-Pauncefote Treaty: Anglo-Saxonism Emerges as an Influence on Anglo-American Relations	95
6 The Spanish-American War: The Apex of Anglo-Saxonism	112
7 Anglo-Saxonism and the American Response to the Boer War	130
8 Dealing with the Russians in the Far East: The Slavic Threat to Anglo-Saxon Supremacy	148
Conclusion: The Decline of Anglo-Saxonism	174
Notes	179
Bibliography	216
Index	232

Acknowledgments

In writing this book, I have benefited from the friendly assistance and enlightening criticism of many individuals and institutions. Most of these I have tried to indicate in my citations. I must single out for special thanks, however, Professor Charles S. Campbell of Claremont Graduate School. It was he who first suggested to me that Anglo-Saxonism might be a subject worth investigating; and in the time that I devoted to research and writing, he was a regular source of inspiration, aid, and reassurance. Others who have studied with him, and benefited from his scholarly example, will understand how large a debt I owe to him.

I would also like to thank Professors John Niven, Robert Dawidoff, and Charles Lofgren, all of whom read an earlier draft of my manuscript and offered their encouragement and suggestions. A fellowship from the John Randolph Haynes and Dora Haynes Foundation made possible a full year of uninterrupted study. In a slightly different version, chapter seven of this book appeared in *Diplomatic History*, Vol. 2 (Summer 1978); I am grateful to the publishers of this journal for permission to use this material. A note of gratitude is also due to Harvard University Press for permission to reprint material from *The Letters of Theodore Roosevelt*.

Finally, I offer my abiding thanks to Anne, who supported me in more ways than even she knows.

Introduction

> The sympathy of race does not often affect the relations of states, but when it does it is a force of tremendous potency; for it affects not so much governments as the people themselves, who, both in America and in England, are the ultimate depositaries of power, the ultimate controllers of policy.
>
> James Bryce, 1898[1]

> Neither do I think that the exchange of complimentary phrases which has become customary, about kinship, common origin, common love of liberty, common language, common literature, about blood being thicker than water and so on, is merely worthless stage claptrap and flummery. There is enough truth and sincerity in it to create and keep alive a real sentiment; and while those are mistaken who think international relations may be wholly governed by mere sentiment, those are equally mistaken who think that sentiment is no force at all in international relations.
>
> Carl Schurz, 1898[2]

Most historians agree that in a relatively brief period around the turn of the century, Anglo-American relations underwent a deep and enduring transformation. After well over a hundred years of American Anglophobia and British condescension toward Brother Jonathan, distrust and hostility gave way to a relationship that was close and fundamentally friendly.

A number of capable scholars have told the story of the Anglo-American rapprochement, and it is not the purpose of this book to reiterate their findings.[3] Rather, the present study is an attempt to examine some of the intellectual convictions and emotional attachments that linked the British and American peoples at the turn of the century, and that helped to make the diplomatic rapprochement possible. Specifically, we are here concerned with the influence on British-American relations of the doctrine known as "Anglo-Saxonism." At the risk of oversimplification, this doctrine may be defined as the belief—part of the prevailing orthodoxy in Great Britain and the United States in the late nineteenth and early twentieth centuries—that the civilization of the English-speaking nations was superior to that of any other group of people on the planet; and that the primacy of English and American civilization was largely due to the innate racial superiority of the people who were descended from the ancient Anglo-Saxon invaders of Britain. The members of the "Anglo-Saxon race," it was said, held in common a certain set of characteristics which were biologically as well as culturally determined. These characteristics, which included such worthy attributes as industry, intelligence, adventurousness, and a talent for self-government, constituted a unique racial endowment which accounted in large part for the economic, political, and cultural successes of the English-speaking peoples.

Closely associated with this belief in the racial uniqueness of the Anglo-Saxons was another conventional wisdom of the age, the Darwinian concept of unavoidable competition and conflict among unlike peoples. Under the influence of this notion, many Britons and Americans held that the Anglo-Saxon race was in a state of continual struggle with other racial and national groups for advantage in the world. The struggle for supremacy among the most advanced peoples took many forms, economic rivalry and military confrontation being only the most obvious. But in the end the lessons to be drawn from the application of Darwinism to international relations were clear to most of those who subscribed to the Anglo-Saxonist creed: the two leading branches of the Anglo-Saxon race should work together for their mutual benefit, and should be constantly on guard to protect their varied and worldwide interests against the ambitions of rival races and nations.

This, in slender outline, is the doctrine of Anglo-Saxonism which, by the closing years of the nineteenth century, had come into great favor in both the United States and Great Britain. It is the contention of this book that Anglo-Saxonism, as an intellectual construct, provided the primary abstract rationale for the diplomatic rapprochement between the two countries. Anglo-Saxonism linked the British and American peoples, or at least that segment of the population in both countries that had the most direct influence on foreign policy, in a kind of larger patriotism of race. While the notion of Anglo-Saxon superiority provided these people with a sense of shared racial heritage and a vision of a common destiny, the Darwinian overtones of Anglo-Saxonism forcibly suggested that Great Britain and the United States were natural allies who should stand together against the rest of the world. Many of the men who helped to shape British and American foreign policy in these years, including such important figures as Theodore Roosevelt, John Hay, Arthur Balfour, and Joseph Chamberlain, believed in the function of race in world politics, and often acted accordingly in their dealings with one another. Thus, through its influence on both public and official opinion, Anglo-Saxon racism helped to draw the two nations together at a time when each had much to gain from a friendly understanding.

This study begins in 1895 because that was the year in which Anglo-Saxon race sentiment, during the brief war scare produced by the Venezuela boundary dispute, first became evident as an element of prime importance in promoting fellow-feeling between the British and American peoples, and an amicable relationship between their two governments. The study ends in 1904 because Anglo-Saxonism as an intellectual vogue was already in decline by then, and because the outbreak of the Russo-Japanese War in February of that year marked the end of the last occasion on which Anglo-Saxonism contributed significantly to the development of improved British-American relations—the effort to contain the "Slavic" (Russian) threat to Anglo-Saxon interests in the Far East.

One must not, of course, underestimate the absolutely essential part played by sagacious and skillful diplomacy, on the part of statesmen in both Great Britain and the United States, to bring about the new cordiality in Anglo-American relations. Without the hard work, patience, and determination of politicians and diplomats on both sides of the Atlantic, to narrow the differences between the two countries and resolve the difficult issues that separated them, no Anglo-American rapprochement could have occurred at the turn of the century. Equally so, however, one must not underestimate the benevolent influence that Anglo-Saxonism had on the relationship between the two English-speaking powers. Anglo-Saxonism, too, was essential to the vast improvement in their relations. If the British and American peoples had not held in common the ideas contained in Anglo-Saxonism, it is likely that the great rapprochement would not have happened; and if that had been the case, the course of world history in the twentieth century might have been very different indeed.

Race
and Rapprochement

1

The Cult of Anglo-Saxonism

Surveying the state of the world in 1905, while the Russo-Japanese War raged in the Far East, Major Stewart L. Murray of the British Army thought he perceived a metamorphosis occurring in international relations. The old rivalry of states, cabinets, and armies was rapidly giving way to a modern rivalry of races. The peoples of the world no longer gave their loyalty just to nations and governments. Today their loyalty was to a blood-unit, a race. Deep in each nation the blood-feeling was stirring and working, bringing into being new ideals and new tasks for the future. Before long the constituent units of the international system would be not rival nation-states, but rival races, each eager to assert and fulfill new race loyalties. Murray could see the transformation happening all over the globe.[1]

Race-thinking like that of Major Murray was common in Britain at the time, and not only in Britain but throughout most of the Western world. The twin forces of burgeoning nationalism and the new imperialism gave an enormous impetus to race-thinking in the late nineteenth century. No major Western nation escaped the influence of speculations about the role of race in history. In France, where the self-esteem of Frenchmen was flattered by talk of the nation's *mission civilisatrice* in Africa, Asia, and the Pacific, considerable credence was given to theories concerning the supposed Celtic or Gallic racial origins of French grandeur. In the newly established German Empire, ideas of Teutonic supremacy and Pan-Germanism bolstered Germany's national conceit and lent additional vigor to its aggressive imperial program. Adherents of Pan-Slavism in Russia encouraged the expansion of Russian influence in the Balkans as a means to the eventual unification of the entire Slavic race.[2] People in all segments of British and American society spoke smugly of the achievements of the Anglo-Saxon race and frequently equated the "white man's burden" with the racial mission of the Anglo-Saxon peoples. By the 1890s, nationalism, imperialism, and racism were so intertwined in Western thought that it was difficult to separate the intellectual strands. Each of the three great "-isms" had helped to fashion and vitalize the other two, and to some extent was dependent upon them. Taken together, they had become part of the psychological pattern of the age.[3]

By tying racism to national aspirations, late nineteenth-century society accorded it eminence and importance. However, the purveyors of racist notions in the late nineteenth century, like racists at most times in human history, eschewed precision of thought. Asked to define exactly what was meant by the expression "Anglo-Saxon race," few persons in Britain or the United States could have given a definite answer.

This imprecision had its uses; it allowed those who believed in the primacy of race in the development of human societies to adjust their definitions of racial terms to fit almost any circumstance. Sometimes they spoke as if there were only three great races in the world, the whites (or Aryans) of Europe, the yellow race of Asia, and the blacks of Africa. At other times they spoke of the English, German, French, and Russian nations as if they were really distinct races. Englishmen and Americans were usually thought of as members of the Anglo-Saxon race, but if they were at odds, one might speak of divergent English and American races; while in other circumstances one could relate the Americans to the entire British Empire by asserting the existence of a great worldwide racial stock called, for want of a better term, the English-speaking race. Race, in other words, was so loosely defined that a person could draw racial lines wherever it fitted his purposes to do so. As a result, disorder, confusion, and nebulosity of thought surrounded the idea of race.[4]

Much of the mental disarray in nineteenth-century race-thought in the United States and Great Britain arose from the confusion of such unlike concepts as race, culture, and nation. In the strict sense of the term, race is only a biological classification used to denote a division of humanity having certain inherited *physical* characteristics. That has never been the sense in which racists have used the word, however, and it was not the sense in which Anglo-Saxonists used it.[5] Race, a term of biological science, and nation, a term used in the social sciences, were often used synonymously. In 1898, former Brish Prime Minister Lord Rosebery declared that when a nation had "inhabited certain boundaries without disturbance for a considerable number of centuries," and had developed a national "name and language and laws," it was evident "that for all practical purposes you have a nation and a race." Scholars and public alike spoke of the German race, the French race, the Russian race, as if race and nationality were semantically interchangeable.[6]

Race-thinking also attributed to inherent racial characteristics a whole range of cultural peculiarities that modern scientists think of as learned, not inherited. "The constructive ideas of our civilisation are Anglo-Saxon ideas," the Reverend Washington Gladden told an English audience in 1898, as though the cultural heritage of Britain and the United States were racial in nature.[7] Captain Alfred Thayer Mahan believed that the "political ideas, fundamental laws, and habits of thought" of the English-speaking peoples were largely genetically determined, "inborn" as well as "inbred."[8] Other Anglo-Saxon race supremacists incorporated such diverse features of Anglo-American culture as the English language, democratic ideals, individualism, Protestantism, libertarian political system, and liberal economics within the inherited characteristics of the Anglo-Saxon race.

Thus, for Anglo-Saxonists, the concept of race had innumerable associations. That which was racial in nature might include almost any aspect of human behavior. Such an amorphous conception of race had no basis in scientific fact, and might have appeared ludicrous to many exponents of Anglo-Saxon superiority if they had thought about race in a deliberate and rational manner; but, for the most part, their prejudices precluded deliberate and rational thought.

Rather than detracting from the power of race-thinking, in fact, the vagueness which surrounded it tended to add to its mystical attraction.[9] Politicians have long realized that sweeping, blurry-edged generalizations have great mass appeal, while careful logic lacks political vitality. Anglo-Saxonism drew much of its power from its very superficiality, its lack of need for proof. It could be believed without proof, because so many people in Britain and the United States wanted to believe it. They enjoyed being told that as

Anglo-Saxons they belonged to a superior race. Such statements flattered individual as well as national pride, and when repeated often enough gained a degree of certitude. Anglo-Saxonism was so widespread largely because it provided Englishmen and Americans with the illusion that they were inherently superior to the other peoples of the earth. It was a comforting illusion.

The superior qualities that lay imbedded in the genes of the Anglo-Saxon were much discussed by race-thinkers.[10] The characteristic most frequently attributed to the race was love of liberty. Prominent Columbia University sociologist Franklin H. Giddings assumed that the Viking ancestry of the Anglo-Saxon accounted for this trait. "After all, it is the blood of the old untamable pirates that courses through his veins," Giddings said.[11] While the Anglo-Saxon was personally independent, he demanded order in his society.[12] His ideal was liberty within the law, and he carried this ideal with him wherever his restlessness took him. For the Anglo-Saxon was also an adventurer. He "does not shrink from loneliness and unknown perils," as one writer put it, "but finds stimulus and excitement in them."[13] The Anglo-Saxon was a person of action, of energy, strong will, and tenacity of purpose. His hunger for new lands and new challenges had carried him in the fifth century from the forests of northern Germany to the shores of Britain, and in the centuries since to America, Africa, Asia, and the islands of the Pacific. The colonial possessions of Great Britain and the immense land area of the United States served as monuments to the fearless energy and sturdy determination of the Anglo-Saxon race.[14]

Although love of ordered liberty and a voracious appetite for new adventures in new lands were the most frequently cited characteristics of the Anglo-Saxon, other racial traits were often mentioned by British and American race-thinkers. Some thought the Anglo-Saxon naturally truthful, logical, and patient, as well as considerate of others and loyal to friends and country. He was given to moral uprightness, generosity, and humaneness, and he had a notable capacity for work. He was punctual, practical, and commonsensical. His overall intelligence was high and his morals were impeccable.[15] All in all, he was a most admirable fellow; and he was proud of it, as Sir Walter Besant affirmed when he declared:

"We are, then, as we always have been, a masterful race; we are a stiff-necked, unyielding race; a tenacious race; we are a race which cannot change its own mind—as regards law and manners—for the mind of any other race; we are a people which if it settles down anywhere, means to go on living as before and to make other people live in the same way."[16] For novelist and philanthropist Besant, as for many others, the tenacity and intractability that could sometimes be observed in Englishmen and Americans provided one more example of the blood legacy of the race.

For those looking for proof of their Anglo-Saxonist suppositions, the facts of international life in the late nineteenth century provided ample evidence that the British and the Americans were superior peoples. Many persons found one spin of the globe sufficient to confirm the proposition. "The whole round world," wrote Besant, "is dotted here and covered there with the possessions of the Anglo-Saxon race; all that is best, most temperate, most fertile, best fitted for the white man's permanent residence, is ours."[17] There was a large element of truth in the claim. In the fifteen years between 1885 and 1900, the area of the British Empire increased by fully one-third. By 1900, one-fifth of the globe was governed from London, and there were few who did not believe that there was something grand and wonderful about all that territory colored red on the map. The British Empire was more than four times the size of the Roman Empire at its greatest extent, and forty times the size of the contemporary German Empire. Queen Victoria was one of the greatest monarchs in history, reigning over fully one-fourth of all mankind. The German, French, and Russian empires combined were not much more populous; and in no other colonial domain were there such large, prosperous white populations as in Britain's temperate-zone colonies of Canada, Australia, New Zealand, and South Africa. The British, moreover, still dominated the seas and controlled the world's strategic points, from Gibraltar to Cape Town and from Suez to Singapore. Finally, even critics of British imperialism admitted that the British colonies were the best governed in the world. British colonists enjoyed more civil liberties than the colonists of any other country, and as a result a sentimental bond of surprising strength united much of the British Empire. Such large achievements seemed clear evidence to Anglo-Saxonists that there was no more intelligent or virile race than that which had moved out over the world from the home island of Britain.[18]

If further proof was needed, the American branch of the race could provide it. The United States in 1900 was larger than any European state except Russia, and boasted the second largest population (again behind Russia) in the Western world. It had the world's most extensive network of roads and railways, and it easily led all competitors in the production of such essentials of modern civilization as wheat, coal, iron, and steel. The total value of American manufactures surpassed that of Great Britain and Germany combined. Americans had subdued a continent in a single century, and in 1898 they crushed Spain and took possession of an island empire in the Caribbean and the Pacific. Thus they joined the further expansion of the Anglo-Saxon race, an expansion considered by one of America's foremost historians to be "in itself the most wonderful of all time."[19] Most people in Britain and the United States agreed, and concluded that a race which ruled so much of the world so efficiently must carry within itself an innate superiority to other peoples.

For many, however, wealth and empire alone were not sufficient proofs of superiority. They required some less tangible evidence of racial preeminence, and they found it in Anglo-Saxon political institutions. It was the "English-speaking race" alone, declared *New York Tribune* editor Whitelaw Reid, that had "secured individual rights" and "created constitutional government among men." Wherever this race had expanded, from North America to South Africa to India and Egypt, it had "carried the principles of... ordered liberty under law." Reid believed the people who spoke English must have liberty and self-government bred in their bone and fibre to have devised the finest political institutions in the history of man.[20] Senator Henry Cabot Lodge, too, thought there must be a racial reason why "representative government has been a full success only among the English-speaking people of the world."[21] It was taken for granted, of course, that representative democracy as practiced in Great Britain and the United States was superior to all other forms of government, just as it was assumed that it was a racially inherent intelligence, morality, self-restraint, and governmental efficiency

THE CULT OF ANGLO-SAXONISM 23

that made possible the unique political institutions of the English-speaking countries. Thus their faith in representative government and libertarian institutions strengthened the conviction of the British and American peoples that they represented the most progressive race in the world, "a concrete, colossal force in the world's progress."[22]

If Britons and Americans had been willing to conclude merely that they were doing very well, without attributing their success to racial factors, there could have been little argument with their contention. However, the concept of race was central to the thinking of many people about the progress of the English-speaking countries. Not content with explaining the unquestionable achievements of Great Britain and the United States in terms of cultural attributes, historical circumstances, or even the workings of inscrutable fate, they embraced the belief that the success of the two countries was determined by the racial characteristics of the Angles and the Saxons. This belief was a central tenet of Anglo-Saxonism.

Having concluded that they were genetically superior to the other peoples of the earth, Anglo-Saxonists frequently carried the idea one step further and persuaded themselves that it was their duty to extend their superior civilization to less fortunate races. The concept of national mission was a venerable one in both English and American history. England had been a nation with a mission at least since the time of Cromwell's Puritan Commonwealth, and perhaps as far back as the struggle against Catholic Spain in the sixteenth century. The American sense of mission was as old as John Winthrop's vision of a city upon a hill. In the climate of opinion existing about the turn of the century, this sense of national mission could be easily transformed into a racial mission, a conviction that it was the duty of the Anglo-Saxon race to regenerate the earth through the extension of its institutions and ideals.

In Great Britain, the appeal to the mission of the race provided one of the chief rationales for imperialism. "We are Imperialists in response to the compelling influences of our destiny," proclaimed a Liberal member of Parliament in 1899. " . . . The basis of Imperialism is race."[23] During the great expansionist surge near the end of the nineteenth century, the justification for imperialism was found more and more in the popular belief that it was the mission of Anglo-Saxon Britain to rule and reform as much of the world as possible.[24] This sometimes led to extraordinary flights of rhetoric. "Never since on Sinai God spoke in thunder has mandate more imperative been issued to any race, city, or nation than now to this nation and to this people," Professor J. A. Cramb told his students at Queen's College, London.[25] Edward Dicey, an author and journalist well known in both the United States and Great Britain, likened the Anglo-Saxon race to the ancient Romans. With both there was "an innate conviction, sometimes suppressed but never abandoned, that it is our mission, our manifest destiny, to rule the world." Dicey held that this was a belief "entertained at heart by ninety-nine Britons out of every hundred."[26]

Americans, particularly during the imperialistic eruption following the outbreak of the war with Spain, shared the British faith in a racial mission. They believed that, more than any other race, the Anglo-Saxon represented civilization and Christianity. A great responsibility went with the Anglo-Saxons' mental and moral excellence, however. It was their duty to elevate and enlighten the rest of mankind, to mitigate suffering and promote social progress. To be sure, when it came to deciding exactly how these duties might best be carried out, Americans frequently differed among themselves. Many anti-imperialists believed the country should do no more than work to improve its own domestic political and social institutions, so that the United States might continue to stand as a beacon and an example for all the rest of the world. Other Americans were of the opinion that the mission of the race was best pursued by missionaries and teachers sent out to redeem the non-Christian peoples of the earth. For strident American imperialists, on the other hand, nothing less than outright political domination of "backward" peoples was sufficient for the carrying out of the Anglo-Saxon mission. Whatever their position on the specific actions required of them as a result of their superior racial endowments, however, most American Anglo-Saxonists were agreed on the general principle that it was the duty of their race to do what it could to preserve and extend the area of freedom, establish peace, and open up new roads to human happiness.[27]

Carried to extremes, the ideas of Anglo-Saxonism and racial mission could lead to a conviction that the division of mankind into races and the superior qualities of the Anglo-Saxon were part of the all-wise plan of the Creator. Divine appointment was implicit in the sense of mission. Many persons in Great Britain and the United States believed that the events of history represented the manifestation of the will of God. Therefore, it was God's will that the British and Americans should go out into the world to uplift and enlighten. The Anglo-Saxon was peculiarly endowed with intelligence and courage in order to carry into the dark regions of the earth the sacred principles of peace, Protestantism, liberty, and justice. "God has not been preparing the English-speaking and Teutonic peoples for a thousand years for nothing but vain and idle self-contemplation and self-admiration," Senator Albert Beveridge of Indiana told the Senate during the debates on organizing a government for the Philippines. "No! He has made us the master organizers of the world to establish system where chaos reigns .... He has made us adepts in government that we may administer government among savage and senile peoples.... We are trustees of the world's progress, guardians of its righteous peace."[28] Beveridge's words expressed the thoughts of many American and British imperialists. J. A. Cramb, one of the most extreme British imperialists, thought he perceived in the empire of Anglo-Saxon Britain an incarnation of the divine idea.[29] Lyman Abbott, Congregationalist minister and exponent of the Social Gospel, reconciled his religious faith with his imperialism by imagining that a world dominated by the Anglo-Saxons would see the kingdom of God established on earth through the workings of Anglo-Saxon liberty and progress.[30]

The Anglo-Saxonist, then, commonly believed that his innate superiority was no accident, and that there was more than good fortune and foresight involved in the empire-building and worldwide influence of his race. "Such facts are God's great alphabet with which he spells for man his providential purposes," wrote Josiah Strong, one of America's most respected clergymen.[31] The Anglo-Saxon was superior for no other reason than that God had willed it so. This thought was the ultimate mystical extension of Anglo-Saxon racism, and one of the most potent conclusions in the web of ideas that constituted the cult of Anglo-Saxonism.

2

Historical and Intellectual Antecedents

Glorification of the Anglo-Saxon was not a new development in the late nineteenth century. Indeed, the idea of Anglo-Saxon excellence was a popular one in England as early as the sixteenth century, when supporters of the break with the Roman Church contended that they were merely returning the country to the older, purer religious practices that predated the Norman conquest. In the sixteenth and early seventeenth centuries, upholders of Parliament in its conflict with the Crown sought to establish the legitimate rights of the national legislative body by tracing its historical roots to the assemblies of the ancient Anglo-Saxons. By the late eighteenth century, it was a popular idea in England that the country derived its free institutions from the Anglo-Saxons. This early type of Anglo-Saxonism, however, was for the most part nonracial; Englishmen lauded Anglo-Saxon institutions, but without the implication that the Anglo-Saxons were innately superior to other peoples.[1]

The concept of free Anglo-Saxons came to America with the English colonists, and was a familiar idea to many of the men who made the American Revolution; Thomas Jefferson once proposed that the Great Seal of the United States be adorned on one side with representations of two fifth-century Anglo-Saxon heroes, Hengist and Horsa.[2] Later, in the first half of the nineteenth century, the idea of Anglo-Saxon freedom began to take on more clear-cut racial overtones in the United States. An organ of the Democratic Party declared in 1839 that it was "the peculiar duty" of the "Anglo-American race" to establish and maintain a civilization in which the highest ends were "the rights, freedom, and mental and moral growth of individual man."[3] Twenty years later, Carl Schurz told a Boston audience assembled at Faneuil Hall that the unparalleled growth and development of the United States was chiefly attributable to the undaunted spirit of the Anglo-Saxon race.[4] The rhetoric of racial Anglo-Saxonism was frequently employed by expansionists in the 1840s and '50s to buttress the concept of "manifest destiny." Supporters of the war with Mexico justified the conflict on racial grounds, alleging that the Mexicans were an inferior race that must inevitably give way before the superior vigor of the Anglo-Saxon. Senator Thomas Hart Benton predicted at the war's outset that the incontestable force of the "Celtic-Anglo-Saxon" division of the Caucasian race would soon carry it all the way across the Pacific and into Asia, where the race would revive and regenerate the inferior yellow-skinned peoples.[5]

Despite superficial similarities, the antebellum brand of Anglo-Saxonism in the United States differed considerably from what it was to become in the late nineteenth century. It had none of the comprehensiveness and symmetry which was to develop later. Nor was it influenced by the elaborate, finely executed race theories of Court Joseph Arthur de Gobineau, whose *Essai sur l'inégalité des races humaines* first appeared in an English translation in Philadelphia in 1856. Gobineau, a disgruntled aristocrat of the Second Empire, was the first European thinker to construct an entire philosophy of history around the idea of race. He was not widely read in the United States, however, partly because of his antidemocratic bias and partly because his *Essai* was reputed to be proslavery propaganda. When his theories did come to prominence, many years later, it was not in the United States, but in the Germany of Wilhelm II.[6]

Unlike Gobineau, antebellum Americans were less interested in defining the role of race in history than in characterizing their own nationality. They used race for its emotional impact, to help communicate the profound faith of Americans in the virility of their countrymen and the beneficence of their institutions. While the Anglo-Saxonists of the 1890s often stressed their duty to rule benighted peoples, antebellum Anglo-Saxonists emphasized the duty of Americans to set people free. The American empire was to be the "empire for liberty" envisioned by Jefferson, not an empire in which a superior race ruled despotically over inferior peoples. Nor was antebellum Anglo-Saxonism used to promote amity between the United States and Great Britain. Americans were Anglo-Saxons, but they were a unique branch of the race, possessed of special merit by virtue of their democratic political processes. American Anglo-Saxons tended to regard the British as decadent monarchists, far removed in blood and spirit from their progressive American cousins. In short, antebellum Anglo-Saxonism was primarily an emotional statement of American nationalism and a call for the extension of American democracy. It appealed to the buoyant optimism of the time, but it lacked the intellectual foundation on which the Anglo-Saxonism of the later period was constructed.[7]

It was the laying of a strong intellectual basis by thinkers on both sides of the Atlantic that made it possible for Anglo-Saxonism later in the century to become a major element in the mental outlook of Britons and Americans. A long process was required to transform the nationalistic pride and vague antiforeign hostility of the earlier period into the full-blown Anglo-Saxonist doctrine that had emerged by the 1890s. The process was a gradual one, and drew on the inspirations of many thinkers in both countries. As with so many of the intellectual developments of the period, the starting point in the creation of a refined Anglo-Saxonism was the work of Charles Darwin.

Darwin inadvertently provided race-thinkers with a scientific explanation for the assumed superiority of some races to others. The subtitle of *The Origin of Species* pointed the way: *The Preservation of Favoured Races in the Struggle for Life*. By "races," Darwin had meant species or varieties of animal life; but his meaning could be easily extended to include human races, and to make these as much subject to the struggle for existence as other forms of life.[8] Darwin himself believed human races were subject to evolutionary laws, and that less fit races would inevitably be eliminated as the more highly developed peoples extended their influence in the world. Writing to an acquaintance in 1881, Darwin said: "Looking at the world at no very distant date, what an endless number of the lower races will have been eliminated by the higher civilized races throughout the world."[9] Darwin also believed that the Anglo-Saxon race, and its American branch in particular, was a superior race. The Anglo-Saxons of the United States would inevitably overcome competing races, and in the process establish an advanced type of society. In his second major work, *The Descent of Man*, published in 1871, Darwin wrote that there was "apparently much truth in the belief that the wonderful progress of the United States, as well as the character of the people, are the results of natural selection." The United States had gained its measure of superiority because over the past dozen generations it had attracted "the more energetic, restless, and courageous men from all parts of Europe." Darwin went on to endorse the view of F. B. Zincke, who had predicted three years earlier that future events would show that all the past history of Western civilization had purpose and value only "when viewed in connection with, or rather as subsidiary to ... the great stream of Anglo-Saxon emigration to the west."[10]

Hence the theory of evolution, which began as an effort to explain changes in the biology of plants and animals, was extended even by Darwin himself to the realm of men and nations. As Herbert Spencer was able to fashion Social Darwinism by analogy, applying Darwinian and pseudo-Darwinian terms to the competition among individual men in society, so other thinkers might carry the analogy to other spheres and apply the idea of natural selection to the competition among nations and races on the international scene. Since the theory of evolution was a dominant theme in British and American thought in the last third of the nineteenth century, it is not surprising that Darwinism influenced thinking on international relations, and that international rivalries were transformed into manifestations of the Darwinian struggle for existence.

After Darwin, the first British thinker to move in this direction was Walter Bagehot, a brilliant economist, sociologist, and political analyst, and a friend of some of Britain's most influential political figures. In 1872, Bagehot published *Physics and Politics*, the first major work to apply the evolutionary hypothesis to society and offer a theory of history organized around the principle of natural selection. The book was favorably received and widely read in both Great Britain and the United States. Bagehot contended that there existed an inescapable law of history which mandated that "in every particular state of the world, those nations which are strongest tend to prevail over the others, and in certain marked peculiarities the strongest tend to be the best."[11] Bagehot thus applied to international relations biological formulas similar to those that Herbert Spencer was concurrently applying to the internal affairs of societies. He told his readers that the rich and powerful nations were rich and powerful because they were the fittest.

Once Darwin and Bagehot had indicated the direction, more refined versions of racial Darwinism began to appear. The man who probably did the most to promote the development of a Darwinian theory of international relations was Benjamin Kidd. When he published *Social Evolution* in 1894, Kidd was a minor civil servant in Great Britain's Inland Revenue Department. The book had tremendous impact and won him instant fame in Britain and the United States. The American edition went through ten printings in less than a year and was reviewed and discussed throughout the country. Theodore Roosevelt reviewed the book at length in the *North American Review*, criticizing Kidd for his "dogmatism and superficiality" while agreeing with his major contention that a race survived only if it was able "to attain a high degree of social efficiency."[12] In Great Britain, too, Kidd's book went through edition after edition. By 1900 a quarter of a million copies had been sold. Kidd resigned from his civil service post to devote full time to his writing, and was soon recognized as one of Britain's leading sociologists. Although his later books, the most notable of which was *Control of the Tropics* (1898), did no more than repeat and extend his earlier theories, they were eagerly studied by Englishmen and Americans seeking a scientific endorsement of imperialism.[13]

Kidd believed that human societies were organic in nature and subject to the same biological laws that governed living organisms. Because social systems "develop and decline like organic growths," the social sciences must be based on biological science, that is, Darwinism.[14] Kidd argued that in the rivalry among races, the feature that acted as the instrument of natural selection was warfare. Races competed for survival through continual war, and those that survived did so because they were the fittest.[15] Kidd measured fitness in terms of a race's "social efficiency," a subjectively defined combination of character, energy, and economy. The race that demonstrated a high degree of social efficiency, Kidd said, invariably triumphed over the less efficient.[16] Refining this conclusion, Kidd broke down the human species into a number of competing races and assigned a degree of social efficiency to each.

The socially inefficient "lower races" included all the various colored races, black, brown, yellow, and red. They were all doomed to eventual extinction. The "progressive peoples," on the other hand, included most of the "energetic, vigorous, virile" white nations, headed by the Teutonic race. The sternest conflict of all, Kidd indicated, occurred among these superior peoples, as each struggled for supremacy against all the others. Kidd had no doubt that for the present the leading race of the world was the Anglo-Saxon branch of the Teutonic race. Its social efficiency was much higher than that of any competitor. No other race had so firmly and permanently established its position. Kidd was certain that no limits could be set to the expansion of the Anglo-Saxons in the twentieth century, saying that it was "almost inevitable that they must in future exercise a preponderating influence in the world."[17]

While Kidd's influence in the development of Anglo-Saxonism in Great Britain and the United States was considerable, the classic formulation of the biological conception of international relations was left to another British thinker, Karl Pearson. After studying at Cambridge, Heidelberg, and Berlin, Pearson returned to England in the early 1880s a fervent exponent of both the socialism of Marx and Lassalle and the evolutionary theory of Darwin. He assumed a chair in mathematics at University College, London, in 1884, and before long was applying statistical analysis to biology to try to prove the validity of evolution. Pearson managed to reconcile his socialistic leanings with Darwinism by opposing Herbert Spencer and arguing that the real struggle for existence as it applied to humankind took place not among individual members of society, but among rival nations and races. In order for Great Britain to continue competing successfully in the international struggle, he said, it ought to end debilitating internal dissension by guaranteeing equality for all men at home.[18]

Pearson's most famous work was *National Life from the Standpoint of Science*, published in 1900 while he was suffering an excess of patriotic enthusiasm as a result of the war in South Africa.[19] Like Kidd, Pearson held that a nation was a vast organism, "subject as much to the great forces of evolution as any other gregarious type of life." Every nation was engaged in a continual struggle against all others, a struggle that sometimes took the form of war, but generally was carried on by means of technological and economic competition.[20] The military and economic power of an advanced race was nearly always sufficient to ensure its triumph over backward races; but when advanced nations competed among themselves, the entire "organized brainpower" of each went into the struggle, and the victor was the one which was most "fit" in mental as well as physical power.[21] The intensity of the struggle, of course, brought terrible suffering to individual members of society, but this was an unavoidable law of life. The suffering produced progress, and progress was the redeeming feature of the pain. Individual suffering was "the fiery crucible out of which comes the finer metal," a higher state of civilization.[22]

The racial Darwinism of Kidd and Pearson sounded very fine and scientific, which increased its appeal in a materialistic age. To many persons, though, it appeared too coldly materialistic; for all its philosophical comprehensiveness, nowhere did it take into account the presence of God in the world. This was a serious deficiency. Fortunately for the race-thinkers, a remedy was at hand. God, too, could be fitted into the theory of racial Darwinsim.

The man who best exemplified the effort to reconcile racial Darwinism with popular religious beliefs was Josiah Strong, the well-known Congregationalist pastor and Social Gospeler from Ohio. Strong read Darwin, Spencer, Kidd, and the Darwinian essays of John Fiske, and unlike many other American clergymen, found little in Darwinism that necessarily had to conflict with Protestant theology. The two books in which Strong most clearly set forth his Christian version of racial Darwinism were *Our Country*, published in 1885, and *The New Era*, which appeared eight years later. Both proved very popular, at least among that segment of the population which took an interest in evangelical Christianity. Between 1885 and 1893, *Our Country*, the book which transformed Strong from an obscure representative of the American Home Missionary Society into an international figure, sold over 160,000 copies; it was translated into several foreign languages, and the vainglorious chapter on "The Anglo-Saxon and the World's Future" was excerpted and published in Great Britain under the title *The United States and the Future of the*

Anglo-Saxon Race. Strong's later work, *The New Era*, repeated many of the arguments found in *Our Country*, and was published simultaneously in Great Britain and the United States; thirty-eight thousand copies were sold within a year, and by 1901 there were 49,000 copies in print.[23] After 1885, Strong was frequently asked to lecture and deliver speeches in the United States, and he was a well-known figure also in Great Britain; he was received with much applause when he visited London in 1904.

Throughout the period of his greatest notoriety, Strong's writings and work were directed primarily towards social reform and the evangelization of people living in the United States. The main purpose of *Our Country*, for example, was to argue the imperative need for home missions to save Americans from the perils of intemperance, socialism, Romanism, Mormonism, the maldistribution of wealth, and the corruption that was rampant in America's cities. Strong did not neglect the nation's place on the international scene, however, and both *Our Country* and *The New Era* stand as prominent examples of the manner in which Anglo-Saxonists in the late nineteenth century managed to bring together racial Darwinism and the Christian religion. In his striking passages on race and international relations, Strong disseminated an optimistic theology that portrayed the Creator as the inventor of, and moving force behind, the process of evolution, and the kingdom of God as the end result of the struggle for existence.

Strong's starting point was his assertion that the recent discoveries of biological science, far from contradicting religion, were actually revelations of the manner in which God was working in the world. "The truths of science are God's truth . . . its laws are God's laws," Strong told his readers. " . . . If God is really the ruler of the universe, the laws and processes of nature are only the divine purposes and methods." Like all other processes in the physical world, the process of evolution was conceived by God, and for a very good purpose; hence there was no reason why the divine presence should be absent from the Darwinian worldview.[24]

As Strong described it, evolution was the cosmic method by which God's plan for humanity was played out. The discovery by science that superior races inevitably displaced inferior ones was a revelation of God's plan for ensuring human progress; evolution was nothing less than His consummate method for bringing about the perfection of humanity.[25]

Strong believed that the Anglo-Saxon race, particularly its American branch, was God's agent on earth.[26] The Anglo-Saxon represented mankind's two most important ideas, civil liberty and "pure *spiritual* Christianity." The fact that these ideas were deeply ingrained in the psyche of the race peculiarly fitted the Anglo-Saxon to be "the great missionary race," destined to serve as exemplars and spiritual advisers to the world.[27] Only divine guidance, Strong continued, could account for the superior endowments of the race and the enormous vitality of its civilization. There must be a grandiose purpose behind Anglo-Saxon superiority. In a passage much quoted by later historians, Strong described what was in store for the race in years to come:

> It seems to me that God, with infinite wisdom and skill, is training the Anglo-Saxon race for an hour sure to come in the world's future.... The time is coming when the pressure of population on the means of subsistence will be felt here as it is now felt in Europe and Asia. Then will the world enter upon a new stage in its history—*the final competition of races, for which the Anglo-Saxon is being schooled.* Long before the thousand millions are here, the mighty *centrifugal* tendency, inherent in this stock and strengthened in the United States, will assert itself. Then this race of unequaled energy, with all the majesty of numbers and the might of wealth behind it . . . will spread itself over the earth. If I read not amiss, this powerful race will move down upon Mexico, down upon Central and South America, out upon the islands of the sea, over upon Africa and beyond. And can any one doubt that the result of this competition of races will be the "survival of the fittest"?[28]

Unlike many other racial Darwinists, however, Strong did not envision war and conquest as the instruments of Anglo-Saxon expansion. In fact, it was not until after the war with Spain in 1898 that Strong came to endorse imperialism as a proper national policy for the United States.[29] In his earlier writings, Strong asserted that the extension of Anglo-Saxon culture and ideals could be accomplished peacefully. Markedly inferior races, he said, would eventually be wiped out by disease and by contact with such vices of civilization as alcohol and tobacco. This was unfortunate, but probably inevitable. Stronger races would either be assimilated by the world's burgeoning population of Anglo-Saxons, or, in order to compete politically and economically with the latter, would be forced to adopt the ways of Anglo-Saxondom.[30] In any case, Strong said, the end result of the struggle for existence and the evolutionary process would be a world in which all mankind was Anglo-Saxonized. A "single supreme civilization," manifesting the Anglo-Saxon's pure spiritual Christianity, would then be established on the earth. This would be the realization of the Christian commonwealth, clearing the way for "the coming of Him who should inaugurate among men the kingdom of God."[31]

Josiah Strong thus successfully reconciled Protestant religious beliefs with an intellectual movement based primarily on biological science and scholarly tracts. In so doing, he showed that a religious sanction could be applied to racial Darwinism. Strong told his readers that there was a divine purpose behind Anglo-Saxon superiority and the process of evolution. For His own hallowed purposes, God had conceived of both.

Aided by thinkers like Strong, racial Darwinism by the turn of the century had become a pervasive concept in popular thinking on international relations in the two English-speaking powers. Highly respected individuals in England like Lord Charles Beresford spoke of the future of the Anglo-Saxon race in Darwinian terms.[32] An acute French observer of British thought regretted that racial Darwinist attitudes had "entered into the very bones" of the British nation.[33] He might have spoken similarly of the United States. American expansionists after the war with Spain commonly used the pseudoscientific language of racial Darwinism to defend or promote expansion. "The rule of the survival of the fittest applies to nations as well as the animal kingdom," wrote an American diplomat in an article supporting annexation of the Philippines. "It is a cruel, relentless principle being exercised in a cruel, relentless competition of mighty forces; and these will trample over us without sympathy or remorse unless we are trained to endure and strong enough to stand the pace."[34] Brooks Adams studied the thoughts of Benjamin Kidd and incorporated them into his essays urging Americans to fight with cunning and ferocity for world economic supremacy. "Nature has decreed that animals shall compete for life, or, in other words, destroy or be destroyed," Adams warned. "We can hope for no exemption from the common lot.... In these crucial moments races either develop genius or sink into imbecility."[35] Other American imperialists avowed that expansion was both inevitable and necessary—inevitable because the expansion of superior races was unavoidable, and necessary in order that the United States might be better prepared to survive the pitiless struggle for supremacy that would soon take place among the advanced, imperial nations.[36]

The development of a refined Anglo-Saxonist ideology benefited mightily from the association of race-thought with the supreme scientific concept of the age, the theory of evolution. Few persons in Great Britain or the United States were inclined to question the wisdom of the scientists, who during the course of the nineteenth century had inherited much of the authority and intellectual leadership that had once belonged to the theologians. As for Darwinian notions specifically, so pervasive and influential were they by the latter years of the century that any social theory based on Darwinian analogy stood a good chance of winning widespread acceptance. Indeed, for some Britons and Americans, the struggle for existence was a universal formula; they habitually blurred the distinction between the organic development of plants and animals and the social development of human groups. "The basic principles of evolutionary science can and should be applied to the solution of all social questions," declared one writer, "and it is the fault of our own short-sightedness and lack of mental grasp if we limit their application to the study of biology."[37] Applying Darwinism to races and nations was especially tempting, since racial Darwinism flattered the egos of Britons and Americans while it provided "scientific" evidence confirming age-old prejudices. Nationalists, militarists, and racists seized upon the idea. It told them that Anglo-Saxon superiority was biologically determined, and that conflict between the Anglo-Saxon and alien races could no more be avoided than the lion could "avoid" pursuing the antelope. More than any other single idea, the theory of evolution shaped Anglo-Saxonism.

Darwin's work thus marks an intellectual watershed separating the ill-defined prejudices of the first half of the nineteenth century from the elaborate Anglo-Saxonist race theories of the late nineteenth century. Racism was garbed in scientific language, and prejudice was elevated to a respectable scientific principle. A pseudoscientific race theory now existed which could be applied to almost any question where men of different ethnic backgrounds came into conflict.[38]

While racial Darwinists were formulating their suppositions about Anglo-Saxon superiority, British and American historians and political scientists were developing a related and equally enticing theory to bolster Anglo-Saxonism. This was the Teutonic origins theory of history, which was derived from the venerable English idea that the ancient Anglo-Saxons had brought free institutions to England. British historians in the second half of the nineteenth century picked up this tradition, expanded it into a theory that explained much of the history of the English-speaking world, and passed their ideas on to their American counterparts. In the last two decades of the nineteenth century, the Teutonic origins theory dominated American historiography.

Romantic nationalism stimulated historical research and writing in the nineteenth century and invested the results with unprecedented authority. The educated readers of Europe and America were prepared emotionally and intellectually for exaltations of the national past, and they eagerly welcomed the new outburst of historical works that treated nations almost as living entities.[39] France produced Michelet and his disciples. In Germany, a host of great figures, Niebuhr, Ranke, and Mommsen among them, embellished the ranks of historians. In the first half of the century, Great Britain produced Carlyle and Macaulay, and the United States, George Bancroft. In the second half of the century, the historical profession in both English-speaking countries was increasingly dominated by advocates of the Teutonic origins theory.

Roughly summarized, this theory held that the democratic, libertarian institutions of Great Britain and the United States had developed from an institutional germ which originated in ancient Germany and was transported to Britain by the Teutonic tribes that invaded the island in the fifth and sixth centuries. The institutional germ was the democratic social organization supposedly developed by the German forest tribes at some time in the remote past. They carried this democratic system with them intact to Britain, maintaining its pure form (and their racial purity as well) by wiping out rather than absorbing the undemocratic and racially inferior Celtic Britons. From the democratic seed thus planted by the Teutonic conquerors, English freedom and gift for self-government evolved. In the seventeenth century the descendants of the ancient Teutons carried the seed to America, where it gained renewed vigor in the forests of New England. As one historian put it, "The old Teutonic assembly . . . which had not long died out in the Frisian sea-lands, which still lived in the Swabian mountain-lands, rose again to full life in the New England town meeting."[40] Those who adopted the theory believed it was possible to trace a direct evolutionary line from the ancient tribes of northern Germany to modern Britain and the United States.

The first important work of the Teutonic origins school was John Mitchell Kemble's *The Saxons in England*, published in 1849.[41] Kemble, while only mildly racial in his thinking, did attempt to demonstrate that the stability of English institutions was owing to the Anglo-Saxon inheritance of the English people. Later scholars, such as Frederick Maitland, James Anthony Froude, William Stubbs, John Richard Green, and Edward Augustus Freeman, placed greater emphasis on the racial connection between modern Englishmen and the various Teutonic peoples, especially the Saxons, who had invaded the island. Ancient Anglo-Saxon poetry and chronicles were unearthed and venerated as part of the heritage of the race. William Stubbs, the greatest English medievalist of his time, learned the Anglo-Saxon language while still a schoolboy. As the first professionally trained historian to occupy the Chair of Modern History at Oxford, he wrote several influential works indicating that English regard for human dignity and independence was largely derived from primitive Teutonic attitudes and institutions. He sharply differentiated the Anglo-Saxon influences in English history, and those of their racial cousins, the Normans, from the influences of the Celtic and Latin peoples.[42] John Richard Green, while less race-minded than Stubbs, traced the origins of Parliament back to the German forests and insisted that English literature was almost purely Teutonic in structure and spirit. "With the landing of Hengest . . . English history begins," he wrote in his *Short History of the English People*. This book, published in 1874, was the largest selling historical work in Great Britain since

Macaulay. In the United States, it outsold all other history books in the last years of the century, including those dealing with American history. Henry Adams, himself one of America's foremost historians, thought Green "the flower of my generation."[43]

The best-known and most influential English exponent of the Teutonic origins theory was Edward A. Freeman, Regius Professor of Modern History at Oxford. Dubbed "the prince of Teutonists" by critics resentful of the strong element of racism in his scholarly works, Freeman devoted his career to promoting the role of race in English history and expounding the need for solidarity among all speakers of the English tongue. In his masterpiece, the fifteen-volume *History of the Norman Conquest* (1867–76), Freeman's sympathies were clearly with King Harold and the Saxons. He changed the name of the Battle of Hastings to the Battle of Senlac out of regard for the Saxons, and declared that he would gladly have fought there at Harold's side. In later historical works, Freeman indicated that he considered modern Germany less purely Teutonic than England, because the German race had suffered an infusion of Latin blood and had failed to preserve Teutonic democratic institutions.[44] He rejected the term "Anglo-Saxon" to describe modern Englishmen and Americans, however, as it offended his historical sense; he preferred "English folk."[45]

Freeman's influence in the United States resulted largely from the seven months he spent there in 1881–82, lecturing before large audiences in a number of eastern cities on the subject "The English People in Its Three Homes." In his lectures, Freeman spoke of northern Germany as Old England, England itself as Middle England, and the United States as New England. "The oldest England sent forth her sons to the shores of the isle of Britain, as in after-times the isle of Britain sent forth her sons to the vaster mainland of America." Praising the common English blood, speech, and traditions that united Britain and the United States, Freeman called for racial brotherhood among all English folk, but especially between the Americans and the British. The sweep of his words thrilled audiences in Boston, New York, and Baltimore, as he told them that Americans and Englishmen shared a common race-memory. "For thirteen hundred years our forefathers and yours lived together, worked together, suffered together, conquered together," he declaimed. " . . . Speakers of the tongue of

Caedmon and of Milton, inheritors of the freedom for which Godwine strove in one age and Hampden in another, I claim you as brethren." Ignoring the large non-English element which had been present in the American population almost from the beginning of settlement, Freeman repeated the same theme over and over: that Englishmen and Americans were of one race.[46]

Returning to England, Freeman wrote about his trip in a book entitled *Some Impressions of the United States*. The travel book was for him another vehicle for advocating Anglo-American solidarity. The Americans must not forget that they were "simply one part of the great English folk," he said. They were attached to Great Britain by "everlasting ties of blood and speech." In later years, Freeman would even praise George Washington as "the expander of England."[47]

The Teutonic germ theory fell on fertile ground in the United States, where interpretations of national history based on race were not entirely new. John Lothrop Motley, the great historian of the Dutch Republic, had held that Americans should take a special interest in the Dutch fight for independence because the Dutch were racial kinsmen of the Anglo-Saxons and traced their liberties back to the same Teutonic wellspring. Francis Parkman had relied to a considerable extent on race theory to explain the triumph of the British colonists over the French in the eighteenth century. He sharply contrasted the "peculiarly masculine" Anglo-Saxons of British North America with the passionate, impulsive, and excitable "French Celts" of Canada, and implied that Americans were free today because of their racial qualities.[48]

The support of the Teutonic origins theory by the most eminent British historians, together with the ever increasing number of American scholars who were being trained in Britain and Germany, foreshadowed the theory's acceptance in the United States. Its Darwinian connotations, too, increased its attractiveness to Americans. The idea of a maturing institutional germ was borrowed, by analogy, from biology, and it was obvious that the twin notions of racial heritage and institutional evolution owed much to Darwin. To the Teutonists, the life and evolution of the Teutonic peoples recapitulated the life and evolution of a biological species, while the peculiar skill of the English and Americans in the art of self-government provided clear evidence that the two Anglo-

Saxon nations were at the top of the evolutionary scale. These intellectual links to Darwinism aided in the wide dissemination of the Teutonic origins theory.[49]

Significantly, Teutonism found the majority of its leading American exponents among well-to-do New Englanders, and among those patrician intellectuals of the Northeast and the Old Northwest who traced their lineage to New England antecedents. These people were generally proud of their English heritage, fearful of the decline in Brahmin leadership, and predisposed to Anglophilia by their upbringing and education. Naturally, they were drawn to a theory that praised their ancestors as the builders of an ideal democracy, and themselves as the keepers of the Anglo-Saxon legacy. Although this genteel group formed but a tiny part of the total American populace, in the last years of the nineteenth century its members still played a greatly disproportionate part in the nation's social, cultural, and intellectual life.[50]

The Teutonic origins theory arrived full-blown in the United States when Herbert Baxter Adams, one of the greatest historians of his generation, introduced it, along with the German seminar method, at the opening of Johns Hopkins University in 1876. Born in western Massachusetts of a family that traced its roots back to the seventeenth-century settlers of the Bay Colony, Adams attended Phillips Exeter Academy and Amherst before going to Germany for graduate training. He took his doctorate at the University of Heidelberg, where he heard the ancient Teutons lauded in seminars presided over by Treitschke. On his return to the United States, Adams became the chairman of the graduate department of history at newly established Johns Hopkins.[51] In 1882 Johns Hopkins began publication of its *Series in Historical and Political Science*, under his general editorship. The theme of most volumes in the series was the Teutonic element in the American experience—the contention that American political institutions were the end product of an evolutionary process that began with the ancient Germans. In his own historical works, Adams undertook to trace many of the institutions of colonial New England back to their origins in northern Germany. He described the New England town meeting as the direct institutional descendant of the ancient Teutonic councils, revitalized in the forests of New England.[52]

Adams's influence went far beyond his writings. He always

maintained close contact with English scholars, and in 1882 he played host to Edward A. Freeman when the great English Teutonist visited Baltimore. Adams was the guiding hand in the founding of the American Historical Association in 1884. By that time he was probably the most influential historian in the United States. He was a great teacher as well; for a generation his seminars turned out young scholars imbued with the Teutonic origins theory. One of these was Woodrow Wilson, who learned his lessons well. In 1889, while still a professor at Wesleyan, Wilson wrote: "It is not the result of accident merely . . . that the English race has been the only race . . . that has succeeded in establishing and maintaining the most liberal forms of government. It is, on the contrary, a perfectly natural outcome of organic development."[53]

In the last two decades of the nineteenth century, the Teutonic origins theory swept the American historical profession. Wilson took it to Princeton. Albert Bushnell Hart insisted that his students at Harvard accept it as a basic tenet of American history. George Burton Adams taught it at Yale. At Cornell, it was taken up by Andrew D. White and Moses Coit Tyler. James K. Hosmer of Washington University wrote a popular *Short History of Anglo-Saxon Freedom*, in which he traced two thousand years of democratic government from its supposed origins on the Elbe and Weser plains. John W. Burgess, although he differed from his colleagues in that he emphasized the German-American rather than the Anglo-American connection, taught Teutonism at Columbia.[54] And during his tenure at Harvard in the 1870s, the redoubtable Henry Adams taught himself the Anglo-Saxon language and established, at his own expense, a special class of Ph.D. candidates to carry out research on Anglo-Saxon institutions; Adams's own research culminated in a long essay on Anglo-Saxon courts of law that became a classic of legal history.[55]

The primary appeal of these professional scholars, for all their fame, was to the academic communities of Great Britain and the United States. The great popularizer of the Teutonic origins theory was John Fiske, whose ideas, through his books and his hundreds of lectures, reached thousands of educated Britons and Americans. Fiske was the best-known and most widely read American historian of his day. His efforts helped to disseminate Teutonism widely among members of the American (and, to a lesser extent, the British) upper and middle classes.[56]

Like Herbert Baxter Adams, the Connecticut-born Fiske was of old New England Puritan stock. He was intensely proud of his ancestry. While still a student at Harvard he traced his genealogy back to fourteenth-century England; in 1900 he declared that he was a lineal descendant of Alfred the Great.[57] At Harvard in the early 1870s, Fiske stayed at the same boardinghouse as Henry Adams; undoubtedly the two men discussed the Teutonic theory over the dinner table and during the evenings of scholarly conversation in the sitting room. Fiske became absorbed both in the historical works of John Mitchell Kemble, William Stubbs, and Edward A. Freeman and in the Social Darwinism of Herbert Spencer. He quickly perceived the linkage between evolution and the Teutonic doctrine and began to apply Spencerian phraseology to Teutonist history: the institutions of Great Britain and the United States, he insisted, were the "fittest" in human history.

Fiske made himself a familiar figure in England as well as the United States. He toured England four times between 1873 and 1883, lecturing before enthusiastic audiences and meeting with members of the English intellectual community. He made the acquaintance of Charles Darwin, Thomas Huxley, and Sir Charles Lyell, and he fulfilled a dream by meeting Herbert Spencer ("our God," Fiske called him). He was widely recognized in England as the great American popularizer of Darwinism and as one of Spencer's major American disciples. By the time of his second trip to England, in 1879, Fiske's friends and acquaintances included a good part of the intellectual elite of the country. His lecture series was delivered in a packed hall at University College, London. He wrote to his wife that at the conclusion of his lecture on "Manifest Destiny," his audience "fairly *howled* applause," the men standing up on benches to wave their hats, and the women standing in the aisles waving handkerchiefs. Simon Newcomb, the noted American astronomer, said after Fiske's 1879 tour that the English scientific community regarded him as the deepest thinker America had yet produced.[58]

"Manifest Destiny" was Fiske's most popular lecture. It was repeated no fewer than fifty times in the United States and Great Britain. He delivered it seven times in Boston alone, four times in New York, and three times in London. In 1880, the lecture was delivered at Washington at the express request of President Hayes, several members of the Cabinet, Senators Hoar and

Dawes of Massachusetts, Chief Justice Waite, and a number of other prominent public figures.[59]

The theme of "Manifest Destiny" was Fiske's hopeful forecast of a future millenium, to be brought about primarily by the benign influence of the "English race." Fiske held that "the conquest of the North American continent by men of the English race was unquestionably the most prodigious event in the political annals of mankind." It was clear to him that the English occupation of North America foreshadowed English domination of the world, since this occupation not only proved once and for all the superiority of English civilization, but at the same time provided the race with a new homeland in which there was room for a population of hundreds of millions—so many that the race would someday dominate all others through sheer force of numbers. Fiske cited population statistics to support his contention that the birth rate in countries inhabited by men of the English race was the most prodigious in the civilized world. Within a century, Fiske said, the power of English ideas and the force of English numbers would mean "every land on the earth's surface that is not already the seat of an old civilization shall become English in its language, in its political habits and traditions, and to a predominant extent in the blood of its people." Fiske foresaw the day when 600 million Americans, together with several hundred million members of the English race in the British Empire, would command the world's seas and the world's commerce. They would be so formidable an economic power that the leading nations of Europe, in order to free their energies for the economic competition, would disband their armies, scrap their weapons of war, and enter into a political federation. Eventually the entire world, inspired in large part by the success of American federalism, would form a single federation, and a world government, based on English democratic principles, would be established. By that time, "four-fifths of the human race will trace its pedigree to English forefathers," and perpetual peace would be assured.[60]

In addition to being a well-known lecturer and visionary, Fiske was the most popular American historian of his generation, and the only one whose books could compete with works of fiction for a place on contemporary best-seller lists.[61] Fiske's historical

HISTORICAL AND INTELLECTUAL ANTECEDENTS

studies, too, helped disseminate the Teutonic origins theory. "The government of the United States is not the result of special creation, but of evolution," he said. "... In the deepest and widest sense, our American history ... descends in unbroken continuity from the days when stout Arminius in the forests of northern Germany successfully defied the might of imperial Rome." This basic concept infused all Fiske's historical writing. Edward A. Freeman was one of Fiske's warmest admirers. On reading Fiske's two best-known historical works, *The Critical Period of American History* (1888) and *The Beginnings of New England* (1889), Freeman wrote to Fiske to express his esteem. "Seldom, if ever," he said, had he "seen any part of English history, that part of it which happened on American soil, treated so thoroughly as part of the history of one English people."[62]

John Fiske's lectures, historical works, and philosophical speculations were far from original. They were derived from the ideas of a large assortment of thinkers, among them Spencer, Kemble, Stubbs, and Freeman. Fiske's audience among the thinking public of the United States, however, was much larger than any of these men could attract; and because of his popularity, he was probably the most effective publicist of the Teutonic origins theory that the United States produced.[63]

By the 1890s, the Teutonic origins doctrine was the dominant historical viewpoint in Great Britain and the United States. The implications of this for the development of race theory were enormous, because Teutonism suggested, when it did not flatly state, that the institutions of the two countries were biologically as well as historically determined, that they were part of the genetic as well as the historical heritage of the race. Moreover, by emphasizing the Anglo-American connection, the historians and political scientists promoted a view of the peoples of the two countries as of one polity and one race. The scholars might call this race "Teutonic" or "English" or "English folk," but most persons in the United States and Great Britain preferred to call it by the name with which they were more familiar: Anglo-Saxon.

Racial Darwinism and Teutonist history provided the essential intellectual underpinning for Anglo-Saxonist doctrine. However, in the late nineteenth and early twentieth centuries, there were three important developments in Great Britain and the United States which also contributed substantially to the growth of race consciousness and the dissemination of Anglo-Saxonist ideas, and which cannot be overlooked here. The first of these was the emergence of the imperial federation movement in Britain; the second was the large influx into the United States of new immigrants from southern and eastern Europe; and the third was the adoption, by popular storytellers and novelists in both countries, of overtly Anglo-Saxonist literary themes. As will be seen, each of these developments encouraged the growth of race-thinking in the two English-speaking countries, and helped to bring about the widespread public acceptance of Anglo-Saxonist notions.

In Great Britain, the propagandists of the imperial federation movement often phrased their arguments in racial terms, and continually called attention to the presumed racial affinity of all the English-speaking peoples.

The goal of the imperial federationists was the transformation of the loosely bound British Empire into an integrated, world-encircling state. They called for a free union, on equal terms, of the white, self-governing colonies—Canada, Australia, New Zealand, and South Africa—with the mother country. A single imperial parliament would be established, and the various member-states of the federation would send parliamentary representatives to London to take an equal share in the central government. Great Britain and the white colonies would become constituent units in a new federated state which stretched around the globe.

The goal of the imperial federationists was a splendid one, and they believed its realization would bring substantial benefits to Great Britain: stronger economic ties with the Empire (through a preferential tariff), a centralized imperial defense system, and increased success in carrying out Britain's civilizing and peace-keeping "mission."

The imperial federation movement was at its height in the late 1880s. The chief agency of the movement, the Imperial Federation League, was founded in 1884, and quickly established branches throughout the Empire. Under the leadership of Lord

Rosebery, the League flourished for the next several years, promoting the general idea of federation while its membership debated the best way to bring Britain and the colonies together. Over the years, attainment of the League's goals was consistently frustrated by internal disagreements and by increasing colonial nationalism and the reluctance of the mother country to surrender exclusive control over foreign policy. The periodic colonial conferences held at London to promote the constitutional union of the Empire could produce no definite scheme of federation. In 1893, Prime Minister William Gladstone denounced the Imperial Federation League's plan to replace free trade with imperial preference duties, and the League collapsed. Though the hope for imperial federation remained alive for many years thereafter, the movement never regained the vitality it had evidenced prior to the League's dissolution.

During its heyday, the imperial federation movement drew much of its strength from Anglo-Saxon racism. Lord Rosebery, who made imperial federation the "dominant passion" of his life, believed strongly that the achievement of this end would be a major step toward establishing the complete predominance of the Anglo-Saxon race all over the world.[64] The three books which furnished much of the propaganda for the federationists, Charles W. Dilke's *Greater Britain* (1868), J. R. Seeley's *The Expansion of England* (1883), and James Anthony Froude's *Oceana* (1886), all contained strong doses of Anglo-Saxonism.

Dilke, a Radical Liberal member of Parliament who might have become prime minister in the late 1880s except for his involvement in a notorious divorce case, wrote his book after a round-the-world tour that took him to the United States, Polynesia, Australia, and India. He was a strong believer in the superiority of the "Saxon" race, and in its essential unity despite its dispersion over the globe. He returned from his tour of "Greater Britain" convinced that "the dearer are, on the whole, likely to destroy the cheaper peoples, and that Saxondom will rise triumphant from the doubtful struggle." It seemed the inevitable destiny of the race, he said, to spread over the globe, extirpating backward peoples and disseminating the English tongue and Saxon institutions. The Americans, one of the most vigorous branches of the race, one day soon would join in its expansion. Saxons would overrun Africa, China, Japan, and most of Latin America, turning those areas into new racial homelands and setting the stage for "universal rule." Eventually, the other Great Powers would be reduced to pygmies by the side of the Saxon.[65]

J. R. Seeley's *The Expansion of England*, one of the classic expositions of British imperialism, contained many of the same racist notions as Dilke's work. Seeley, a professor of Classics at Cambridge, believed the most pronounced trend of modern history was the extension of the English race and English institutions to the farthest reaches of the earth. The white colonies, he said, were distinct from England only in the geographical sense; in race, spirit, and institutions, they were mere extensions of England. He urged that the mother country and the colonies be merged in a federal union on the American model, creating a world state of the English race. Seeley left open the possibility of the United States, a country "English in race and character," and only separate from the remainder of the race because of an unfortunate misunderstanding in the eighteenth century, one day joining the federation. He would warmly welcome such a development.[66]

James Anthony Froude's *Oceana* also left open the possibility of future American affiliation with an imperial union. Froude, a noted historian of the Teutonic origins school, was also one of Britain's leading imperialists. His book was part travelogue and part propaganda piece for the imperial federation movement. Like Dike, he published his volume after a round-the-world tour that took him to several of the major British colonies and to the United States. Among the countries he visited were South Africa, Australia, and New Zealand, and he returned home convinced that public sentiment in those countries was favorable to federation. As for the Americans, Froude took great pride in the fact that "fifty million Anglo-Saxons" now occupied North America, making that vast continent English in its language, laws, religion, and manners. He did not believe the United States would be likely to join any federation in the near future, but he did believe it would be a valuable friend of a federated British Empire.[67]

The movement for imperial federation attracted many of the same individuals who later joined in promoting Anglo-American friendship. In the late 1890s, Lord Rosebery became one of the leading advocates of close cooperation, based on racial affinity, between the United States and Great Britain. Charles W. Dilke wrote several articles in 1898 in support of a military alliance between the two great branches of the Anglo-Saxon race. Joseph Chamberlain, the foremost Anglo-Saxonist and friend of the United States in the third Salisbury government, actively promoted imperial federation.

It is not difficult to explain the parallel support for imperial federation and Anglo-American amity in the minds of many Britons. The racial arguments for friendship with the United States and for federation were often identical, and supporters frequently transferred into the sphere of Anglo-American relations ideas originally developed in connection with the federation movement. Promoters of imperial federation often pointed out that the addition of the United States to the countries supposed to participate in the imperial union would mean the unification of all the Anglo-Saxon states in the world. Then the ideal of race unity would be fully realized.[68]

Two of the best-known and most influential advocates of both imperial federation and Anglo-American friendship were W. T. Stead and Cecil Rhodes. Stead, the founder and editor of the Liberal periodical *Review of Reviews*, was an odd combination of imperialist and humanitarian reformer. In many ways, he was the Victorian idealist *par excellence*: eager, honorable, forthright, intensely moral, and vividly cognizant of the duties incumbent on the English race. When he founded his review in 1890, he took for his starting point "a deep and almost awe-struck regard for the destinies of the English-speaking man," and dedicated himself and his periodical to promoting fraternal union with the United States.[69] Stead sincerely believed that the best way to elevate mankind and ensure world peace was for the English-speaking race to occupy as much of the world as possible, and he hoped that a world-dominating English-speaking federation would bring about a permanent *Pax Anglo-Saxon*. An ardent admirer of the United States, Stead thought that "the creation of the Americans" was the greatest achievement of the race. His personal plan for an imperial federation called for Great Britain and the colonies to join the American Union as states in a new United States of Anglo-Saxondom. The new race union, which would allow the British and American peoples to carry out their racial mission more effectively, would be governed on the principles of the American Constitution. "If . . . we substitute for the insular patriotism of our nation the broader patriotism of the race," Stead said, "and frankly throw in our lot with the Americans to realise the great ideal of Race Union, we shall enter upon a new era of power and prosperity the like of which the race has never realised since the world began."[70]

Until Stead turned anti-imperialist during the Boer War, he was a close friend and confidant of Cecil Rhodes, the colossus of South Africa and another champion of imperial federation, race union, and Anglo-American amity. Rhodes was above all else a British nationalist, and his chief loyalty was always to the Empire. Unlike his friend Stead, who thought the United States the most powerful Anglo-Saxon country and advocated Britain's merging with the American Union, Rhodes always hoped that federation of the race might take place under the Union Jack, with the United States somehow "recovered" by Great Britain. (Rhodes rarely missed an opportunity to excoriate the "insensate folly" of George III in driving the Americans from the Empire.) Despite his reservations, however, in February 1891 Rhodes grudgingly told Stead that he would be willing to see Great Britain and the self-governing colonies join the United States if that was the only practicable way of satisfying the great need for the unity of the "elect race."[71] Rhodes thought that a federal government, perhaps meeting alternately five years at Washington and five years at London, would be the greatest instrument for establishing Anglo-Saxon peace, liberty, and justice in the world.[72]

In his continual efforts on behalf of imperial federation and race unity, Rhodes regarded himself as the agent of the divine purpose. No man took the concepts of national and racial mission more seriously than Rhodes.[73] In the first of his famous wills, drawn up at Kimberley when he was just twenty-four and had not yet accumulated his later stupendous wealth in gold and diamonds, he directed that his estate should be used after his death to endow a secret society with the following aims:

> The extension of British rule throughout the world . . . and especially

the occupation by British settlers of the entire continent of Africa, the Holy Land, the Valley of the Euphrates, the islands of Cyprus and Candia, ... the whole of the Malay Archipelago, the sea-board of China and Japan, the ultimate recovery of the United States of America as an integral part of the British Empire, ... colonial representation in the Imperial Parliament, which may tend to weld together the disjointed members of the Empire, and finally the foundation of so great a Power as to hereafter render wars impossible and promote the best interests of humanity.[74]

Rhodes never lost sight of his plan, although it was occasionally modified to meet changed conditions. The Rhodes scholarships were part of his efforts to further race unity. They were established for colonial students in his will of 1893 to promote imperial federation, and extended to American students in his will of 1899 to help provide a common education for potential leaders of all the Anglo-Saxon countries. (In 1901, Rhodes provided for five annual scholarships for German students; Parliament ended the German scholarships during the First World War.) Rhodes seldom doubted that one day his hope for a mighty world empire would be realized, and at times he was left breathless with the sweep of his scheme. "What a dream!" he wrote in one of his wills. "But yet it is probable. It is possible."[75]

The linkage between Anglo-Saxon racism and hopes for imperial federation in the minds of the federationists is plain to see. For many, imperial unity, the immediate goal, was a giant step in the direction of the ultimate goal, race unity. As one prominent federationist put it not long after the collapse of the Imperial Federation League, a "United States of Great Britain" would be a mighty achievement, but the "crowning stone of the whole edifice" must be representation of the United States in an Anglo-Saxon parliament. Once that was brought about, the race would be an irresistible force, well on the way to carrying out its mission of "girdling the globe with beneficent influences."[76]

The educated public of the United States, while generally unenthusiastic about the movement for a federation of the British Empire, and—at least prior to 1898—hostile to talk of a race union, was certainly aware of the ideas being discussed in Great Britain. Indeed, the United States had its own early proponent of a race federation. Andrew Carnegie made an effort to keep the idea before the American public in the early and mid-1890s, years before the popular feelings engendered by the war with Spain made it respectable. Carnegie was never able to forget that though the United States was his chosen country, Scotland was the land of his birth. He loved Great Britain, "the mother of nations," and believed that no other country had done as much for the progress of the world. He frequently took extended vacations in England and Scotland, and over his 30,000-acre Scottish estate, Skibo, he always flew his "United flag," the Stars and Stripes and the Union Jack sewn together.[77]

Though he was passionately attached to Great Britain, Carnegie loathed imperialism, monarchism, the established Anglican Church, and British involvement in European politics. In the early 1880s, he used part of his wealth to buy up a string of British newspapers, and mounted a campaign to abolish the monarchy and House of Lords and transform Britain into a republic. The effort was a dismal failure, of course; the very fact that it was made indicates the depth of Carnegie's ingenuousness about national and international affairs. He never understood that differences in British and American institutions and interests could be formidable barriers to an Anglo-American union. If the British people could only be convinced of the wisdom of such a course, he thought, Great Britain could overnight, through simple acts of Parliament, become a republic, withdraw from its tropical colonies, and disentangle itself from European power politics. The way would then be cleared for the mother country to apply for statehood in the American Union.[78]

Carnegie expected the British to follow this astonishing course out of race sentiment. He himself was extremely race-conscious; he believed race sentiment "the strongest sentiment in man," and "the real motive which at the crisis determines his action in international affairs." In 1903, he confidently predicted to Arthur Balfour that in the not-too-distant future, race patriotism would be as potent a force as love of country: "As the Virginian of today supplements State Patriotism by the wider Patriotism of the Union, so are the American and the Briton some day to cherish Patriotism of the whole Race." Carnegie insisted that all British-American differences were only temporary, and that in the end nothing could keep apart the sundered halves of the great

Anglo-Saxon race. Someday soon, Americans and Britons would be one people.[79]

Believing as he did, Carnegie found the imperial federation movement in Great Britain a wonderful sign of what the future might bring, but he believed also that the federationists aimed too low. It was shortsighted of Britons to work for a federation of the Empire, he told them, and not include in their plans the largest and potentially the most powerful English-speaking state in the world. They ought to raise their sights above an imperial federation and aim instead for a great race union among Great Britain, the self-governing colonies, and the United States. Somewhat in the manner of W. T. Stead, Carnegie believed that the logical way to achieve this was for the colonies and the constituent units of the United Kingdom—England, Scotland, Wales, and Ireland—to apply for American statehood. Each of the new states would then set up its own legislature—England could keep Parliament—and elect representatives to attend an expanded Congress at Washington.[80]

Carnegie's ideas were extremely naïve, and many people found it hard to take them seriously. Alfred Thayer Mahan dismissed Carnegie's thinking as "rather vaporous," while Carnegie's Liberal friends in England maintained a discreet, shocked silence after the first publication of his project for uniting Anglo-Saxondom. The Tory press had a field day accusing the steel king of wanting to see Great Britain added to the American empire.[81]

The artlessness of Carnegie's scheme, however, could not wholly detract from the nobility of his ends; for Carnegie, the great champion of world peace, sought from the realization of his hopes something more than an Anglo-Saxon reunion. As he envisioned it, the true purpose of such a union was the establishment of a permanent world peace. Like Stead and Rhodes, he believed an Anglo-Saxon union would be so powerful that no other country would ever dare go to war without its permission. "A reunion of the Anglo-Americans...would dominate the world and banish from the earth its greatest stain—the murder of men by men," he said. "It would be the great arbiter between nations, and enforce the peaceful settlement of all quarrels." "If ever the parent-land and all her children unite..., it need not be feared that a shot will be fired or a sword drawn. The writ of that race union will run the circle round and ensure peace."[82] Carnegie sincerely believed that an Anglo-Saxon union, establishing a single, federated Anglo-Saxon state, would banish for all time the scourge of war. "For such...a destiny," Carnegie said, "even Queen Victoria on bended knee might pray."[83]

Andrew Carnegie devoted much of his time after 1890 to publicizing his ideas on a race federation and world peace. His articles on the subject appeared in some of the most prominent British and American periodicals of the day, and helped to keep the idea of a race union, often written or talked about in Great Britain in connection with the imperial federation movement, before the reading public of the United States. Few Americans were well acquainted with the imperial federation movement, but many educated people knew about the ideas of Andrew Carnegie.

One other factor that increased considerably the race-consciousness of Americans after 1890 was the tremendous influx of new immigrants from the poverty-stricken lands of southern and eastern Europe. The change in the sources of immigration first became noticeable in the 1880s. In 1896, for the first time, immigrants from southern and eastern Europe constituted a majority of new arrivals. In succeeding years, the influx of Italians, Poles, Jews, Russians, Armenians, Greeks, Syrians, Czechs, and Slovaks rapidly overshadowed the dwindling numbers of immigrants from the traditional sources in Great Britain, Germany, Scandinavia, and the Low Countries. The most dramatic increase in the new immigration occurred after the turn of the century: three hundred thousand came in 1900, 600,000 in 1903, and nearly a million (eighty-five percent of total immigration) in 1907.[84]

Conservative citizens were horrified at the new trend in immigration, especially since it coincided with disturbing developments in American society. As the millions of impoverished immigrants poured into urban slums, sweatshops proliferated, labor violence increased, city and state governments grew more corrupt, and many persons turned to socialism as the answer to the gross injustices in American society. Americans of the old stock were usually unwilling to admit that complex social and economic forces were responsible for unsettled conditions. They sought simpler explanations, and often settled upon the racial character of the new immigrants as the cause of poverty, corruption, and festering unrest in the United States. The immigrants were easy targets for racial prejudice, since they were alien in custom, appearance, religion, and class as well as ethnicity. American conservatives, especially those in the Northeast, where most of the newcomers were concentrated, blamed the nation's troubles on the biological traits of the immigrants. Anglo-Saxon America was being overrun, they said, and the invaders were poisoning the social organism. Unless Anglo-Saxons united to turn the tide, America was lost. By the turn of the century, race was by far the most powerful source of objection to the new immigrants.

The changed character of immigration thus increased considerably the race feeling of large numbers of Americans, leading these people to draw more clearly the line separating Anglo-Saxons from other European peoples. The trend was resisted by a distinguished minority of the nation's social and intellectual elite—men like William James, Edward Everett Hale, Josiah Royce, Charles W. Eliot, and Thomas Wentworth Higginson, who continued to believe in the efficacy of the melting pot and in America's role as a refuge for the oppressed.[85] However, in the face of the tide of new immigrants, most old-stock Americans came to see Anglo-Saxonism as a defense against the destruction of traditional American society. The tenets of Anglo-Saxonism provided this segment of the Protestant, Anglo-Saxon community with a convenient rationale for its race prejudice.

Opponents of the new immigration asserted that the maintenance of a democratic, libertarian society depended on continued Anglo-Saxon dominance. Disregarding the contributions of non-English elements to American history, these people declared that Anglo-Saxons had created the United States, and only Anglo-Saxons could sustain it. "As regards political freedom," the historian James K. Hosmer cautioned, "every people but the Anglo-Saxons has been at some time crushed and become spirit-broken. To Anglo-Saxons alone can our American freedom be safely intrusted." John W. Burgess declared that political responsibility must be based upon capacity to discharge it; the "Teutonic" element in the United States must determine when and where the capacity existed. The economist Edward A. Ross sternly warned that old-stock Americans would be committing race suicide if they continued to admit large numbers of people representing the lower races. Whitelaw Reid expressed dread of what might become of the country when Americans ceased to be an Anglo-Saxon people.[86]

Opposition to continued immigration was particularly strong among the Brahmin elite of New England. In 1894, a number of monied Bostonians initiated a major campaign aimed at securing federal statutes restricting immigration. They formed the Immigration Restriction League, elected John Fiske its first president, and named an executive committee composed almost solely of wealthy Harvard graduates, including George F. Edmunds, Robert Treat Paine, and Leverett Saltonstall. The League prospered and attracted hundreds of members. Although it never succeeded in securing restrictive legislation, it continued to operate until the First World War.[87]

The rhetoric of immigration restriction drew heavily on ideas of racial Darwinism and Anglo-Saxon superiority. Francis A. Walker, president of the Massachusetts Institute of Technology and a vice president of the Immigration Restriction League, referred to the vast throngs of peasantry crowding into the country as "beaten men from beaten races; representing the worst failures in the struggle for existence." They had none of the ideas and aptitudes of "those who are descended from the tribes that met under the oak-trees of old Germany to make laws and choose chieftains." Other restrictionists were more brutal in their statements: the new immigrants were "human gorillas," said the patrician editor of the *Atlantic Monthly*, Thomas Bailey Aldrich. In his famous poem "Unguarded Gates," published in 1892, Aldrich urged that the gates to America be closed to the "wild motley throng" that was entering, "flying the Old World's poverty and scorn." It was because the gates were left unguarded, he reminded his countrymen, that "the thronging Goth and Vandal trampled Rome."[88]

HISTORICAL AND INTELLECTUAL ANTECEDENTS 57

The new immigration thus stimulated Anglo-Saxon racism among the influential elite of the Northeast. Anglo-Saxonist doctrine justified hostility to the immigrants and provided ideas around which Americans of Anglo-Saxon heritage could rally in the face of a perceived threat to American society. Fear of the immigrant was one more stimulus to the growth of race-consciousness in turn-of-the-century America.

○ ○ ○

Popular authors of the period also helped to disseminate race theories and reinforce racism in the public mind. Novelists and storytellers were both publicists of race theories and purveyors of the Anglo-Saxon creed in the 1890s and 1900s. Fictional characters often were delineated in racial terms, and race-thinking was one of the most obvious underlying philosophical currents in much of British and American fiction.[89]

Rudyard Kipling contributed much to the cult of Anglo-Saxonism. Probably no other writer in the English-speaking world caught so well the spirit of nineteenth-century imperialism. Kipling was, indeed, the poet laureate of empire; his work epitomized a literature glorifying the strong man and extolling national mission and imperial power.[90] His whole literary career, one contemporary critic observed, was "one unflagging appeal to the fighting instincts of the race.... His breath has stirred the veins, not of hundreds of men, nor of thousands, but of a cluster of nations." H. G. Wells recalled in later years that the prevailing intellectual force during his undergraduate days was "Kiplingism."[91]

Kipling's beliefs were in accord with the philosophical tenets of Americans as well as Englishmen. In Kipling's romantic, sentimental stories and poems, the reading public in both countries recognized popular notions concerning the harshness of nature, the duties of superior peoples, and the instincts of race. The English craze for Kipling reached the United States at the beginning of the 1890s, and by 1898 there were thirty-five American editions and reprints of his works. American critics praised him as the greatest living English writer of fiction. His poem "Recessional" was adopted as the official hymn of the Chicago public schools. When Kipling lay seriously ill in a New York hotel in February 1899, hushed crowds gathered in the street outside, blocking traffic. Many people kneeled to pray before the hotel door, and special prayers were offered in the city's churches. His recovery was greeted with widespread expressions of relief.[92]

Kipling's own feelings toward Americans were mixed. He sometimes deplored the vulgarity, materialism, and lack of culture in the United States. He married an American woman, however, and lived for four years in Vermont, and he had many American friends. Though they often criticized Kipling's satiric indictments of their society, Americans loved his stories, and considered themselves brothers in blood and spirit with his English heroes. After all, they, too, were Anglo-Saxons, members of the elect race. The French author Victor Bérard paid grudging tribute to Kipling's influence in all English-speaking countries when he observed: "Wherever penetrated the works of Rudyard Kipling—that is to say, among the one hundred or one hundred and twenty millions of Anglo-Saxons scattered throughout the world—a mighty stream arose which swept away everything."[93] Even allowing for the evident hyperbole in Bérard's statement, there can be no doubt that Rudyard Kipling helped to popularize Anglo-Saxonist notions in all parts of the English-speaking world.

Two noted American novelists, Jack London and Frank Norris, repeated Kipling's success on a more modest scale. Both were familiar with the race theories of the day, and both translated those theories into literary works that had a considerable audience.

Jack London idolized Rudyard Kipling. While developing his talents as a writer, London undertook to improve his style by spending day after day laboriously copying Kipling's stories in longhand. London was familiar as well with the racial Darwinist works of Benjamin Kidd and with the Teutonic origins theory of history.[94] Such ideas were in accord with the racial prejudices he had acquired as a boy growing up on the brawling San Francisco waterfront, and he happily adapted them to his literary purposes. The heroine of one of his early novels frankly declared: "We are not God's, but Nature's chosen people, we Angles and Saxons, and Normans, and Vikings, and the earth is our heritage. Let us arise and go forth."[95] Though a socialist, London did not believe that inferior races were fit for life in a socialist society; socialism could only be made to work by Anglo-Saxons. In London's novels, the heroes were nearly always tall, muscular, blonde and blue-eyed Anglo-Saxons, sober-minded, clean living, and highly moral. Typical of London's heroes was Billy Roberts of *The Valley of the Moon*, whose appearance reminded one of the female characters of a painting she had cherished for years:

> Between tall headlands of rock and under gray cloud-blown sky, a dozen boats, long and lean and dark, beaked like monstrous birds, were landing on a foam-whitened beach of sand. The men in the boats, half naked, huge muscled and fair-haired, wore winged helmets. In their hands were swords and spears, and they were leaping, waist-deep, into the sea-wash and wading ashore.... One fair-haired invader lay across the gunwale of a boat.... In the air, leaping past him into the water, sword in hand, was Billy. There was no mistaking it. The striking blondness, the face, the eyes, the mouth were the same.[96]

Frank Norris, like London, was strongly influenced by Rudyard Kipling, whose works Norris discovered during his freshman year at Berkeley. The great Anglo-Indian was, said Norris, his "adored and venerated author." Also while at Berkeley, Norris developed an interest in ancient Anglo-Saxon literature, especially the heroic sagas. In his later novels, Norris displayed an obsession with race and the popular Anglo-Saxonism of the day.[97] He wrote often of the "instincts of race," and in his first full-length novel, published in 1898, one of the characters declared: "Somewhere deep in the heart of every Anglo-Saxon lies the predatory instinct of his Viking ancestors—an instinct that a thousand years of respectability and tax-paying have not quite succeeded in eliminating."[98] In his most famous work, *The Octopus*, Norris sharply contrasted the simplicity, directness, honesty, beauty, and strength of the Anglo-Saxon farmers of the San Joaquin Valley with the degenerate attitudes and appearance of their Portuguese and Mexican employees. And here, as elsewhere, Norris idealized the westward movement of the Anglo-Saxons, from the forests of Germany to the shores of Britain, to America, and across the Pacific to Asia. "The Anglo-Saxon started from there [Asia] at the beginning of everything," one of the book's minor characters states, "and it's manifest destiny that he must circle the globe and fetch up where he began his march.... Tell the men of the East to look for the men of the West."[99]

It is impossible to state with any degree of precision how much authors like London and Norris helped stoke American race feeling. It is certain, however, that both writers—London in particular—reached a large audience. Norris's *The Octopus* was received with admiration by the critics, and had a very respectable sale of over 30,000 copies. Its successor, *The Pit*, was the third best-selling novel in the United States in 1903, and, like *The Octopus*, was popular in Great Britain as well.[100] As for Jack London, the years between 1900 and 1905 were his most spectacularly successful, as he moved from virtual anonymity to a position as one of the country's most celebrated and successful authors. Almost everything he published during this five-year period was received with both critical and popular acclaim, the highlight coming with the appearance of *The Sea-Wolf* in 1904; featuring as its protagonist the Nordic superman Wolf Larsen, *The Sea-Wolf* quickly outdistanced its competition to become the best-selling American novel of the year.[101] It seems likely that part of the appeal of both London and Norris was their explicit allegiance to popular ideas of race. They reflected public attitudes while at the same time reinforcing and publicizing them.

By the mid-1890s, Anglo-Saxonism permeated the mental outlook of Britons and Americans. This was hardly a surprising development, considering the extent to which Anglo-Saxonism had won the acceptance of the intellectual communities on both sides of the Atlantic. Over the years, race theories had attracted some of the best minds in the English-speaking world, and these people had lent their considerable intellectual and moral support to the cult of Anglo-Saxonism. Biologists joined with historians, theologians with politicians, Boston Brahmins with military officers, business entrepreneurs with poets and novelists, to spin a web of seemingly irrefutable arguments in support of race prejudice. Anglo-Saxonism was a mature intellectual doctrine by the mid-1890s, ready to influence the way Britons and Americans looked at each other and the world in the years of the Anglo-American rapprochement.

3

International Rivalry and the Struggle for Existence

Since most Anglo-Saxonists subscribed to a Darwinian view of world politics, they believed that the principle of natural selection operated in international relations, that weak and "unfit" peoples inevitably went down before strong and "fit" ones. This viewpoint, of course, provided a convenient rationale for imperialism: imperialists perceived the black, brown, and yellow peoples who were subjugated by whites as the losers in the Darwinian struggle. It is interesting to note that the Darwinian conception of world affairs also furnished a strong argument for Anglo-American solidarity. Many Anglo-Saxonists believed that if the two branches of the race failed to cooperate, the Anglo-Saxons themselves might someday become victims of the struggle for existence.

In the years surrounding the turn of the century, the idea was widespread in Great Britain and the United States that racial competition would go on until some one race had grown so powerful that it could dominate all the others, and impress its ideas, arts, and institutions on the rest of the world. For the time being, the Anglo-Saxons might lead all rivals in the struggle for existence, but Anglo-Saxon supremacy could not be guaranteed in the future. The Anglo-Saxon nations had to be constantly on their guard to fend off the challenges of other peoples.

The need for Anglo-American solidarity was a logical corollary of the belief in a continuing racial struggle for supremacy. For over a century, the Anglo-Saxons of England and America had been badly divided and often at each other's throats. During this time, the British had carried almost the entire burden of providing for the defense of the various Anglo-Saxon homelands, including the contribution of the Royal Navy to the defense of the Americas. Yet, as the nineteenth century drew to a close, it was increasingly evident that the British no longer had the resources to stand alone against the Continental powers. The British, it seemed, needed the aid of their fellow Anglo-Saxons in the United States.

For many Anglo-Saxonists, the question of British-American solidarity to maintain the position of the Anglo-Saxon race was of paramount significance. The respected Yale historian George Burton Adams told his countrymen in 1896 that if Anglo-Saxondom were threatened in the future, "there is only one place for us. We must be on the side of our own ideas and institutions and race." Alfred Thayer Mahan had adopted a similar view four years earlier, writing to the British Army officer George Sydenham Clarke in November of 1892: "To work together for our mutual good and if necessary against the rest of the world, would be the highest statesmanship—for in political traditions as well as by blood we are kin, the rest alien." David Mills, Canada's minister of justice, told Americans: "In the highest sense the United States has not, and cannot have, an independent existence. Her fortune is inseparably associated with the race to which she belongs, in which her future is wrapt up, and in which she lives and moves and has her being." In the eyes of men like Adams, Mahan, and Mills, the foremost aim of British and American statesmen should be the promotion of race unity, to insure the well-being and the future success of Anglo-Saxon civilization and all it represented.[1]

To the Anglo-Saxonist, it was obvious which nations, or "races," were serious rivals for power. As one American wrote in 1903: "The world is now, in a practical sense, owned or controlled by five nations: the British Empire, the United States of America, Russia, Germany, and France .... the ... small sovereignties of the world are mere satellites, revolving around these great political planets."[2] The statement was an exaggeration, but an understandable one. Among them, these five nations controlled four-fifths of the earth's land surface and ruled two-thirds of its population. Smaller countries seemed doomed to sink to an ever lower international position in comparison. Anglo-Saxonists naturally concluded from this that their primary competitors for world position were the French, the most virile and energetic representatives of the so-called "Latin race"; the Germans, Teutonic cousins of the Anglo-Saxons; and the Russians, champions of the "Slavic race." These, with the Anglo-Saxons, were the peoples who had proved their fitness in the struggle for existence.

Just as they had fairly definite ideas about their own supposed racial traits, Anglo-Saxonists commonly assigned certain racial characteristics to their Latin, German, and Slavic rivals for power. The stereotypes of these peoples greatly affected the manner in which each was assessed as a potential challenger for world supremacy. A detailed look at the Anglo-Saxonist perception of these rivals as racial types, and as Darwinian competitors, provides insight into the Anglo-Saxonist world view.

The Anglo-Saxonist perception of the so-called Latin race is a familiar one. Latins were held to be sentimental, highly emotional, incontinent, irresponsible, and undisciplined. They were also credulous and superstitious people, who often mistook appearance for reality. They were playful and exceedingly fond of creature comforts; and although they sometimes displayed great physical bravery, they were wanting in perseverance and tenacity. In the realm of politics, Latins were dangerously enamored of the military type of individual, and consequently their governments tended to Caesarism.[3]

Most articulate Britons and Americans considered the Latin race to be the least vigorous of the world's advanced races, and the one least likely to pose a serious threat in the future to Anglo-Saxon predominance. It was a common assumption that the Latin nations were decadent. As a British editorialist observed in 1898:

> Latin Europe—that is to say, roughly, France, Spain, and Italy—sees itself year by year more closely restricted to its boundaries. Italy has been obliged to resign her only foreign possessions; Spain's dependencies daily threaten either to break away or to rot off; France alone...retains her vitality, but in spite of a feverish activity in acquisition shows no real power to expand.[4]

It is not difficult to discover the causes for the widespread belief in Latin decadence. To anyone viewing international politics in the late nineteenth century, it was evident that certain nations, notably Great Britain, Germany, Russia, and the United States, were either holding their own or increasing their influence in the world. The Latin nations, on the other hand, seemed to be on the decline. "Latin Europe has rotted from end to end of the Continent," wrote Brooks Adams.[5] Portugal had not been a significant factor in world affairs for centuries. Italy, poverty-stricken and debt-ridden, could not even manage to defeat the Ethiopians. Spain had been a declining power since the destruction of the Armada, and Spanish impotence, evidenced in the country's feeble campaigns in Morocco and inability to quell the Cuban insurrection, was underscored in the Spanish-American War. The various setbacks suffered by France in the nineteenth century seemed to foreshadow an analogous fate for that country. Beaten at Waterloo and Sedan, France had lost its paramountcy on the Continent. Now it was hampered by a static population, unaggressive industry, shrinking merchant marine, and unprofitable colonial empire. Moreover, France was clearly the junior partner of Russia in the Dual Alliance.

Race theorists found it easy to explain such developments in racial terms: the Latin race, they said, had lost its vigor, and the corruption, steadily spreading from one Latin nation to another, had finally reached the French. "In France, as in the later Roman world, population is decreasing, and there is gross sensuality and licentiousness," wrote Theodore Roosevelt. "France is following Spain in her downward course." The famed Columbia University sociologist Franklin H. Giddings looked down contemptuously on the French as "a people that idly sips its cognac on the boulevards as it lightly takes a trifling part in the *comédie humaine*." Such a nation, Giddings said, "can only go down in the struggle for existence with men [i.e., the Anglo-Saxons] who have learned that happiness, in distinction from idle pleasures, is the satisfaction that comes only with the tingling of the blood, when we surmount the physical and moral obstacles of life."[6]

Even some Frenchmen conceded their inferiority to the Anglo-Saxon powers and set out to find the explanation. The distinguished economist Edmond Demolins, in his study of *Anglo-Saxon Superiority*, said that the root cause lay in the differing educational systems of Latin and Anglo-Saxon countries. Demolins's book was published in Paris in 1897 and went through five editions in two months. Many Frenchmen thought his conclusions were outrageous, but the English translation of the study enjoyed a wide vogue in Great Britain and the United States. Reviewers in British and American periodicals were particularly taken with Demolins's judgment that the Anglo-Saxons were "destined to succeed the Roman Empire in the government of the world."[7]

Thus, on the basis of the seeming decline in France's international fortunes and the prevailing stereotype of the Latin race, Anglo-Saxonists discounted France as a major threat to their supremacy. The day of the Latin was over, and the French, with neither genius nor liking for the tasks which fell on the shoulders of an expanding nation, would soon succumb to the racial decay that had previously ruined the Italians, Spaniards, and Portuguese.[8]

Anglo-Saxonists perceived the alleged "German race" as a much more serious rival for power than the Latins. The Germans, after all, were fellow Teutons, and many of the racial traits commonly attributed to them—frugality, ambition, industriousness, adaptiveness, loyalty, and caution—were characteristics that Britons and Americans admired and often credited to themselves.[9]

Anglo-Saxonists nearly always portrayed the Germans as a powerful and virile race, and for a very good reason: Germany's rising power presented a serious challenge to Great Britain, in particular, and to the United States as well. Not content with being the greatest military power in Europe and Britain's most formidable competitor for foreign trade, Germany began the construction of a big navy at the turn of the century with which to challenge British maritime supremacy. With their security and economic well-being resting almost solely on their foreign trade and control of the seas, the British gradually developed an obsession with the German threat. Occasionally, they expressed their fears in racial terms. In March of 1903, a writer in a British periodical declared:

> When we consider the spirit of irreconcilable hostility against Anglo-Saxondom that pervades the countless expansionist manifestations in Germany emanating from official and semi-official quarters, from professional and mercantile circles, from the clergy and the proletariat, we cannot help being struck by the unanimity of hatred and by the unflinching determination of Germany to erect a German world empire upon the ruins of Anglo-Saxondom.[10]

Americans, too, viewed German power with nervousness and distrust. The so-called "German menace," Tyler Dennett has pointed out, "haunted nearly every [American] diplomatic negotiation of the period."[11] Statesmen in Washington thought it would be a disaster for American interests if Germany won mastery of the seas. Clashes in Samoa, in China during the Boxer uprising, and in Venezuela, as well as a rumored clash at Manila Bay, increased American anxiety. American naval planners kept the fleet concentrated in the Atlantic to meet a feared German attack. John Hay absorbed the Germanophobia of his English friends and declared in 1898: "The Vaterland is all on fire with greed and hatred of us."[12] Rumors of German ambitions in Latin America were constant. Henry Cabot Lodge, for example, told Henry White in February 1900 that he understood the chief object of German naval expansion was the seizure of Brazil as a colonial empire and the breaking down of the Monroe Doctrine.[13] When Theodore Roosevelt came to the White House in 1901, he was convinced that Germany had serious designs on South America and that Berlin intended to test the American fleet at the first opportunity.[14]

The Germans obviously were seen as enemies of the Anglo-Saxon countries, despite the theoretical racial affinity of all Teutonic peoples. This divergence of theory from the facts of international life presented a problem for race-thinkers. Some of them tried to come to terms with the difficulty in a fashion consistent with the tenets of Anglo-Saxonism. They suggested that the Germans and Anglo-Saxons had been separated for so long that they should no longer be thought of as kin. Or they argued that Germany had been seduced by absolutism and had lost the freedom-loving Teutonic spirit; or that the Germans had been corrupted through intermarriage with Latin peoples. Most race-thinkers, however, got around the problem by simply refusing to speak of competition with Germany in racial terms.[15] The Latins and Slavs were frequently referred to as racial enemies, but the Germans, for all their competition with the British and Americans, were only occasionally spoken of in this fashion in either country. In this way, Anglo-Saxonists avoided facing one of the embarrassing defects in their theoretical framework.

Germany was a powerful rival, but in the early years of the twentieth century few Anglo-Saxonists considered Germany to be the greatest menace to the Anglo-Saxon world position. The Germans, after all, faced severe geographical and strategic handicaps. They were squeezed between the allied French and Russian armies on the Continent, and their fleet in 1900 was no match for that of Great Britain, or even those of Russia and France. The German overseas empire was a good deal smaller than the land area of the United States, and almost insignificant when compared with the British, French, and Russian empires. In short, while Germany was clearly a power to be reckoned with by the English-speaking countries, it was not the most serious challenger for racial preeminence and world domination.[16]

That distinction went to the Slav.

It is difficult to overestimate the horrific fascination with which many Britons and Americans, particularly the former, regarded the Russian colossus. They viewed expansion of the Russian Empire almost as a cosmic movement, a gigantic, elemental, irresistible force that overwhelmed anyone and anything that stood in its way. Statesmen and philosophers alike compared Russian expansion to the movement of a glacier, rolling out of the north and each year building a greater volume and a more crushing weight. Prior to the startling revelations of Russian weakness in the Russo-Japanese War, many articulate persons thought the great problem of Europe and of Western civilization was how to contain the Russian Bear.[17]

A look at the map of the world in 1900 defines the problem as Anglo-Saxonists saw it. All across the Asian land mass, in a continuous line of front extending 8,000 miles from the Bosporus to the Sea of Japan, Anglo-Saxon Britain confronted Slavic Russia. A belt of weak, semi-independent buffer states—Turkey, Persia, Afghanistan, Tibet, China—separated Russian territory from Britain's Asian empire and British spheres of influence. In the Crimean War and at the Berlin Conference in 1878, Russia's southward march had been checked; but still the British feared that the Czarist empire might someday succeed in absorbing the buffers, as it had absorbed so many other Asian territories. That would bring the Russians face to face with the British, jeopardizing Britain's positions in the Mediterranean, the Persian Gulf, India, Burma, Malaya, and the Yangtze Valley. Some people thought the very existence of the Empire would be imperiled.[18] The Anglo-Russian duel was continuous in the late nineteenth century, and placed tremendous pressure on the British Empire as it strove to bolster the buffer states. In 1890 the War Office concluded that without allies, Great Britain could not hope to wage a successful war against Russia in defense of Asia. The Czar's armies were too huge, and the Russians were almost immune to Britain's most potent weapon, sea power, because their empire was a continuous land mass, lacking in good harbors and practically self-sufficient economically.[19] No peace seemed possible with such an unrelenting foe. Shortly before the Japanese attack on Port Arthur, the invariably pessimistic Cecil Spring Rice wrote to Mrs. Theodore Roosevelt: "Russia is not a government, it is a growing organism . . ., and you can't get an organism to promise not to grow, though you can, if you like, cut off its extremities."[20] If the Russians succeeded in rolling over Asia, they would weld their conquests into a single, massive power with which to confront the scattered Anglo-Saxon communities. The prospect was as simple—and as terrifying—as that.

Adding to the sense of menace was the anomalous racial character attributed to the Russians. Although their success as a world power seemed to attest to their racial superiority, most Anglo-Saxonists could not help but conceive of them as only semicivilized. They were not quite European; they did not fit into Western civilization. It was part of the Russian enigma that a people so alien to the other dominant races could seemingly pose the gravest threat to the welfare of Anglo-Saxondom.

Many persons thought of the Russians as the latest wave of barbarians out of Asia. After all, wasn't it true that the Russians had once been ruled by Mongols? Josiah Strong belived that the average Russian, despite his European veneer, was an Asiatic at heart. He recalled Napoleon's famous dictum: "Scratch a Russian and you will find a Tartar." Franklin H. Giddings compared the Russians to the "hordes of Asiatic barbarism" that Attila had thrown against Rome. The English author and journalist Edward Dicey drew parallels between the contemporary Russian advance and the westward movements of the Goths, Huns, Tartars, and Turks in centuries past. The blood of all these barbaric peoples flowed in Russian veins, he said, making the Russian presence incompatible with the progress of civilization. Many other observers of world affairs voiced similar sentiments: The Russian, if he was civilized at all, was only partly so.[21]

Of course, the racial characteristics attributed to the Russian people were not at all flattering. Anglo-Saxonists assumed that the stereotyped personality of the Russian peasant—slow, stupid, uncomplaining, superstitious, and intensely loyal to Czar and Church—was racial in nature. Paradoxically, "the Slavic race, ignorant and strangely docile, full of patience and fortitude, is characterized also by a mighty energy, sluggish, indeed, but enduring to the end, and submitting itself readily to outside guidance."[22] It seemed to the Anglo-Saxonist that the very traits that made the Russians so unappealing also made them a formidable foe. The Russian peasant was easily molded by the military class into a mindless cog in the country's immense military machine; and once such soldiers began to move, their patience, stolidity, and unquestioning obedience to their leaders made them almost impossible to stop. Eventually, they wore down resistance.[23]

It appeared to most persons that the clash between Anglo-Saxon and Slav was a contest between freedom and despotism. Everyone knew that the foundation of Anglo-Saxon civilization was individual liberty, and that the Russian government historically was one of the most despotic on earth. "The Anglo-Saxon is the supreme representative of civil and religious liberty; the Slav is the supreme representative of absolutism, both in state and church," said Josiah Strong.[24] Anglo-Saxonists generally portrayed the encounter with the Slav as an ideological conflict between democracy and absolutism, a clash of incompatible ideals.[25]

Russia's conception of its national and racial mission broadened the ideological implications of the rivalry. The Russians, like the British and Americans, were imbued with a sense of destiny and a mystical faith in the superiority of their institutions. Important elements in the society were chauvinistic toward the West, and believed deeply in Pan-Slavism and Russia's civilizing mission in Asia. A number of influential Englishmen worried that Pan-Slavism would result ultimately in Russia's absorbing the Slavic nations of eastern Europe, and then dominating the rest of the continent. Arthur Balfour feared for the future if the Czar's empire were not blocked. "What kind of Europe will it be," he asked W. T. Stead in 1898, "dominated by the Slavs...?"[26] Indiana Senator Albert Beveridge returned to the United States from a 1901 tour of Siberia and the Far East to report that he had been told by a

Czarist official: "Yes, you may be stronger now, richer now, than we are, but we shall be stronger tomorrow than you—yes, and all the world; for the future abides with the Slav!" Beveridge believed St. Petersburg was intent on Russianizing all Asia, from Jerusalem to Peking.[27] Other men in public office, including Theodore Roosevelt, applauded Russian efforts to bring order and stability to the shaky Chinese Empire, but feared that the government of Nicholas II might be plotting to annex northern China and man Russian armies with millions of Chinese peasants. The prospect, said Roosevelt, was "very appalling."[28]

What the future seemed to hold was a death struggle between the Anglo-Saxon and the Slav. To some people, it seemed as if two thousand years of history, from the time of the Greek wars against the Persians, had been leading up to this consummation. Henry Adams recalled Tocqueville's famous prophecy that the future would be divided between Russia and the United States.[29] Other Americans consulted works of Teutonic history and learned that for fifteen hundred years their race had been moving steadily westward. The Anglo-Saxons began their journey in ancient Germany, crossed the cold waters of the North Sea in the fifth and sixth centuries, and reached North America in the seventeenth. In the next two hundred years, they subdued the North American continent and moved on to the Pacific. Meanwhile, on the other side of the world, the Slavs had been rolling eastward across Asia for generations, conquering barbarian tribes and laying claim to the vast, sparsely populated regions of Siberia and Central Asia. Now, as the nineteenth century drew to a close, these two masterful races were coming face to face for the first time, in China. China would probably be the scene of their fight for supremacy. Americans began to adopt this view as soon as it became apparent that the United States was about to become more deeply involved in Far Eastern affairs. Josiah Strong reported an incident that occurred at a dinner in New York City a few months after the Battle of Manila Bay. Benjamin Kidd was the honored guest. Rising to deliver a brief speech, Kidd remarked that he believed "the gun fired by Admiral Dewey in the Bay of Manila was the most important historical event since the Battle of Waterloo." Professor Franklin H. Giddings interrupted to go Kidd one better. Dewey's victory, he said, "was the most important historical event since Charles Martel turned back the Moslems, because the great question of the twentieth century is whether the Anglo-Saxon or the Slav is to impress his civilization on the world."[30]

The idea of an irrepressible conflict between Anglo-Saxon and Slav infected many British and American intellectuals and politicians in the years between the Spanish-American War and Japan's stunning victories of 1904-5. The fact that four of the six homelands of the Anglo-Saxon race—the United States, Canada, Australia, and New Zealand—were ranged around the Pacific basin served to bolster the confidence of some people, as did Anglo-Saxon supremacy on the seas. These advantages would be nullified, however, if the race were not united—if it were not, as a British military officer remarked, "strong in the strength of union."[31] The United States and the British Empire had to support each other, because in the struggle for life among the great and growing races, a defeat suffered by one Anglo-Saxon state would weaken the race as a whole, while a victory would increase the security of all its members and promote the influence of Anglo-Saxon principles and ideals. In the cruel and dangerous world of power politics, the salvation and perpetuation of the Anglo-Saxon race was a powerful motive for cooperation between the United States and Great Britain.

4

Anglo-Saxonism and the Shapers of Foreign Policy

Anglo-Saxonism could not have significantly affected Anglo-American relations if important diplomats, government officials, and foreign policy theoreticians in both countries had not adopted Anglo-Saxonist precepts. In Great Britain, two leading figures in the third Salisbury cabinet, Joseph Chamberlain and Arthur Balfour, were enthusiastic proponents of Anglo-Saxon solidarity. Cecil Spring Rice, because of his close personal connections with a number of powerful American political figures, was one of the most influential Anglo-Saxonists in the British diplomatic corps. Many other important British officials subscribed to Anglo-Saxonist ideas, but out of them all, Chamberlain, Balfour, and Spring Rice had the most direct effect on Anglo-American relations.

Most members of the imperialist elite in the United States were believers in the racial affinity of Englishmen and Americans. This elite was a closely knit little group of intellectuals and politicians who provided powerful support for a more active American role in international affairs. The leading members were Theodore Roosevelt, Henry Cabot Lodge, John Hay, and Alfred Thayer Mahan. These men moved in the same social circles, shared similar ideas, and frequently corresponded or consulted personally with one another. Mahan contributed to the group his abilities and reputation as a widely respected advocate of a more vigorous American foreign policy; while Roosevelt, Lodge, and Hay all occupied positions from which they could either make national policy or influence its direction. All of these individuals were able and energetic, and all of them, in varying degrees, accepted Anglo-Saxonism and desired an improvement in Anglo-American relations. Hence some of the same people who helped lead the nation into foreign war and overseas expansion at the end of the nineteenth century, also actively promoted the rapprochement between Great Britain and the United States.[1]

Any discussion of Anglo-Saxonism within the American foreign policy community should begin with Theodore Roosevelt. Roosevelt's racism was not of the conventional sort. In principle, he maintained that people should be judged on their individual merits. A good man was a good man, whatever his race, said Roosevelt—although he held that superior races produced "good men" in larger proportions than did inferior races.[2] Roosevelt had no doubts about the virtues of Booker T. Washington, though he considered the Negro race generally to be primitive. He had enormous respect for the Japanese, but thought most Orientals inferior. Roosevelt also opposed the intolerant nativism of many of his contemporaries, while at the same time personally favoring immigration restriction. When Roosevelt spoke of northern Europeans as members of the "higher races," it was in a relative rather than an absolute sense. As he wrote in 1905: Two thousand years ago, "to the Greek and the Roman the most dreaded and yet in a sense the most despised barbarian was the white-skinned, blue-eyed and red or yellow-haired barbarian of the North.... It would not seem possible to the Greek or Roman of that day that this northern barbarian should ever become part of the civilized world—his equal in civilization. The racial differences seemed too great."[3] For Roosevelt, evolution was a continuous process that went on throughout history. The races that were "superior" today would decay and decline tomorrow, and new races would rise to take their places.

Although he used the word "race" as loosely as most of his fellow Americans, applying it indiscriminately to nations, ethnic groups, and language families, Roosevelt was aware of some of the pitfalls of this practice. He refused to use the term "Anglo-Saxon" to describe modern Englishmen and Americans, saying that the appellation was legitimate only when applied to the peoples who dominated England between the fifth and eleventh centuries. In part because he himself was of Dutch rather than English descent, he preferred to describe the modern inhabitants of Britain and the United States as the "English-speaking people" or the "English-speaking race." He held that this "race" was united by blood, culture, and world view, as well as by language.[4]

Roosevelt recognized that the United States was a nation made up of many races and ethnic groups. While he was opposed to the intermixture of "higher" and "lower" races, he believed the intermixing of peoples of northern and western European blood, as had happened in the United States, was a healthy thing. The English themselves were the descendants of Celts, Germans, Scandinavians, Normans, and Dutchmen (he had to include the Dutch in order to include himself), he said, so the interbreeding of these peoples in the United States only repeated the original interbreeding that created the English-speaking people. Roosevelt held that the new intermixing actually strengthened the American racial stock.[5]

Granting that Roosevelt's racism was more refined than that of many of his contemporaries, and based on a more thorough knowledge of English and American history, Roosevelt can still be seen as one of the leading proponents of the superiority of the race that he preferred to call "English-speaking." In books, articles, letters, and speeches, he lauded the virtues of this race and spoke proudly of its achievements. In 1889 he declared that "the spread of the English-speaking peoples over the world's waste spaces" was "the most striking feature" of the past three hundred years. In 1897 he told Augustus Lowell the same thing. Four years later, he proclaimed the expansion of the English-speaking race "perhaps the greatest fact in all history."[6] He was still of the same opinion when he left the White House in 1909.

The origins of Roosevelt's pride in the English-speaking race lay in his intellectual background. He was trained in history at Harvard during the heyday of the Teutonic origins theory, and later he sat in the front row at John W. Burgess's lectures at Columbia, listening with rapt attention to Burgess's extolling of Teutonic virtues. By the time he began work on his six-volume study *The Winning of the West*, Roosevelt was thoroughly convinced of the validity of the Teutonic interpretation. The "English race," he believed, possessed "a perfectly continuous history," stretching from its beginnings in northern Germany down to the present day. He portrayed the conquest of the Great Plains and the Far West by American pioneers as a chapter in the race expansion of the English-speaking peoples, and the culmination of two thousand years of westward movement.[7]

Roosevelt was also deeply influenced by the racial Darwinism that was a common intellectual property of his generation. Born just one year prior to the publication of *The Origin of Species*, he grew up in a society permeated with ideas derived from Darwin and Spencer. He read Darwin, Huxley, Fiske, and other evolutionists. Asked to deliver the Romanes Lecture at Oxford University the year after he left the White House, Roosevelt spoke on the subject "Biological Analogies in History." His words to the faculty and students at Oxford were explicit. "Of course there is no exact parallelism between the birth, growth, and death of species in the animal world and the birth, growth, and death of societies in the world of man," he declared. "Yet there is a certain parallelism. There are strange analogies; it may be there are homologies."[8] Roosevelt firmly believed that international rivalry was a Darwinian struggle for existence, and that force determined the final outcome. The nation or race that was unwarlike inevitably went down before more adventurous and combative rivals.[9] However, Roosevelt thought the greatest source of strength in a people was "character"—loosely defined by him as a blend of self-mastery with a high sense of morality. Character gave rise to hardihood and virtue. A people with character demonstrated decency, vitality, courage, fair dealing, and moral uprightness. An enemy could not easily overcome such a people. Roosevelt had no doubt that, for the time being at least, character was most highly developed in the English-speaking race. He worried incessantly, however, that overconfidence and the profusion of material prosperity would undermine the race's character and lead to decadence.[10]

Like many other Anglo-Saxonists, Roosevelt had clear ideas about the racial rivals of the English-speaking people. He was not worried about the Latin race, he said, because the day of the Latin was over. Henceforth the Latin peoples would have to look to the past for their glories.[11] His feelings about the Germans tended to fluctuate with developments in German-American relations. He admired German military power and imperial ambitions, but he was determined that German expansionism should not imperil American interests. Basically, Roosevelt was confident of the ability of the English-speaking people to beat back any challenge from Germany. He believed the Germans were a superior people who might, for a generation or two, be formidable competitors of Britons and Americans. But ultimately, he said, the character, opulent empires, and military prowess of the English-speaking race would decide the outcome of the rivalry. In a hundred years, the Germans would be of small consequence.[12]

Roosevelt's most serious concern was with the Russians, or Slavs. He thought the Slavs clearly the second most powerful race in the world, and he expected them to rise to first place if the English-speaking peoples grew effete. For the time being, though, as he told Cecil Spring Rice in 1901, "the Russian growth—the growth of the Slav—is slow.... Russia's day is yet afar off. I think the twentieth century will still be the century of the men who speak English."[13] While conceding a brilliant future to the Slavs, Roosevelt held that Englishmen and Americans could still "outbuild, out-administer and out-fight any Russians you could find from St. Petersburg to Sebastopol or Vladivostock [sic]." The Russians might be expanding in Asia, but there were still great waste spaces in Australia, South Africa, and North America which the English-speaking peoples would eventually fill with vigorous populations.[14]

Roosevelt's beliefs on the subject of race inevitably influenced his dealings with Great Britain. One of the most careful students of Roosevelt's foreign policy has concluded that his conduct of foreign relations cannot be understood without a comprehension of his faith in "the oneness of the American and British interest and his conviction that in combination the Americans and the British could dominate the world—to the advantage of civilization."[15]

Roosevelt's many British acquaintances strengthened this intellectual predilection. Like many other young, upper-class Americans, he visited England regularly in the 1880s and 1890s. His visits, and his reputation as a historian and political reformer, brought him into contact with such notables as Joseph Chamberlain, James Bryce, John Morley, and Viscount Goschen. His second marriage took place in London, with Cecil Spring Rice as best man. Roosevelt met Rudyard Kipling in 1890, and continued to see him at irregular intervals for the next ten years. His tentmate during the Cuban campaign was the British military observer, Arthur Lee. In later years, Lee served as an M.P., a cabinet minister, and as one of Roosevelt's private lines of communication to the British government. Significantly, most of Roosevelt's British friends were Anglo-Saxonists.[16]

It cannot be denied, however, that Roosevelt's attitude toward the English was not always friendly. In fact, until the conduct of the English during the Spanish-American War convinced him of their good intentions, Roosevelt was sometimes given to anti-English outbursts. Such outbursts reflected in part his expansive American nationalism, and in part his disdain for the Anglomania of many of his upper-class countrymen. In 1895, on hearing of his sister's engagement, he was thankful that it wasn't to an Englishman. He was willing to go to war over the Venezuelan question in 1895–96, and as late as February 1898 he could speak of driving the English out of Canada. Rudyard Kipling recalled that on his first meeting with Roosevelt, the latter had thanked God that he himself had not one drop of English blood.[17]

Roosevelt was always an American first, but after 1898 he never doubted that Englishmen and Americans had more in common than any other two peoples, and that the fate of each was caught up in the fate of the other. "I believe in the expansion of great nations," he told his friend Spring Rice in 1899. " . . . In the long run I suppose all nations pass away, and then the great thing is to have left the record of the nation that counts—the record left by the Romans—the record that will be left by the English-speaking peoples."[18] The welfare and greatness of the race was one of Roosevelt's chief concerns, as a historian, a publicist, a politician, and as president of the United States.

Henry Cabot Lodge, Roosevelt's closest personal friend since they worked together in 1884 to try to block the nomination of James G. Blaine for the presidency, won a reputation during his Senate career as an unrelenting Anglophobe. The reputation was only partly deserved. Lodge had sharply conflicting feelings toward Britain; sometimes he admired the British, more often he distrusted them. These conflicting feelings gave rise to a tug of war in Lodge's mind that, in the opinion of one historian, warped

Lodge's judgment where Anglo-American relations were concerned.[19]

Lodge's career abounds with examples of his animosity toward the British. In the 1890s he warned the Senate repeatedly of British efforts to encircle the United States with naval and military strongpoints. He accused the British during the Venezuela boundary dispute of deliberately violating the Monroe Doctrine, and welcomed the opportunity to seize Canada if war came. In 1896 he wrote to Arthur Balfour complaining that England had pursued a policy "of almost studied unfriendliness" towards the United States ever since the American Revolution.[20] When the British refused to ratify the first Hay-Pauncefote treaty in 1901, Lodge charged them with double-dealing, and urged unilateral abrogation of the Clayton-Bulwer treaty by the United States. As a member of the tribunal charged with settling the Alaska boundary question in 1903, Lodge seemed to take malicious pleasure in saying that Britain, not Canada, was delaying a settlement.

Such incidents illustrate one side—the most obvious side—of Lodge's feelings toward Britain. Yet the other side exercised almost as great an influence on his thoughts and actions. Lodge was a Boston aristocrat, the son of a wealthy China-trade merchant and a descendant of the Massachusetts High Federalist George Cabot. As his friend and teacher Henry Adams pointed out, Lodge, like many other genteel Bostonians, was "English to the last fibre of his thought—saturated with English literature, English tradition, English taste."[21] He disdained the vulgar masses and the vulgar plutocrats alike, and was much more comfortable with English friends like Arthur Balfour and Cecil Spring Rice than with the poverty-stricken Irish laborers who comprised a large part of his Massachusetts constituency.[22] His anti-English tirades were in part an attempt to appeal to this constituency, and in part a reaction against the sometimes condescending attitude of the British upper class toward the United States. Like Roosevelt, Lodge was a fervent American nationalist, and he resented British pretensions of superiority. He was also envious of Britain's dominant position in international politics, and uneasy about the extent to which English values dominated his own life. Hence he could manage to manifest at one and the same time a pride in English culture and traditions, and acrimony toward Great Britain.[23] The former tendency came to the fore during the Anglo-American good feeling of 1898, and for several years thereafter exercised a strong influence on Lodge's perception of the international scene. In 1900, Alfred Thayer Mahan rejoiced that Lodge's opinion "concerning the community of interest between outselves & Great Britain in some of the great questions of the future" coincided with his own.[24]

Lodge's fitful support for the British-American rapprochement after 1898 resulted in part from a prideful Anglo-Saxonism he acquired early in life. Like Roosevelt, Lodge was trained in history at Harvard during the years when the Teutonic origins theory dominated American historiography. His formal training went far beyond that of Roosevelt, however. He took a doctorate in history, writing a dissertation on Anglo-Saxon land law. In his dissertation, which was researched and written under the direction of Henry Adams, Lodge purported to find direct links between ancient Anglo-Saxon legal doctrines and modern constitutional liberties.[25] The Teutonic origins theory was an intellectual load Lodge carried with him ever after. His later historical works were fine examples of the Teutonic interpretation.[26] At times the influence of his historical training was evident in his speeches on the Senate floor, as when he embellished the 1900 debates on establishing a government for the Philippines with a discussion of the contrasting racial histories and tendencies of Anglo-Saxons and Filipinos.[27]

Lodge's Anglo-Saxonism was accentuated during his long fight to secure passage in the Congress of legislation restricting immigration from southern and eastern Europe. Lodge was a warm supporter of unrestricted immigration in the 1870s and early 1880s, when Massachusetts factories required cheap labor and the old immigration from northern and western Europe still predominated. As the sources of immigration changed in the late 1880s, however, Lodge reversed his position and became one of the most powerful adversaries of the unrestricted flow of new immigrants. As a congressman in 1891, he introduced a bill which would have required that all immigrants be able to read and write their own language. The effect of such a measure, as Lodge well knew, would have been to exclude most of the new immigrants from entry into the United States. Lodge directed public attention to his literacy bill by publishing two articles in leading periodicals, explaining the alleged dangers of unrestricted immigration. In one article, "The Distribution of Ability in the United States," Lodge used the six-volume *Appletons' Cyclopaedia of American Biography* to classify by "race" about fourteen thousand successful Americans. He pointed out that over seventy percent of these successful people were of English descent, while nearly all the rest traced their ancestry either to other parts of the British Isles or to other "Teutonic" countries. Only nineteen individuals were of southern or eastern European descent. Lodge concluded from these figures that Americans must cease letting into the country hordes of people who were practically incapable of major achievement, and who contributed little or nothing to the national well-being.[28]

Lodge's 1891 bill failed to become law, but for years thereafter he continued to work for a literacy requirement as a tool for blocking the new immigration. His determination increased in 1895, when, during a summer tour of Europe, he came across the works of the French race theorist Gustave Le Bon. Le Bon said that the English were the purest and noblest European race, and the great hope of mankind. He warned, however, that the continued vitality of the English would be endangered if they intermingled with inferior races. Such intermingling would inevitably degrade English society and produce a nation of morally deficient half-breeds. Lodge was fascinated by Le Bon's theories, and wrote to Roosevelt recommending that he read some of the Frenchman's writings.[29]

On his return to the United States, Lodge, now the junior senator from Massachusetts and a member of the Committee on Immigration, introduced a new literacy bill drawn up by the Boston-based Immigration Restriction League. During the fierce debate that followed, Lodge made clear his conviction that the new immigrants represented alien races threatening the Anglo-Saxon race of the United States. Relying heavily on Teutonist history and on Le Bon, Lodge praised the racially inherent energy, willpower, religiosity, and morality of Anglo-Saxons, and warned against the "breeding out" of these qualities through intermixture with "lower races."[30]

The Lodge literacy bill finally passed the Senate in December of 1896, and, having met the approval of the House, was sent to President Cleveland. The President, however, vetoed the bill. The frustrated Lodge reintroduced the literacy measure in 1898, 1902, 1903, and 1904, but it never again won congressional approval.[31]

Lodge's efforts to maintain the racial purity of Americans undoubtedly heightened his Anglo-Saxonism, and thus contributed to his willingness to pursue rapprochement with Great Britain after 1898. His support was important for two reasons. First, from the mid-1890s onward, Lodge was widely recognized in the Senate as an intelligent and articulate "specialist" in the area of foreign affairs, and as a leading voice on the Foreign Relations Committee. Second, with the accession of Theodore Roosevelt to the presidency in 1901, Lodge took on the role of intimate friend and trusted adviser of the president. Frequently, in matters affecting the relations between the United States and Great Britain, the Anglo-Saxonist Roosevelt sought out the opinion of the Anglo-Saxonist Lodge.[32]

If Henry Cabot Lodge was sometimes not above giving a spiteful twist to the lion's tail, John Hay was the most pronounced Anglophile among the shapers of American foreign policy. An associate of Lodge since 1887, and an old friend of the Roosevelt family, Hay was a product of rural Illinois who adopted the tastes and prejudices of the Eastern gentry. He married into great wealth, and his wife's money allowed him to set himself up as a "gentleman of culture." His Washington residence at 800 Sixteenth Street was run on a modified British pattern.[33] He made frequent trips to Great Britain in the 1880s and 1890s, often staying at the Scottish estate of his friend Andrew Carnegie. Through his association with Henry Adams and Cecil Spring Rice, Hay came to know the English political leadership well. Among his English acquaintances were William Harcourt, James Bryce, Arthur Balfour, Joseph Chamberlain, and Lord Curzon. Hay was a witty and charming man, much in demand by English socialites as a dinner guest. He found the attention flattering, and was so taken with the country and its titled ruling class that at one point he considered following in the footsteps of Henry James and going to live in England permanently.[34]

Hay worked hard in the campaign of 1896 to secure the election of William McKinley, in hopes that his reward might be the London ambassadorship. When his hopes were realized, he made the most of the opportunity. One of his biographers states that Hay's seventeen months as ambassador to the Court of St. James were "the happiest months of his life."[35] When he was called home in the summer of 1898 to become secretary of state, he was full of regrets. He wrote to his wife to say it was a pity he should have to abandon the charms of England so soon; it grieved him deeply.[36] Hay's departure from England had no lessening effort on his regard for that country, however. Theodore Roosevelt probably would have been seriously affronted if he had known that his secretary of state wrote to Arthur Balfour on Balfour's becoming prime minister in 1902 to congratulate him on his "accession to the most important official post known to modern history."[37]

There was a significant amount of Anglo-Saxonism underlying Hay's love of England. Many of his English acquaintances were outspoken proponents of Anglo-Saxon superiority and racial mission. Hay knew Rudyard Kipling well enough to play host to him at his New Hampshire summer house in 1892. At about this same time, Hay, who was a poet of some reputation, composed a sonnet hailing England as "the cradle of our race."[38] Like most of his countrymen, however, Hay felt his Anglo-Saxon pride most deeply during the Spanish-American War. Addressing the guests at the Easter banquet of the Lord Mayor of London in April 1898, he declared that "a sanction like that of religion" underlay British-American friendship: "We are bound by a tie which we did not forge and which we cannot break; we are joint ministers of the same sacred mission of liberty and progress, charged with duties which we cannot evade by the imposition of irresistible hands."[39]

Hay thus looked at American foreign policy through the eyes of a passionate Anglophile and a convinced Anglo-Saxonist. These beliefs helped shape his policy toward Great Britain in the years he ran the State Department. One of his biggest regrets as secretary of state was that public and Senate opposition made a treaty of alliance between the United States and Great Britain "an unattainable dream." But, as he wrote to Henry White in September of 1899: "As long as I stay here no action shall be taken contrary to my conviction that the one indispensable feature of our foreign policy should be a friendly understanding with England."[40]

Alfred Thayer Mahan's military background set him apart from political figures like Hay, Lodge, and Roosevelt. This professional naval officer, whose brilliantly articulated views on sea power and expansion provided much of the intellectual rationale for the extension of American power beyond the country's continental boundaries, was an early convert to Anglo-Saxonism. His own lineage was predominantly Irish, and he was only one-fourth English; but he insisted that as far as he understood his own personality, the English strain usually predominated. Mahan was not a "pure" Anglo-Saxon, but he wanted to be.[41] Five years before the publication of his first and most famous work, *The Influence of Sea Power upon History*, he was already convinced that "the best hope of the world" lay in the union of the two branches of the Anglo-Saxon race.[42]

Mahan first met Theodore Roosevelt in 1887, when Roosevelt came to the Naval War College to lecture on the War of 1812. The two found that they held many views in common, and they soon became fast friends. Through Roosevelt, Mahan met Henry Cabot Lodge. After the publication of *The Influence of Sea Power* in 1890, these three men became mutual advisers and proponents of an expansive American foreign policy. Roosevelt published reviews of all four of the books that Mahan wrote between 1890 and 1897, heaping praise on all of them.[43]

Prior to the Spanish-American War, Mahan was better known in Great Britain than he was in his home country, and his ideas were certainly a good deal more effective there in influencing governmental policy. The *Sea Power* book was largely a telling of the heroism of British seamen and the glories of the British Navy, and while it was not widely read in the United States, it created a sensation in Britain. Lord Rosebery, the Liberal prime minister, declared that no literary work in his time had aroused such enthusiasm in the British people. Mahan's theories stimulated naval building programs in several European countries, but nowhere were they more important than in Britain. When Captain Mahan visited England as commander of the cruiser *Chicago* in

1894, he was lionized by the most eminent persons in the country. Queen Victoria herself received him, as did Prime Minister Rosebery, most members of the cabinet, the First Lord of the Admiralty, the Prince of Wales, the Duke of York, the Lord Mayor of London, and a host of naval and military officers. He was proclaimed a genius and a prophet. Oxford and Cambridge presented him with honorary degrees. He was credited with having discovered the source of Britain's national success: sea power.[44]

Mahan was thus a theoretician whose ideas were known and respected in both Great Britain and the United States, and whose writings provided an intellectual basis in both countries for a closer understanding between them. His primary influence on the shaping of American diplomacy after 1890 was as an influential expositor of what he called the "one true policy" for the United States. This one true policy contained two elements. The first and best-known was Mahan's call for the expansion of American naval power and the acquisition of overseas bases to serve the ships. The second was Mahan's "great desire," as he put it in 1897, "to promote a unity of feeling, and a sense of common interest," between the United States and Great Britain.[45] He was, he said, a race patriot. He believed that the United States and Britain shared a common racial heritage and a common destiny, and that they should work together to safeguard and promote the interests of the race as a whole.[46]

Through his contacts with Roosevelt, Lodge, and other imperialists, the popularity of his ideas with expansionist senators and congressmen, his following in Great Britain, and the influence of his many books and newspaper and periodical articles, Mahan became a highly effective advocate of Anglo-American cooperation. "It is not by directly forcing this thought [of the general integrity and beneficence of British expansion] down their throats," he told one of his English friends in 1897, "... but by a frequent recurrence to it in various connections that I seek this aim"—an Anglo-American understanding. The technique was a potent one.[47]

Mahan's desire for an Anglo-American understanding was in part the result of his belief in racial Darwinism. His writings were filled with references to the "struggle for existence" among nations and races, and the role of warfare as the means of eliminating the weak from international competition.[48] Mahan's military background made such ideas all the more congenial to him.

Mahan was likewise convinced that the future welfare of mankind would best be served by the advancement of the Anglo-Saxon race. The Anglo-Saxon, he believed, uniquely embodied the principles of political freedom, self-government, and the rule of law. In Mahan's eyes, the worth of these principles, and of the race that adhered so tenaciously to them, had been proved through centuries of continuous existence and onward development. The two great branches of the race owed it to mankind to work together to preserve and extend their singular racial heritage. Human happiness depended on it.[49]

Thus, while Mahan consistently deprecated talk of a formal treaty of alliance between the two Anglo-Saxon powers, he was always a proponent of diplomatic and military cooperation wherever he deemed the overall interests of the race to be at stake. He believed a formal alliance was both a political impossibility and a hindrance to freedom of action, but he also believed that an alliance was not necessary to a good understanding. Britons and Americans were of one race and one race spirit, and gradually they would move toward a common racial outlook and a recognition of common interests. He thought that both sentiment and sound policy mandated such a course, and he was determined to do what he could to move the United States in that direction.[50] His deep Anglo-Saxonist convictions underlay many of the writings that were read so eagerly by Americans looking for guidance after 1898 as their country joined the ranks of the world powers.

The leading Anglo-Saxonists among British officials lacked the group coherence, but none of the influence, of the American imperialist elite. The Unionist cabinet responsible for the formulation of British policy throughout the years of the rapprochement was formed in June of 1895. The Marquess of Salisbury was prime minister and foreign secretary. His nephew Arthur Balfour was First Lord of the Treasury and leader of the Conservative party in the House of Commons. Balfour also handled the Foreign Office during his uncle's frequent illnesses; he became prime minister in 1902 and served until the Liberals returned to power in 1905. Joseph Chamberlain, who had broken with Gladstone over Irish Home Rule in 1886 and led a group of Liberal-Unionists into a political merger with the Conservatives, was colonial secretary in the Salisbury cabinet. These three men—Salisbury, Balfour, and Chamberlain—were the primary shapers of British foreign policy, although Lord Lansdowne became an increasingly important figure after he took over the duties of foreign secretary from the ailing Salisbury in October of 1900.

Lord Salisbury himself was no Anglo-Saxonist. Old and set in his ways (he was already 65 when he became prime minister for the third time), Salisbury took a firmly realistic view of international relations. He could see no place for sentiment in foreign policy. In his opinion, friendship and cooperation between nations could be based only on mutual interests. Any other attachment was fleeting.[51] Moreover, Salisbury disliked and feared the racial animosities he saw developing among the Great Powers. Just as he believed that sentiment had no place in international amity, so he held that unreasoning hatred had no place in international rivalry. As far as relations with the United States were concerned, Salisbury was not prepared to pursue actively an Anglo-American understanding. He was a resolute defender of Britain's traditional policy of "splendid isolation"; and besides, he doubted the reliability of the American government and felt slightly disdainful toward American society. A calm, reserved, aristocratic, and cynical man, Salisbury thought American society vulgar, and he distrusted the emotionalism that often found its way into American foreign policy. Fortunately for Anglo-American relations, Salisbury usually let subordinates take the initiative in dealings with the United States.[52]

Perhaps the ablest of Salisbury's subordinates, and the chief exponent of collaboration with the United States, was Joseph Chamberlain. Chamberlain's personal character—erratic, impulsive, emotional, and flamboyant (his personal emblems were an orchid in the lapel and a monocle)—was just the opposite of Salisbury's, as were his views on a number of important foreign policy topics. He was convinced that Britain could no longer stand alone in a Europe increasingly dominated by two opposing alliance systems. Hence he advocated a federation of the Empire, the abandonment of isolation, and the forging of alliances to secure Britain's far-flung interests. Two of his most consistent beliefs were in the efficacy of sentimental attachments between nations, and in the important role which an Anglo-American alliance was to play in the future history of the world.[53]

Chamberlain was probably the most popular figure in British politics when he entered the cabinet in 1895, and undoubtedly he was the most outspoken and persuasive imperialist. A consummate politician, he could have had any of the more important cabinet posts (except, of course, prime minister), but his long involvement with the expansion of the Empire and with the imperial federation movement led him to request the Colonial Office. With his enormous talents, Chamberlain soon turned that traditionally secondary post into a sort of "co-premiership" with Salisbury. At times he dominated the cabinet, and at one point in 1898 he almost wrested control of policy from Salisbury's hands.

Chamberlain was one of the most zealous Anglo-Saxonists in Britain. While not an extremist like Cecil Rhodes, he readily accepted the prevailing race theories of the day and unceasingly preached the superiority of the Anglo-Saxon race and its obligation to extend Anglo-Saxon civilization to "backward" peoples. "I am an Imperialist, and proud of the name," he declared.[54] He read the works of the Teutonist historians, and of racial Darwinists like Benjamin Kidd. Kipling delighted him. As a sponsor of the imperial federation movement, he was familiar with the racial arguments in favor of federation with the white colonies. Chamberlain was convinced that the Anglo-Saxon race was the great governing race of the world; that it was called to empire; and that the unity of all its branches was essential both to its future security and to the fulfillment of its mission.[55]

As might be expected from a fervent Anglo-Saxonist, Chamberlain was a warm friend of the United States. His American acquaintances included Roosevelt, Lodge, Hay, and Mahan. His third wife, Mary Endicott, was the daughter of Grover Cleveland's first secretary of war. He met her while in Washington in 1887, where he negotiated an abortive treaty on the North American fisheries. Long before he took an American wife, however, Chamberlain had developed a sentimental attachment to the United States. He was much moved by the ideas concerning Anglo-American racial affinity that appeared in books like Charles W. Dilke's *Greater Britain* and J. R. Seeley's *Expansion of England*. In the 1880s he held out the hope that imperial federation might lead eventually to a federation of all Anglo-Saxon states. "I refuse to speak or think of the United States as a foreign nation," he told a Toronto audience in 1887. "They are our flesh and blood."[56]

Chamberlain believed that race feeling was one of the strongest sentiments binding nations together, and he hoped that eventually race feeling would draw the United States and Great Britain together in an Anglo-Saxon alliance. He appealed to the race patriotism of both countries during the Venezuela boundary dispute, and he was delighted at the explosion of race feeling that occurred in 1898. In a widely noticed article, he told Americans that the day was at hand for the realization of his dream of an Anglo-Saxon alliance. Such an accord, he said, would guarantee the security of Anglo-Saxon civilization and the peace of the world. It would establish Anglo-Saxon military and naval supremacy so firmly that no power or combination of powers would dare challenge it.[57] From 1898 until his resignation from the cabinet in 1903, Chamberlain consistently spoke out in favor of an alliance, or at least an informal understanding, between the United States and Great Britain. At one point, as will be seen in a later chapter, he favored inclusion of Germany in the scheme, and the forging of a grand alliance to block Russian expansion in Asia.

Arthur Balfour was the other leading Anglo-Saxonist in the Unionist cabinet. An aristocratic "philosopher-statesman," Balfour was charming, self-confident, and intellectually brilliant. He was also the indispensable figure in the third Salisbury cabinet. The prime minister trusted him implicitly, and Chamberlain liked and admired him. Balfour tempered the relationship between Salisbury and the colonial secretary, and helped keep their personal disagreements over policy from developing into a split within the Unionist coalition.[58]

Like Chamberlain, Balfour was a devotee of Anglo-Saxon superiority and a supporter of Anglo-American friendship and collaboration. He was, he told Henry White, "the most earnest advocate of a harmonious co-operation between the two great Anglo-Saxon States."[59] Apparently he first awoke to the need for an understanding between the two countries during the Venezuela boundary affair, when he declared that war between them would be a racial civil war. From that time onward, Balfour was determined that friendship with the United States should be a touchstone of British foreign policy. He worked continually for good feeling and collaboration between the two powers, emphasizing in his speeches and correspondence the ties of race, language, law, literature, and world view that united them.[60] Balfour was always "an American," his associate John S. Sandars said in 1909: "he never allows the expression 'foreigner' or 'foreign State' to be used in speaking of America or Americans."[61]

Balfour's absorption in racial Darwinist and Anglo-Saxonist doctrine is revealed most clearly in a document he wrote in 1909 entitled "The Possibility of an Anglo-Saxon Confederation." Though composed after the period with which we are concerned, this document reflects his earlier ideas, and marks a culmination of his thinking on the subject of Anglo-Saxon unity. In great detail, Balfour envisioned a near future in which the whole world was divided up into a few great "racial states," representing the Anglo-Saxon, Slavic, German, Latin, Asiatic, Turko-Mohammedan, and South American "races." The Slavic state, an expanded Russian Empire, extended from Hungary and the Balkans eastward to the North Pacific. Germany had absorbed Holland, Denmark, and much of Switzerland, and dominated central Europe. The Latin federation counterbalanced the Germans by loosely uniting Spain, Portugal, France, Italy, Belgium, Greece, and part of Switzerland. China and Japan formed the core of the Asiatic race-state, while the Mohammedan race-state was built around a rejuvenated Turkey. The South Americans were united in self-defense. Finally, the United States and the British Empire were loosely federated to form "a more than equal counterpoise" to the other states. "There will simply be superimposed on English, American, Canadian, South African and Australian national sentiment a common anglo-saxon [sic] patriotism," said Balfour. He expected the Anglo-Saxon federation to control the world's oceans, and through its naval supremacy to establish a *Pax Anglo-Saxon*. Major wars would be unlikely in the new world order, because no other race would dare challenge Anglo-Saxon power. This idea of an Anglo-Saxon union to bring world peace was an old one, but Balfour still had hope for its realization in the not-too-distant future.[62]

Balfour's belief in the racial affinity of Britons and Americans, and his hope for an Anglo-Saxon union in the future, certainly influenced his dealings with the United States from the Venezuela boundary dispute through the end of his premiership in 1905. In January and February of 1896, he spoke in racial terms for peace between the two countries. He joined Joseph Chamberlain in 1898 to quash any manifestation of pro-Spanish sentiments by the British government. He commented frequently on the racial ties uniting the two peoples in the years thereafter. In Balfour's judgment, the best interests of Great Britain were served by courting racial sentiment in Anglo-American relations.

Cecil Spring Rice, the outstanding Anglo-Saxonist of the British diplomatic service, was Theodore Roosevelt's closest English friend. The two met for the first time during an 1886 Atlantic crossing, and "Springy" served as best man at Roosevelt's second wedding, in London, later that same year. During his years with the British legation at Washington (1887–92, 1894–95), Spring Rice visited Oyster Bay a number of times, and one summer shared Lodge's vacated Washington home with Roosevelt. He was an intimate member of Washington high society, and a particular favorite at social gatherings because of his happy blending of intelligence, urbanity, wit, tact, cynicism, and bachelorhood.

Spring Rice's primary influence on Anglo-American relations during the late 1890s and thereafter was through his relationship with Roosevelt. After his departure from Washington in 1895, Spring Rice deluged his friend with correspondence from the distant capitals to which he was assigned: Berlin (1895–98), Constantinople (1898–99), Tehran (1899–1901), Cairo (1901–3), St. Petersburg (1903–6). Roosevelt welcomed his opinions and advice. "You happen to have a mind which is interested in precisely the things which interest me," Roosevelt told him in the summer of 1897, "and which I believe are of more vital consequence than any other to the future of the race and of the world; so naturally I am delighted to hear from you, and I always want to answer your letters at length."[63] Some historians have been guilty of exaggerating Spring Rice's influence on Roosevelt. Roosevelt made his own judgments on important issues affecting the Anglo-American connection, and there is no evidence that he ever let Spring Rice's prejudices overcome his better judgment. He did respect the opinions of his English friend, however, and where appropriate took them into account in his decision-making. The sheer volume of correspondence between the two men, and the frequency with which world affairs were discussed, demonstrates the basic compatibility of many of their views. They gave special attention to the Far East, and in 1904 and 1905, during the Russo-Japanese conflict, Spring Rice served as semiofficial envoy of the British government to President Roosevelt, at Roosevelt's express request.[64] In the spring of 1905, Roosevelt tried unsuccessfully to persuade London to replace its current ambassador, Sir Mortimer Durand, with Spring Rice.

A gloomy, pessimistic brand of Anglo-Saxonism was the dominant element in Spring Rice's view of world politics. Beneath his witty and humorous exterior, Spring Rice was an introspective and reflective man. Henry Adams, an expert on pessimism, thought him "a victim of chronic and morbid terrors."[65] The English diplomat's chief apprehension was that the English branch of the Anglo-Saxon race was in decline, at the same time that the rising power of Slavic Russia threatened the survival of the race as a whole.

Spring Rice first expressed concern about the future of the race during his first winter in Washington. Writing to a friend in England, he said he had been "reading pretty hard" on the subject, and had "made acquaintances and learnt things" in the American capital which he was sure would help him very much in determining the probable fate of the race.[66] In succeeding years, he came to the dolorous conclusion that the English branch of the race was doomed to sink into obscurity, while the United States was fast becoming "the real fortress of our race." He was terrified that the Russians and Germans would forge an alliance to destroy the British Empire, and anticipated such a development at any time. He wrote to Roosevelt from St. Petersburg in 1904 to say that the possibility of the downfall of Britain gave him all the more reason to wish success to the United States, since "whatever happens to the old establishment there is a new branch on a larger scale, which no Emperor, however splendid, can do any harm to." The contemplation of America's growing strength gave him much satisfaction.[67]

Spring Rice despised the Russians, and like many other Anglo-Saxonists, he expected the future struggle for world supremacy to pit Anglo-Saxon against Slav. During the divisive American election campaign of 1896, he worried that the social fissures accentuated by the McKinley-Bryan campaign heralded the disintegration of the United States, in which case "the future of the world is not improbably in the hands of the Slavs."[68] For many years thereafter, Spring Rice seldom missed an opportunity to warn his friend Roosevelt about the Russian peril. The Russians were like the Huns and the Goths at the court of Constantine, he said in 1897: "They like and despise our civilisation and firmly believe it will all be theirs in time. They watch the fruits of civilisation growing, intending when they are ripe, to come and take them." Three years later, he predicted that the Slavs would create a new civilization in Asia, one "which will overwhelm the old as the Greeks did Asia and as Asia did the Romans." The conflict was already forming itself in the struggle for China, he said. Spring Rice's view of the Slavic enemy was probably presented most succinctly, however, in a letter he wrote to his brother Stephen in October of 1898: the Russians, he said, represented "the powers of darkness."[69]

It is impossible, of course, to state precisely how much the doleful forebodings of Cecil Spring Rice may have influenced the thinking of his friends in Washington, Roosevelt in particular. It is safe to say, however, that Spring Rice's opinions at least served to reinforce intellectual predilections that were already prevalent in the United States. His dire warnings about the Russians reflected a widely held view. Roosevelt almost certainly found most of Spring Rice's ideas compatible with his own. After 1898, more Americans in high places came to resent and fear Russian expansion, and to see in it a threat to the safety and welfare of the entire Anglo-Saxon race. By emphasizing repeatedly the putative racial aspects of the Anglo-American–

Russian rivalry, Spring Rice did his part to encourage fellow-feeling between the United States and his own country.

Imbued as they were with Anglo-Saxonist precepts, men like Spring Rice, Chamberlain, Balfour, Roosevelt, Lodge, Hay, and Mahan naturally took a special view of the relationship between Great Britain and the United States. All of them, in varying degrees, believed that the two countries shared a common racial heritage and destiny; and thus they made it one of their priorities to promote Anglo-American friendship. Because these men were firmly entrenched in the foreign policy elites of their respective countries, and capable of influencing or shaping policy in accord with their reflections and suppositions, their Anglo-Saxonist beliefs were of considerable import. Their beliefs had a notable impact on the rapprochement of 1895–1904.

5

The Venezuela Boundary Dispute and the Olney-Pauncefote Treaty: Anglo-Saxonism Emerges as an Influence on Anglo-American Relations

In the time period covered by this study, Anglo-Saxonism first exercised a marked influence on British-American relations during the Venezuela boundary dispute of 1895–96. The brief war scare following President Cleveland's belligerent message of 17 December 1895, and the long negotiations which followed to end the Venezuela squabble and arrange for the arbitration of future Anglo-American disputes, elicited countless expressions of kinship and good feeling from the public of both countries. Much of the public reaction against the prospect of an Anglo-American war and in favor of an arbitration treaty was rooted in the widely held belief that Englishmen and Americans were fellow Anglo-Saxons, and that a war between them would be fratricidal. The emergence of a strong sense of racial brotherhood during 1895–96 meant that an important new factor had been injected into British-American relations. Englishmen and Americans, adversaries and rivals for a century and a quarter, would never look at each other in the same way again.

When Grover Cleveland and his secretary of state, Richard Olney, noisily intervened in the long-standing boundary controversy between Great Britain and Venezuela, they certainly had no intention of provoking a crisis that might lead to war.[1] Indeed, the crisis which followed Cleveland's message of 17 December 1895, to the Congress was more apparent than real. A close examination of the message reveals that it was essentially temporizing in nature, and that Cleveland had written into it a number of devices for avoiding a direct confrontation with the British.[2] The administration apparently made no attempt whatsoever during the course of the dispute to prepare for either offensive or defensive military action. Moreover, a reading of the Senate debates of 19–20 December on the appropriation for Cleveland's boundary commission shows that the mood of the Senate was decidedly unwarlike. Most senators recognized the absurdity of risking hostilities over the boundary between Venezuela and British Guiana, and anticipated a peaceful resolution of the affair. In fact, on 19 December, just two days after Cleveland's message, the Senate heard and had entered into the *Record* a memorial from the House of Commons favoring the framing of an Anglo-American treaty binding the two nations "to refer to arbitration disputes which diplomacy fails to adjust."[3]

It is important to note, however, that the improbability of war was not so plain at the time. For a few weeks in December and January, it appeared to people on both sides of the Atlantic that the crisis was genuine and the possibility of a third Anglo-American war very real. Hence the public response to the Venezuela dispute was based on a perception that war might indeed result from the clash of wills between Lord Salisbury, who was determined that the United States should not be allowed to determine unilaterally the boundary of a British colony, and President Grover Cleveland.

The war scare was fueled by the jingoistic initial response given by Americans to the message of 17 December. No act in Grover Cleveland's career met with such popularity. For a while, politics was forgotten, as members of both major parties cheered the president's challenge to Salisbury. The Senate greeted the message with wild applause, a phenomenon almost unheard-of in Senate history. Both houses of Congress approved unanimously the requested $100,000 boundary-commission appropriation, without a word of criticism being offered. From the depths of the political doldrums, Cleveland was suddenly raised up to being, in the words of the Detroit *Journal*, "the most talked about and lauded man in this country."[4] A poll of twenty-eight state governors showed twenty-six of them giving the president unqualified support. The press in general gave overwhelming support to Cleveland, and editors who opposed him, like E. L. Godkin and Joseph Pulitzer, were condemned as traitors. Theodore Roosevelt pronounced himself "very much pleased" with the president's actions, and welcomed the opportunity to invade Canada.[5] Many people thought hostilities were imminent; the War Department was deluged with letters from veterans offering their services. Julian Pauncefote, the British ambassador at Washington, reported to Lord Salisbury three days after the message: "The Venezuela crisis which is raging here makes all other questions appear ancient history. Even 'Behring Sea' is forgotten for awhile and nothing is heard but the voice of the Jingo bellowing defiance to England. We must wait until the noise has subsided to judge the real attitude of the country."[6]

The British response to the threat of war differed markedly from the pugnacious emotionalism that seemed to sweep the United States. The first reaction in Britain was amazement. The American challenge took the British people "utterly by surprise," James Bryce told Roosevelt. "Not one man out of ten in the House of Commons even knew there was such a thing as a Venezuelan question pending." Britons were more shocked and pained than angry; they could hardly believe that Cleveland was willing to risk an Anglo-American conflict over so petty a question.[7]

During the last two weeks in December, a powerful demand arose in Britain for a quick, conciliatory settlement with the United States. Pleas for a settlement poured into the Foreign Office from churches, arbitration societies, chambers of commerce, public assemblies, and social clubs. The Anglican clergy called on people in both countries to pray for peace. Gladstone demanded a peaceful solution in the name of "common sense," and the Liberal leader Sir William Harcourt announced that he would raise the Venezuelan question in the next session of Parliament. The Prince of Wales and the Duke of York expressed peace sentiments. The London press, while rejecting Cleveland's pretensions to dictate international boundaries, did so in remarkably mild terms, and generally lent its support to those hoping for a quick and amicable denouement to the controversy.[8]

One of the most notable aspects of the British reaction was the citing of race sentiment by peace-minded persons as the basis for a settlement. The British press and public, as well as a number of high officials, tended to adopt the view that any conflict involving Great Britain and the United States would be a racial civil war, pitting Anglo-Saxon against Anglo-Saxon. Lord Rosebery said that he refused to accept the possibility of such a war, "for it would be the greatest crime on record. History would have to relate that the two mighty nations of the Anglo-Saxon race, at a time when they appeared about to overshadow the world in the best interests of Christianity and civilization, preferred to cut each other's throats about a frontier squabble in a small South American republic."[9] General Lord Wolseley, commander-in-chief of the Army, asked God's help in preventing war with the United States. Eight hundred English workers signed a petition saying that a conflict between Britain and the United States would be "a crime against the laws of God and Man." In the first few days after Cleveland's message, scores of Britain's leading men of letters, including Thomas Hardy, George Meredith, Alfred Austin, John Morley, John Ruskin, and Rider Haggard, called on their American counterparts to help end "the present crisis of the Anglo-Saxon race." For the united Anglo-Saxon race, their memorial read, "there is, we trust, such a future as no other race has yet had in the history of the world....We ask you to join us in helping to protect that future."[10] The London press echoed such sentiments, the *Chronicle* declaring that a war between the two kindred peoples would be an "unholy thing," and the *Times* saying it would be a calamity to the civilized world. John St. Loe Strachey, editor of the *Spectator*, said he could hardly conceive of circumstances in which the English people would willingly make war on Americans. Even the ultraconservative *St. James's Gazette* voiced its respect for the Anglo-Saxon pluck and determination of the United States.[11] Indeed, so widespread was the horror expressed at the prospect of war that on 28 December the generally anti-American *Saturday Review* felt compelled to condemn the "obsequious flattery of the American and servile fear of war" so evident in Britain during the past week. "The ineffable vulgarity of Jonathan and the pinchbeck sentiment of John are as sickening as the quarrel is unreal," editorialized the *Review*.[12]

Part of the horror Britons felt at the actions of the United States reflected their shock at discovering that the Americans apparently were willing to spill Anglo-Saxon blood for what they considered a backward, racially inferior people like the Venezuelans. W. T.

Stead, in his *Review of Reviews*, deprecated any action that would tend to sacrifice the interests of the English-speaking peoples to protect "the half-breeds of Venezuela." In the opinion of Joseph Chamberlain, Venezuela was but "a semi-civilised State," while James Bryce told Roosevelt that the government at Caracas was "not a civilised government at all." Sir Richard Bethell informed Canadians fearful of an American invasion that the "murderous man-monkeys" of Venezuela were not worth a single drop of Anglo-Saxon blood. One organ of the Conservative press called on Americans to abjure fighting their British cousins, and instead join with them to end once and for all the "sluttish anarchy" in "that semi-barbarous half-caste Republic."[13]

If there was any willingness in Britain to go to war with the United States, it quickly evaporated after 3 January 1896; for on that day, the Kaiser sent his famous telegram to President Kruger of the Transvaal, congratulating the Boers on their capture of the Jameson raiders. The reaction of the British press and public to the Kruger telegram differed enormously from the reaction to President Cleveland's message. Britons were surprised and dismayed at the misunderstanding with the United States, and overwhelmingly opposed to war. On the other hand, they were infuriated at the Kaiser's audacity, and almost unanimous in their willingness to fight if the government chose to do so. Rarely, in fact, had the British public been so thoroughly aroused. German workers and sailors were attacked on the streets of London, the windows of German shops were broken, the German ambassador was threatened, and letters to newspapers expressed rage at the supposed German insult to the Queen and the British nation. Of course, a number of factors contributed to the sharply contrasting responses of Britons to the American and German actions: the resentment built up over the years at German commercial competition, the Anglo-German rivalry for colonies, the blow to British pride of Jameson's capture, and the more direct threat to British interests presented by German ambitions in southern Africa.[14] Still, it is difficult to avoid the conclusion that a major part of the explanation for the sharp contrast in reactions may be found in the differing ways the British viewed Americans and Germans racially. In the popular view, the Germans, while racial relatives, were essentially alien; but the Americans were fellow

Anglo-Saxons, and therefore deserving of special consideration.

For weeks after Cleveland's message and the Kruger telegram, Britain remained awash in Anglo-Saxonist sentiment. Edward Dicey, the prominent author and journalist, argued that it would be better for the government to surrender to the American position on the Venezuelan question than to risk a war with the United States, for in such a conflict even a British victory "would be only less painful than defeat." W. T. Stead continued to deplore the prospect of a fratricidal war, as did James Bryce. In February, the *Spectator* declared that British friendship for the United States rose "in many minds to something approaching passion." Britons of every class and economic station, the periodical continued, felt the warmest sympathy for their American kinsmen, and believed that one of the primary responsibilities of the British government was to bring into harmony the two great branches of the Anglo-Saxon race.[15]

Arthur Balfour and Joseph Chamberlain, the two most prominent Anglo-Saxonists in the Salisbury cabinet, also appealed to race sentiment to help ease the tension in British-American relations. Because of difficulties Britain was experiencing at this time not only with the Germans and Boers in South Africa, but also with the French in the Niger and Nile Valleys, with the Russians in the Near East, and with the deteriorating situation in China, such appeals were sound policy. Great Britain certainly could not afford a crisis with the United States. On the other hand, there can be little doubt, given the prevailing attitude of the British public and the past utterances of Balfour and Chamberlain regarding the racial affinity of Englishmen and Americans, that the statements the two men made in January and February of 1896 were sincere, and not based merely on consideration of Britain's self-interest.

Balfour was the first cabinet minister to appeal for Anglo-American friendship and racial harmony after President Cleveland's message. On 15 January, in a speech approved in advance by Lord Salisbury, he told a Manchester audience that "the idea of war with the United States carries with it some of the unnatural horror of a civil war." The British people had a pride of race that forbade hostilities with another English-speaking community. Surely, Balfour said, the common sense of Anglo-Saxons could produce a settlement of the dispute without resort to arms. To loud cheers, he concluded: "The time will come, the time must come, when someone, some statesman of authority, . . . will lay down the doctrine that between English-speaking peoples war is impossible."[16]

Balfour's Manchester speech elicited a long letter of praise from Henry Cabot Lodge, who was beginning to have second thoughts about the Venezuela controversy after first endorsing in unqualified fashion the belligerent stand of Cleveland and Olney. Lodge told Balfour that he thought the Manchester speech generous, fair, and high-minded. "I feel as you do about a war between the English-speaking peoples," he said, "and should regard it as a terrible calamity to civilization."[17]

Two weeks after Balfour's oration, Joseph Chamberlain, who had earlier ranked Cleveland's message among "the greatest crimes of the century," delivered one of his most famous speeches on Anglo-American relations.[18] Speaking before an enthusiastic audience at Birmingham, the colonial secretary declared that Great Britain and the United States were "more closely allied in sentiment and in interest than any other nations on the face of the earth." He then insinuated that he would like to see the two countries intervene jointly in Turkey, the government of which had recently shocked and outraged the civilized world by instigating the systematic slaughter of thousands of Christian Armenians. "While I should look with horror upon anything in the nature of a fratricidal strife," Chamberlain said, "I should look forward with pleasure to the possibility of the Stars and Stripes and the Union Jack floating together in defence of a common cause sanctioned by humanity and justice."[19]

Not to be outdone by the colonial secretary, Balfour told a meeting at Bristol a week later that it was time for the two branches of the Anglo-Saxon race to join in an alliance "for the propagation of Anglo-Saxon ideas of liberty, government, and order." Old controversies should be forgotten, and the British and American peoples united to "carry out the duties which Providence has intrusted to us." Between fellow Anglo-Saxons, war was unthinkable.[20]

Such expressions of fellow-feeling by powerful figures in the British government encouraged the development of opinion in the

United States favoring some peaceful solution to the boundary dispute. Indeed, the threat of war implied in the blunt language of Cleveland's special message had already provoked second thoughts in many Americans, and the wild popularity which the president enjoyed in the first few days after issuing his challenge to Salisbury quickly faded. The message was delivered to Congress on a Tuesday; by the following Friday, important segments of the population were beginning to express doubts about the wisdom of Cleveland's action; by Sunday, clergymen across the country, but especially in the heavily populated Northeast, were condemning the president; and by the end of December, the Indianapolis *Journal* could truthfully declare that jingoism had faded, and that the predominant sentiment of Americans was now "as distinctly anti-war as it was at first warlike."[21]

Most aspects of the negative reaction to Cleveland's message are so well-known that they need not be repeated here.[22] More should be said, however, about Anglo-Saxonism's role in turning Americans away from the prospect of war. Race sentiment was doubtless a strong background presence during the initial public protest against Cleveland's policy; but this presence had too little time to produce strong documented results during the short initial reaction. The few organs of the commercial and religious press that pointed to the racial ties between Great Britain and the United States as a reason for their opposition may have been motivated primarily by other considerations. It is reasonable to assume, for example that the Los Angeles *Investor*, which indirectly appealed to Anglo-Saxon race sentiment by attacking the "mongrel" Venezuelans, was actually concerned less with racial amity than with the potential for economic disaster in an Anglo-American conflict. Likewise, it is conceivable that the Presbyterian journal *The Evangelist* was moved as much by pacifism as by ties of race when it declared: "Next to our own country, we love England, the land of our fathers, and the bitterest calamity that could happen to both nations would be a fratricidal and suicidal war."[23] On the whole, there is little evidence that Anglo-Saxonism played an important part in the reversal of American opinion in late December.

But in January, as antiwar sentiment began to assert itself more strongly and as word flowed into the country of the sharp reaction in Britain against the prospect of a conflict, race feeling became increasingly evident in American discussion of the Venezuelan affair. Among those Americans most eager to see the controversy brought to an amicable conclusion was Captain Alfred Thayer Mahan. Writing in early January to his English friend James R. Thursfield, a noted naval historian and an editorialist for the London *Times*, Mahan grudgingly confessed that he would do his duty as a naval officer if war came. "But as a matter of personal feeling and even more of personal conviction," he wrote, "I am absolutely with you in the belief that no greater evil can possibly happen to either nation or to the world than such a war. My own belief has long since passed... from faith in, and ambition for my country alone, to the same for the Anglo-Saxon race. The former first of course, but a sort of *primus inter pares*." A week later, Mahan half-jokingly told another English friend that if war came he would have to ask the Admiralty to fly something other than a British ensign on its ships, for he would be exceedingly reluctant to fire on the British flag.[24] That Mahan spoke for many of his countrymen was made evident by the profusion of American race sentiment during the weeks and months that followed.

On 22 January, Senator Edward O. Wolcott of Colorado took the Senate floor to question the wisdom of a policy that threatened to spill Anglo-Saxon blood for the sake of Venezuela. Echoing similar statements made in Britain, Wolcott attacked Latin Americans in general, and Venezuelans in particular, for their alleged racial inferiority and incapacity for self-government. Having proved to his own satisfaction that Venezuela was not worth a war between Anglo-Saxons, Wolcott turned his attention to England's defiant response to German interference in southern Africa. He thanked God that he was of the same race as the English, and drew loud applause from the galleries when he affirmed that blood was indeed thicker than water. Englishmen and Americans, as the premier representatives of the Anglo-Saxon race, owed it to humanity to stand shoulder to shoulder in world affairs.[25]

Andrew Carnegie, one of the staunchest advocates of Anglo-Saxon unity, joined the refrain in February with a *North American Review* article asking the English branch of the race to end the frightful possibility of a fratricidal war by backing down to the American branch. Carnegie attributed the whole difficulty to the "root passion" of the Anglo-Saxon race to acquire territory, explaining that Great Britain had been driven by a racially inherent aggressiveness to expand its Guiana colony westward. While Americans were happy to see their English cousins acquire all the land they could in Europe, Asia, and Africa, the United States had staked out the western hemisphere as its own domain, and London must defer to Washington on the Venezuelan question. English aggressiveness had met its match, Carnegie said, in the aggressiveness of Americans.[26]

In March, two widely noticed articles by Edward Atkinson and Sidney Sherwood deprecated the prospect of war. Sherwood, a professor of economics at Johns Hopkins, went so far as to endorse the idea of an Anglo-American alliance recently put forward by Joseph Chamberlain and Arthur Balfour, arguing that such a union would guarantee world peace by overshadowing the two rival alliance systems in Europe, the Dual Alliance and the Triple Alliance.[27] A few months later, George Burton Adams added his voice to those urging a prompt settlement of the Venezuelan question on racial grounds. Adams was ready to see the English occupy all the land in dispute if that was necessary to avert a racial civil war. An Anglo-American war would almost certainly result in the collapse of Anglo-Saxon civilization, he said, and "the ruin of the empire of the world which now belongs to our race." Alien races like the Germans and Russians would be quick to take advantage.[28]

Nor did Secretary of State Richard Olney, who spent much of 1896 trying to negotiate a way out of the Venezuela imbroglio, remain unaffected by the Anglo-Saxonist sentiment that was being expressed in America. In September of 1896, shortly before Olney and Julian Pauncefote reached agreement on a compromise settlement, Olney wrote a remarkable letter to Joseph Chamberlain. Chamberlain, who was in Washington at the time to try to help with the negotiations, had sounded out the secretary of state on the possibility of joint Anglo-American action to end the Armenian massacres. In politely declining the proposal, Olney—a Massachusetts native who took great pride in his English ancestry[29]—vividly expressed his belief in the racial affinity of Englishmen and Americans:

There is no general and rooted hatred by Americans of the English people. On the contrary, if there is anything the Americans are proud of, it is their right to describe themselves as of the English race—if there is anything they are attached to, it is to ideas and principles which are distinctly English in their origin and development.... And for like reasons and because of our inborn and instinctive English sympathies, proclivities, modes of thought, and standards of right and wrong, nothing would more gratify the mass of the American people than to stand... shoulder to shoulder with England in support of a great cause—in a necessary struggle for the defence of human rights, and the advancement of Christian civilization.[30]

On the basis of such statements, it can be concluded that race sentiment helped turn Americans away from war in 1896 and toward an amicable accord with Great Britain. The popular belief that the two peoples were racial kinsmen, fellow Anglo-Saxons, contributed significantly to the feeling of revulsion that came over many individuals at the prospect of an Anglo-American conflict. And once the war scare had passed, this same belief helped create an atmosphere conducive to the compromise settlement, ending the Venezuela boundary dispute, that was signed by Richard Olney and Julian Pauncefote on 12 November 1896.[31]

One of the striking consequences of the war scare following President Cleveland's message of December 1895 was the sudden emergence of strong public feeling in both Great Britain and the United States in favor of an arbitration treaty between the two countries. It is highly doubtful whether such a proposal could have progressed very far prior to the reaction against the threat of war. Yet in early 1897, after months of careful negotiation, a general arbitration treaty was actually signed by Olney and Pauncefote. Moreover, only the two-thirds rule and the equal representation in the Senate of both heavily and sparsely populated states, prevented the treaty—albeit in a grossly amended form—from being ratified and put into effect. Few events better illustrate the improved climate in British-American relations, and the role of Anglo-Saxonism in bringing about the new public feeling, than the support given to arbitration in 1896–97.[32]

The leading figure of the movement in Great Britain for an

arbitration treaty was W. T. Stead. Stead was active in the peace movement as well as being one of Britain's most outspoken Anglo-Saxonists and promoters of Anglo-American friendship, and in the cause of arbitration he saw an opportunity to combine his two great passions in a single campaign. As Stead himself described his decision to work for arbitration, he was moved to action during the first two weeks of January 1896 by the urgencies of "the misunderstanding" which had occurred "between the two great sections of the English-speaking race." He thought it was time the two nations stopped "rubbing along," trusting to patience and good fortune to save them from bloodletting whenever their ambitions and interests clashed. "The time has surely come," he said, "when we can as a race declare that war is so terrible a thing we shall never resort to it . . . until the *casus belli* . . . has been duly submitted and solemnly adjudicated upon by an impartial arbitration court."[33]

Largely at Stead's initiative, a conference was held at Sion College, London, on 4 January 1896, to draw up a memorial favoring arbitration. As finally adopted, the memorial read: "Whatever may be the differences between the Governments in the present or the future, all English-speaking peoples united by blood, language, and religion, should regard war as the one absolutely intolerable mode of settling the domestic difficulties of the Anglo-American family."[34]

The Sion College conference marked the beginning of a massive outpouring of feeling in Great Britain in favor of arbitration. So many persons signed the Sion College memorial that when it was eventually forwarded to the Foreign Office, it was contained in a volume nearly two feet thick.[35] Thousands of letters and petitions demanding the working out of a permanent arbitration arrangement poured down on Parliament and the Foreign Office. On 11 February, Arthur Balfour drew cheers in the House of Commons when he declared that the Venezuela controversy would have served a great purpose if the result should be a general system of arbitration insuring for all time "good will between the English-speaking races on the two sides of the Atlantic."[36] By the first of March, the idea of arbitration had been endorsed by 126 members of Parliament and by 82 mayors of British towns. On 3 March, a huge demonstration promoting arbitration was held at Queen's Hall, London. Those in attendance were entertained by a chorus wearing sashes representing the Union Jack and the Stars and Stripes. The organizers of the demonstration read letters of support from William E. Gladstone, Lord Rosebery, Viscount Peel, James Bryce, H. H. Asquith, Herbert Spencer, and many other luminaries. Significantly, most of the letter-writers extolled the ties of race uniting Britons and Americans. One speaker at the Queen's Hall meeting drew sustained applause when he declared that patriotism of race was more sacred than patriotism of country, and that war between England and the United States would be murder. In March and April, under Stead's direction, the arbitration movement was organized on a national basis, and was designated the "Anglo-American Union."[37]

Agitation for arbitration was less noisy in the United States, but was nonetheless on a scale sufficient to attract the attention of President Cleveland and several members of his cabinet, who wrote letters of support. Mass meetings were held during February of 1896 in New York, Philadelphia, Chicago, Boston, and a number of other American cities. The New York State Assembly passed with just one dissenting vote a resolution expressing its earnest support for an arbitration treaty. Thousands of Americans, including powerful businessmen like Cyrus McCormick, George M. Pullman, Marshall Field, and Philip D. Armour, signed proarbitration petitions. In August, the *North American Review* published an article by the noted English novelist and humanitarian Walter Besant, advocating a permanent court of arbitration as a first step toward an Anglo-Saxon race alliance.[38]

In part because of massive public pressure, Secretary Olney and Ambassador Pauncefote enlarged their negotiations on the Venezuela question to include discussions of an arbitration treaty. The final treaty, signed on 11 January 1897, provided for the compulsory arbitration of virtually all outstanding and future issues between the two countries (with safeguards allowing either government to nullify awards on matters affecting vital national interests).[39] President Cleveland sent the treaty to the Senate a few days later with a brief message urging ratification.

There is no doubt that a majority of Americans favored ratification. The Senate received more petitions and memorials from groups supporting the Olney-Pauncefote treaty than it had received for any previous American treaty. Only a dozen petitions opposed the pact, and most of those were from Irish clubs and associations. Senators admitted that their mail ran heavily in favor of ratification, and a number of them voiced loud complaints on the Senate floor about the enormous public pressure they were feeling to approve the treaty.[40] A poll by Pulitzer's *New York World* found the overwhelming majority of commercial organizations, clergymen, college presidents, city mayors, and newspaper editors favoring ratification. Mass meetings of support were held in the nation's largest cities, and several state legislatures passed resolutions favoring the treaty. William McKinley, Cleveland's successor, strongly endorsed the treaty. Most organs of the press were in agreement with the Chicago *Times-Herald*, which stated, "if the question were submitted to the American people, they would decide by an overwhelming vote that the treaty should be adopted."[41]

As in the public reaction against the war scare of December, Anglo-Saxonism was less evident in American support for arbitration than it was in British opinion. A broad reading of Senate documents and journals of opinion makes it obvious that most people supported ratification of the Olney-Pauncefote treaty not because they felt an intellectual and emotional attachment to Anglo-Saxon Britain, but because they believed the treaty marked a giant step forward for the peace movement.

While clearly secondary in importance to pacifism and a general desire for world peace, Anglo-Saxonism was nevertheless an appreciable factor in the backing the treaty received in the United States. Expressions of support citing the racial ties between Britons and Americans came from newspaper editors and commercial organizations in New York, Michigan, Indiana, Iowa, Virginia, Missouri, Tennessee, Texas, and Oregon.[42] Alfred Thayer Mahan, regretting that pacifism and fear of economic dislocation inspired most American backing for the treaty, wished that Americans might instead base their support on "an intelligent appreciation of the great future open to the English-speaking races."[43] The press in all parts of the country cited Anglo-American racial affinity as an important reason why the treaty should be ratified. The Omaha *World-Herald* declared, "it has been left to the Anglo-Saxon race to set the example of peaceful arbitration among the nations." The Lewiston (Maine) *Journal* held that defeat of the treaty would constitute "a blow delivered by the child to the parent, by Anglo-Saxon to Anglo-Saxon." The editor of the Houston *Post* believed the Olney-Pauncefote treaty portended the creation of "an English-speaking league" to further Anglo-Saxon civilization.[44]

Despite public support for the treaty, however, and despite the efforts of Secretary Olney on the treaty's behalf, the Senate refused to ratify.[45] First, the Foreign Relations Committee amended the pact in such a way as to make it likely that no question of substance would ever be arbitrated. Then, on 5 May 1897, the Senate killed the treaty. The final vote was forty-three in favor of ratification, twenty-six opposed—three votes short of the two-thirds required for approval.[46]

More significant than the amending of the Olney-Pauncefote treaty and its defeat in the Senate, however, was how close it came to ratification. Any arbitration treaty between Great Britain and the United States probably would have been unthinkable at any time up to two years before. Yet in 1897 a large majority of the Senate voted for ratification; and of the twenty-six votes in opposition, nearly all came from Southern Bourbons and from silverites representing sparsely populated Western states, whose votes were determined more by hatred of Cleveland and the gold standard than by the merits of the treaty. The heavily populated Northeast voted overwhelmingly in favor of the amended treaty, and except for the equal representation in the Senate of all states, regardless of population, the treaty would have been ratified with ease.[47]

Certainly a majority of the American public was disappointed at the defeat of the treaty. The press reacted with outrage. "The popular will is overborne by a senatorial cabal," fumed the Chicago *Evening Post*. Two days after the Senate vote, Ambassador Pauncefote bitterly informed Lord Salisbury that the Senate action "absolutely disregarded public opinion," which had everywhere received the treaty with acclamation.[48]

Richard Olney, now returned to private life in Boston, reacted to the treaty's defeat with chagrin and frustration. On 8 May, he wrote a long memorandum to Henry White, first secretary at the

American embassy in London, explaining his feelings and asking White to show the memorandum to members of the British government. Olney said that although the rejection of the treaty was a calamity "of world-wide proportions," Whitehall must understand that the vast majority of Americans liked the British and had favored ratification of the agreement. In the future, the British government should ignore the political maneuverings of the "cheap politicians" responsible for the treaty's failure, and predicate its actions on the fact that

> the American people are proud of their lineage; set the highest value upon the laws, the institutions, the literature, and the language they have inherited; glory in all the achievements of the Anglo-Saxon race, in war, in politics, in science, in literature, and in art; and feel themselves to be not merely in name but in fact, part of one great English-speaking family whose proud destiny it is to lead and control the world.[49]

Henry White, on receiving this highly revealing memorandum, immediately showed it to Arthur Balfour, and Balfour found it so interesting that he borrowed it and circulated it among his colleagues in the cabinet. The bewildered White never got it back.[50]

The Olney memorandum, setting forth ideas similar to those he had expressed the previous September in his letter to Joseph Chamberlain, foreshadowed the position Olney was to take in the months to come. In March of 1898, less than a year after the failure of the arbitration agreement, Olney declared in an address at Harvard University that the United States ought to diminish its diplomatic isolation and actively cooperate with Great Britain in world affairs. Among the most prominent reasons Olney gave for advocating this new direction for American foreign policy was his firm belief that "there is a patriotism of race as well as of country." This starkly Anglo-Saxonist notion, as Ernest R. May has suggested, may have been in his mind for some time.[51]

One conclusion to be drawn from the Venezuela boundary dispute and the Olney-Pauncefote treaty is that the dispute and the treaty marked the beginning of a changed relationship between Great Britain and the United States; another is that Anglo-Saxonism had an appreciable effect in bringing about the new feeling of friendship. People in both countries reacted with something akin to horror at the prospect of an Anglo-American war over the Venezuela boundary, and to a considerable extent the reaction was based on the popular belief that Englishmen and Americans were fellow Anglo-Saxons. In the aftermath of the war scare, Joseph Chamberlain and Arthur Balfour began to call publicly for the forging of an Anglo-Saxon alliance, and public opinion in both countries became favorable to a general arbitration treaty. And while the Olney-Pauncefote treaty was not ratified by the United States Senate, the fact that a large majority of Americans supported it, many of them on racial grounds, testified to the new sense of kinship and goodwill in British-American relations.

Ironically, then, Grover Cleveland's veritable ultimatum to the British government in December 1895 had the eventual consequence of moving the two countries toward improved relations; indeed, the dispute showed that at the level of popular feeling, the United States and Great Britain had already moved close to a friendly relationship. Under the stress of the Venezuela boundary dispute, Anglo-Saxon race sentiment emerged as a new and potent influence on British-American relations. Henceforth, the people of each country would tend to see the people of the other as kinsmen, as racial relatives with whom war was not to be considered. Serious questions, to be worked out by difficult and painstaking diplomacy, remained to trouble the Anglo-American relationship; but, in part because of the friendly influence of Anglo-Saxonism, much of the old hostility was gone.

6

The Spanish-American War: The Apex of Anglo-Saxonism

Historians have frequently pointed out that the configuration of world politics in 1898 tended to draw the United States and Great Britain into a relationship of marked cordiality. Each country, at the time of the Spanish-American War, found itself without allies, threatened by several of the great Europeans powers, and needful of the diplomatic support of the other.[1]

While such practical, material considerations did tend to promote a closer diplomatic rapprochement between Great Britain and the United States in 1898, Anglo-Saxon race sentiment fostered vital public support for the growing international friendship. Indeed, as the United States defeated Spain and began to compete actively for world power and prestige, no factor was more important than Anglo-Saxonism in promoting good feeling between the British and American peoples. Anglo-Saxon race sentiment was the most prominent element in the stupendous outpouring of emotional camaraderie that swept the two countries in 1898. As the *Spectator* observed a month before the outbreak of the Spanish-American War, "The difficulties with Spain have increased that sentiment of essential unity which exists, though generally latent and unobserved, among all Anglo-Saxons."[2] Press, public, and government officials in the United States and Great Britain spoke warmly of the putative racial bond between the two countries and cited racial affinity as the deep-rooted basis for a friendly and harmonious relationship. The Spaniards and their supporters on the Continent were frequently condemned as enemies of Anglo-Saxondom, and American victories were hailed as further proof, if any were needed, of Anglo-Saxon superiority. Many prominent individuals on both sides of the Atlantic even welcomed the idea of a formal military alliance between the two Anglo-Saxon powers.

And once the war was won, British and American imperialists alike claimed that the new American expansionist policy marked the fulfillment of the destiny of the race. Such ideas contributed mightily to a new sense of friendship that did not pass away completely with the fading of wartime passions, but remained to ease the way to a permanent Anglo-American understanding.

British partisanship for the United States was clearly evident weeks before the quarrel with Spain erupted into open war. When Hearst's New York *Journal* published the famous De Lôme letter on 9 February 1898, British newspapers were nearly as loud as the American press in their denunciations of the Spanish minister.[3] The destruction of the *Maine* in Havana harbor six days later brought a tremendous outpouring of sorrow in Britain, a phenomenon that was widely regarded at the time as owing to the "community of race" between Great Britain and the United States. Two days after the sinking, the London *Daily Chronicle* stated that the sorrow and sympathy felt by the British people were little different from what they might have been "if the appalling calamity had overtaken one of our own ships." The reason for this, the newspaper said, was that all Britons believed at heart that the United States was on "'our side' in the great game of the world." In the days following the tragedy, a flood of condolences poured into the State Department from such British dignitaries as the Prince of Wales, the Duke and Duchess of York, First Lord of the Admiralty Viscount Goschen, and the Lord Mayor of London. Alfred Thayer Mahan received a number of letters from his English acquaintances expressing horror that such a tragedy should have befallen Americans.[4]

During March and April, as war fever mounted in the United States, British partiality for their American cousins increased also. So much in doubt were the official professions of strict neutrality in the event of war that representatives of the Salisbury cabinet had to answer questions in the House of Commons on 14 March as to whether the government was seeking an alliance with the United States and whether it was planning to lend warships to the United States for use against Spain. The officials flatly denied the latter possibility and refused to reply to the first (Britain was at this time seeking American cooperation in the Far East), but speculation continued on both questions.[5] One Conservative

M.P. announced that many members of his party expected Great Britain and the United States to fight side by side if either were attacked by some power other than Spain.[6] And on 28 March, the London *Times*, the editorial opinions of which often reflected official government thinking, declared that British neutrality in a Spanish-American conflict inevitably would be colored by the fact "that one of them is knitted to us yet more closely by the ties of blood." The next day, the *Times* prominently displayed the new poem, "A Voice from the West," by poet laureate Alfred Austin. The poem's sentimental drift, calling on Englishmen and Americans, as "sons of the self-same race," to act in concert in world affairs, was caught best in its last stanza:

Yes, this is the Voice on the bluff March gale,
"We severed have been too long:
But now we have done with a worn-out tale,
The tale of an ancient wrong,
And our friendship shall last long as Love doth last
 and be stronger than Death is strong."[7]

John Hay, America's ambassador at London, was delighted at such indications of British friendliness. He reported jubilantly to President McKinley on 4 April that Joseph Chamberlain had spoken with him about an alliance, and Earl Grey had indicated that Britain might be willing to lend naval units to the United States "to make a quick job of Cuba."[8] Hay was certainly exaggerating the willingness of the British to involve themselves militarily in a Spanish-American conflict, but his communication nonetheless indicates the confidence of some Americans, even before the war began, in the backing of their fellow Anglo-Saxons. On 24 March, a Pennsylvania congressman, addressing the House of Representatives, dismissed fears that intervention in Cuba would lead to a confrontation with some or all of the great Continental powers by remarking that "any foreign intervention would be met by the two great English-speaking people [*sic*] of the world."[9]

To a considerable extent, the Anglo-Saxon race sentiment evident in British and American attitudes before the war grew out of a common perception of the Spanish as racial inferiors. In the popular mythology of Anglo-Saxon racism, no European people fared worse than the Latin people of Spain. Americans in the late nineteenth century almost invariably portrayed Spanish history as an unbroken record of cruelty and corruption. Henry Cabot Lodge was typical in his assessment of Spanish racial character. During an 1895 tour of Spain, he wrote home to report that the Spanish were a "repellent" race, "a backward, uncivilized people" whose favorite amusements were "brutal, stupid, & bloody."[10] This view of the Spanish, together with a smug sense of Anglo-Saxon superiority, was apparent in the charges in the yellow press and on the floor of Congress in the months before the war that the Spanish were too decadent and bloody-minded to reform Cuba and end the insurrection. Congressman William C. Arnold doubted that peace could ever come to the island as long as it was governed by a people whose predominant traits were "deceit, perfidy, treachery, cruelty, tyranny, and savagery."[11]

The British generally shared this low assessment of Spanish character and potential for improvement, a fact that helps account for their pro-American sympathies both before and during the war. One historian has pointed out that the British press in the months leading up to the war tended to present the situation in Cuba "not as that of a European Power attempting to restore order in a colony, but as that of a barbarous race oppressing its barbarous subjects." The British not only saw Spanish rule as bad, but they expected it to continue to be bad, as the inevitable consequence of Spanish cruelty and incompetence. In these circumstances, it was almost a duty of the United States, representing as it did the power, efficiency, and humane civilization of the Anglo-Saxons, to intervene and end the slaughter and anarchy. Cecil Spring Rice, writing to his friend Theodore Roosevelt in November 1897, probably expressed the feelings of a majority of Englishmen when he said: "I am glad... that the press of England at any rate recognises that it is rather hard for people of our blood to sit quiet with such things going on at the door. I saw one article in the *Manchester Guardian*... which said that if it were jingoism to object to massacre and robbery, it hoped for the credit of the race and language that all America would go Jingo mad."[12]

Given these attitudes, the British people were well prepared, when war actually began during the fourth week in April, to make clear their overwhelming preference for the American cause. Within six hours of the cable from Washington announcing the declaration of war, thousands of American flags and red, white, and blue streamers were flying from shops, hotels, and private homes in London, and a large crowd had gathered in front of the American embassy to cheer for the United States.[13] In the next few days, virtually the entire press of Great Britain and the Empire pronounced its sympathy with the Americans and its hope that all representatives of the Anglo-Saxon race would see the war as a means of promoting friendship and cooperation. "We readily admit that our sympathies are with the Americans as men of our own race," proclaimed St. Loe Strachey's *Spectator* on the day McKinley called for 125,000 volunteers. The London *Daily Chronicle*, having tested the sentiment of the population of the capital, zestfully declared: "If there be any doubt about the feelings of the great majority of the nation, we shall be happy to try the experiment of marching a hundred thousand Londoners through the metropolis with the Union Jack and the Stars and Stripes in combination." The *Daily Mail* collected editorial opinions from colonial newspapers throughout the Empire and published them in a symposium entitled "Anglo-Saxons Solid." The British, sneered *Le Temps*, France's most respected journal, were suffering "an acute fit of Anglo-Saxonism."[14]

Britain's political leadership was as afflicted with Anglo-Saxonism as the press and public, and quickly joined in the applause for the United States. John Hay wrote happily from London that the state of feeling in England was the best he had ever known. Most members of the royal family were sympathetic toward the United States, said Hay, and "among the political leaders on both sides I find not only sympathy, but a somewhat eager desire that 'the other fellows' should not seem the more friendly."[15] Indeed, Hay was correct in his observation that many leaders of both the Conservative majority and the Liberal opposition in Parliament were eager to endorse and promote the new community of feeling between Britain and the United States. Arthur Balfour pronounced himself elated at the new turn in Anglo-American relations, and Joseph Chamberlain called publicly for an "Anglo-Saxon alliance." On the opposition side, perhaps the most significant expositions were those of Sir Edward

Grey and H. H. Asquith, who declared in separate speeches that the coming together of the English and American branches of the race was one of the great events of 1898.[16]

Largely because they perceived American victories as Anglo-Saxon victories, redounding to the glory of the race as a whole, Englishmen took a huge interest in the progress of American arms. The *Spectator* cheered Dewey's triumph at Manila with the words: "We rejoice in the efficiency of the American representative of our race, because we believe that, failing the Anglo-Saxon, the wronged of the world will find no defenders; we exult in his skill, his preparedness, his daring." Henry White reported to Lodge in June that the British public was nearly as interested in developments as the American, and eager for Sampson and Schley to get at the Spanish fleet at Santiago. Washington Gladden, the noted Ohio clergyman and social reformer, spent the summer of 1898 touring England and lecturing on the causes of the war and the benefits of Anglo-American friendship; he recalled later that he was amazed at the enthusiasm of his audiences and their interest in the war.[17]

Some British observers concluded that the Spanish-American conflict marked the culmination of a struggle to the death between Anglo-Saxon and Spaniard that was at least as old as the defeat of the Armada. Cecil Spring Rice, on receiving "the glorious news from Manila," wrote to John Hay expressing wonder at "the continuity of history, the struggle that began 400 years ago of which we are seeing the last chapter." He thought there must be some "divine instinct ingrained in the race" that had led the Anglo-Saxons to batter away at the Spanish Empire so consistently for so long, until the last vestiges of its power had been destroyed. Lord Charles Beresford, a retired rear admiral who currently occupied a seat in Parliament, reminded Englishmen that the Americans, in capturing Manila and invading Cuba, were repeating the feats of much earlier Anglo-Saxon soldiers, sailors, and adventurers who had fought for England.[18]

Great Britain's sympathy for the American cause, together with the numerous British appeals to Anglo-American racial affinity, elicited a warm response in the United States. British Ambassador Julian Pauncefote, astonished at the sudden transition of American opinion from a wary distrust of England to "the most exuberant affection," reported to Salisbury that he was being overwhelmed with addresses and memorials saluting "the supposed Anglo-American 'Alliance.'"[19] Some of the most remarkable expressions of good feeling came from the little group of American expansionists who had long advocated what Henry Cabot Lodge called the "large policy" for the United States. Lodge himself, forgetting his reputation for Anglophobia, declared at the opening of hostilities with Spain that "the heart of America" went to England in grateful recognition of its moral support. "Race, blood, language, identity of beliefs & aspirations, all assert themselves," Lodge said, ending with a declaration of his belief that the drawing together of the two great English-speaking peoples was destined to be one of the most important results of the war.[20] Captain Mahan was equally certain that the new relationship between the two branches of the race would be of enormous consequence in the years to come; and John Hay, who was to become secretary of state in September 1898, confidently asserted that "the interests of civilization are bound up in the direction the relations of America and England are to take in the next few months."[21] Theodore Roosevelt took time off from soldiering in Cuba to write gleefully to Cecil Spring Rice at the British Legation in Berlin: "I rather incline to the view of my beloved friend Lt. Parker of the Gatlings, whom I overheard telling the Russian Naval Attaché at Santiago that the two branches of the Anglo-Saxon race had come together, 'and together we can whip the world, Prince, we can whip the world'!"[22]

Americans as well as Britons frequently portrayed the war with Spain as a virtual "war of races," pitting the robust civilization of the Anglo-Saxon United States against the decadent semicivilization of Spain. The Anglo-Saxons, it was said, had risen to power during the past three hundred years largely at Spain's expense, and the Spanish-American War was the final episode in this centuries-old racial rivalry. Shortly after Admiral Cervera's fleet was smashed off Santiago, an American West Coast writer exulted: "While the Spaniard has been sinking into impotence, the Anglo-Saxon has augmented his power until it fills the earth. The conflict inaugurated by the Armada spread to every continent and every island which Spain has made her own, and victory has been invariably with us."[23]

Such a racial interpretation of the war was indeed encouraged by many newspapers in Spain, Portugal, France, and Italy, which viewed the contest as frankly one between the Latin and the Anglo-Saxon. Of course, the Latin participant received considerably more sympathy in these countries. The French press was virulently pro-Spanish, and given to praising Spain's Latin heritage and condemning the Anglo-Saxon prejudices of the British. France's patronage led some Spanish editorial writers to hope that Spain would be rescued by a great Latin crusade against the arrogant Anglo-Saxon countries.[24]

In the United States, the racial interpretation of the war sometimes led people to portray it as a Darwinian struggle for existence in which the weak and unfit Spanish were doomed to go down before the strong and aggressive Anglo-Saxons. Henry Cabot Lodge concluded that the fundamental nature of the conflict could best be described in Darwinian terms: Spain had "proved herself unfit to govern, and for the unfit among nations there is no pity in the relentless world-forces which shape the destinies of mankind." Lodge also implied that a major cause of the war was the instinctive racial antipathy of free and enlightened Anglo-Saxons toward the tyrannical regime of Latin Spain.[25]

The Anglo-Saxonist fervor stirred up by the war led to many extraordinary demonstrations of fraternal affection in both the United States and Great Britain. In the most ironic demonstration of 1898, the Fourth of July was celebrated as a holiday throughout Britain, and longtime advocates of Anglo-American solidarity like W. T. Stead and Sir Walter Besant proposed that American Independence Day henceforth be celebrated in all Anglo-Saxon countries.[26] Similar Anglo-Saxonist sentiments led a collection of distinguished Englishmen meeting at Stafford House in London on 13 July 1898, to proclaim the formation of a so-called Anglo-American Committee, with James Bryce as chairman. The committee, which numbered among its members the Duke of Sutherland, the Earl of Jersey, Lord Charles Beresford, Lord Brassey, and Earl Grey, unanimously adopted a resolution declaring that since the peoples of the United States and Great Britain were allied by blood, traditions, principles, ideals, and interests, every effort should be made to see that they cooperated in world affairs.[27] Two weeks after the formation of the Anglo-American Committee, an analogous organization came into being in New

York City, with Whitelaw Reid as chairman and such celebrated figures as Lyman Abbott, Cornelius Vanderbilt, Abram S. Hewitt, and Benjamin Tracy as charter members. The American branch of the Anglo-American Committee drew up and sent out to hundreds of prominent citizens an address thanking the British for their sympathy and calling for "an intimate and enduring friendship between these two kindred peoples." The address was ultimately signed by over a thousand of the country's foremost educators, industrialists, lawyers, publishers, religious leaders, politicians, and government officials.[28]

It should be pointed out, nonetheless, that Anglo-Saxonist excitement was not universal in either Great Britain or the United States. Queen Victoria's sympathies were with her beleaguered niece, the Spanish Queen Regent, and indications are that Lord Salisbury preferred the Spanish monarchy to the truculent American republic.[29] In the United States, Irish- and German-Americans protested the prevailing Anglomania, and William James expressed disgust at the "sniveling cant" of the Anglo-Saxonists. The Chicago *Chronicle* said that Englishmen and Americans were of the same race only if the English had plenty of Bohemian, Greek, German, Polish, Hungarian, Celtic, and Latin blood.[30] As was often the case in these years, the most telling critique of the passions of the moment came from Mr. Dooley, who archly said to Hennessy:

> Th' name iv Dooley has been th' proudest Anglo-Saxon name in th' County Roscommon f'r many years . . . . I tell ye, whin th' Clan an' th' Sons iv Sweden an' th' Banana Club an' th' Circle Francaize an' th' Pollacky Benivolent Society an' th' Rooshian Sons iv Dinnymite an' th' Benny Brith an' th' Coffee Clutch that Schwartzmeister r-runs . . . an' th' Holland Society an' th' Afro-Americans an' th' other Anglo-Saxons begin f'r to raise their Anglo-Saxon battlecry, it'll be all day with th' eight or nine people in th' wurruld that has th' misfortune iv not bein' brought up Anglo-Saxons.[31]

Even America's dissenters from the Anglo-Saxonism of 1898, however, must have appreciated the fact that during the course of the war with Spain, Great Britain's official conduct tended to be "neutral" in favor of the United States. London was extremely considerate of American sensibilities in the weeks preceding the war, when the European powers were discussing a possible mediation effort. The British also delayed the official proclamation of the lease of Mirs Bay from China, so that American ships would not have to be ordered out when news came of the declaration of war. After the Battle of Manila Bay, Admiral Dewey was allowed to send messages to Washington on the Hong Kong cable, and the British helped the Americans to contact Filipino guerrilla leader Emilio Aguinaldo; but a Spanish fleet trying to reach the Philippines was refused permission to take on coal at Egypt. Furthermore, London engineered the expulsion of a Spanish agent from Canada on questionable evidence, at the same time that British officials at Gibraltar allowed American espionage activities to go on there unhindered.[32] Such obvious courting of American favor by the British government, while no doubt based primarily on a realistic appraisal of Britain's world position and the value of American friendship, added to the strength of the emotional Anglo-Saxonism that was helping to draw the two countries together.

One of the questions often raised by Anglo-Saxonists during the war, and which continued to be discussed well into the following year, concerned the possibility of a military alliance between Great Britain and the United States. The idea of an Anglo-Saxon alliance, as we have seen in past chapters, was not a new one by any means. It will be recalled that during the Venezuela boundary dispute, Joseph Chamberlain and Arthur Balfour had proposed an alliance for the promotion of Anglo-Saxon ideals and interests. Richard Olney's advocacy of active cooperation based on the "patriotism of race" will also be remembered. Articles calling for an alliance had been appearing occasionally in British and American periodicals for years, but had never been taken very seriously.[33]

What set apart the alliance talk of 1898-99 from past proposals was its ubiquity in journals of opinion and the new seriousness attached to the idea, not only by the population and leadership in Great Britain and the United States, but by the foreign ministries of all the Great Powers. Rumors of a secret Anglo-American accord were incessant in 1898, and turned some European diplomats to contemplating the best means of countering this supposed new force in world politics.[34]

The event that, more than any other, stimulated the discussion of an alliance, was Joseph Chamberlain's famous speech at Birmingham on 13 May 1898. Delighted with America's emergence on the international scene at the very time Britain was seeking a counterweight to Russia in the Far East, and encouraged by John Hay not to let the Liberals monopolize the expressions of goodwill toward the new world power,[35] Chamberlain issued a resounding call for an Anglo-American alliance based on racial affinity. One of the primary duties of the British people, he said, was "to establish and maintain bonds of amity with our kinsmen across the Atlantic.... They speak our language, they are bred of our race." Then, in an apparent reference to the possibility of a world conflagration developing out of the anticipated breakup of China, Chamberlain told his cheering audience: "And I even go so far as to say that, terrible as war may be, even war itself would be cheaply purchased if in a great and noble cause the Stars and Stripes and the Union Jack should wave together over an Anglo-Saxon alliance."[36]

Chamberlain's words received a mixed reception in Britain and the United States, and, as might be expected, were roundly condemned in the Continental countries. The press of stricken Spain accused the colonial secretary of trying to plunge the whole world into war, in hopes that the conflict would end with the Anglo-Saxons straddling the globe.[37] Most organs of the British press, however, were favorable, especially the *Spectator*, which wholeheartedly endorsed "anything that makes for the strengthening of the Anglo-Saxon race."[38] The adverse response in Britain came from public officials fearful that Chamberlain's blunt declaration might actually harm the chances for an alliance, by arousing Irish and other anti-British elements in the United States. One M.P. accused the colonial secretary of having "done more to injure the prospect of an alliance with America" than any man in England.[39]

Chamberlain was unrepentant, however, and defended his speech in the House of Commons by raising the specter of a great coalition of Continental powers threatening "Anglo-Saxon liberty and Anglo-Saxon interests" in the near future. If such a threat arose, no amount of Irish votes would be able to "stand for a moment in the way of the sympathies which bind together the Anglo-Saxon race." Besides, as he told John Hay, he was "greatly pleased" with the reception his speech had received in the United States.[40]

Chamberlain had reason to be pleased. While most of the American press assumed a wait-and-see attitude toward the alliance possibility, and a few journals definitely opposed the idea, a substantial number of newspapers saw such a development as both natural and desirable. They assumed that an alliance would not only protect the common interests of all Anglo-Saxon people, but would promote justice and right in all corners of the globe. As the *Literary Digest* observed, many of the persons who shaped American opinion were ready to "welcome as never before the suggestion of Anglo-Saxon against the world."[41]

Reflecting widespread opinion of this sort in both countries, British and American periodicals blossomed in 1898–99 with numerous articles and editorial comments endorsing the idea of an Anglo-Saxon alliance. Lyman Abbott, the renowned Congregationalist minister and editor of the *Outlook*, held that such a combination would promote the political liberty, ethical spirit, energy, intelligence, and thrift that characterized the Anglo-Saxon race. James K. Hosmer, the historian, and B. O. Flower, editor of the *Arena*, descried in an alliance the first step toward the political federation of all Anglo-Saxon countries and the domination of the world by Anglo-Saxon power and principles. Other American writers held that a pact uniting Great Britain and the United States would lead eventually to a world government organized around Anglo-Saxon constitutional precepts.[42]

British publicists writing in support of an alliance included such distinguished individuals as James Bryce; Professor Albert V. Dicey; Lord Charles Beresford; Charles W. Dilke; George Sydenham Clarke, the noted navalist and student of imperial defense; and Sidney Low, the former editor of the *St. James's Gazette*. Judging from the content and tone of their articles, all of these men would have endorsed the views of a writer in the *Contemporary Review* who stated:

> Whether they [the two Anglo-Saxon peoples] desire it or not, the necessities of the world's life, the preservation of their own political ideals, and the commercial and economic conditions which they confront, must soon compel a closer *entente* between these two great

peoples. They are the peacemakers of the twentieth century, the protectors of the world's liberty, of free economic development, and of the weak nationalities of the earth.[43]

Underlying all the talk of an Anglo-Saxon alliance was the assumption that such a combination would be so powerful that it could guarantee world peace. Supporters held that no other power or combination of powers would dare attack a united Anglo-Saxondom, nor make war anywhere in the world without its consent.[44] Of course, discussion of an alliance was also stimulated by common apprehensions of Germany and the Dual Alliance powers of Russia and France. All three of these countries sympathized with Spain during the Spanish-American War, putting the United States on its guard and heightening American awareness of the value of British friendship. At the same time, both London and Washington were nervous about the growth of German sea power and highly suspicious of German intentions. Finally, with America's entry into the Great-Power rivalry in the Far East, many persons on both sides of the Atlantic recognized a common Anglo-American interest in preserving the open door by countering the aggressions of the Continental powers, especially Russia.

Looking to the possibility of war between the two English-speaking countries and their European rivals, one Englishman went so far as to make a study comparing the real and potential military strength of the United States and the British Empire to the strength of a triple alliance of France, Russia, and Germany. He concluded that an Anglo-American alliance would be decidedly superior and likely to win any war in the near future.[45] At least two popular novels of the day depicted a future conflict between an Anglo-Saxon alliance and a Continental coalition. In each imagined instance, the book's tall, muscular, blonde and blue-eyed Anglo-Saxons triumphed over their malevolent foes and used the occasion to establish peace, liberty, and Christian charity throughout the world.[46]

Nearly all the proponents of an alliance mentioned its supposed military invincibility, and most assumed that it would be able to dictate world peace, assure the triumph of justice and right in all international questions, induce other countries to adopt the superior principles of Anglo-Saxondom, and generally, as former

Prime Minister Lord Rosebery was reported to have told Oscar S. Straus, "control the world for the interests of the world."[47] It was a vision that appealed mightily to the national pride, the idealism, and the smug self-satisfaction of Britons and Americans alike, and its widespread acceptance accounts for much of the popularity of the alliance idea.

Backers of an Anglo-American alliance thus anticipated enormous benefits to both countries, and indeed to all mankind. Even the most enthusiastic supporters of the idea soon came to realize, however, that a formal treaty of alliance between the United States and Great Britain was out of the question at this time; the remnants of American Anglophobia, and the traditional American aversion to foreign entanglements, presented insurmountable obstacles. Recognizing this fact, the *Edinburgh Review* offered the explanation that binding alliances were "naturally distasteful to the robust independence of the Anglo-Saxon race." Sir Charles Dilke, addressing the House of Commons in June of 1898, declared that every Englishman would welcome "an alliance of hearts" between the two countries, "but none of us, and few Americans, think that it would be likely to produce what may be called a war alliance." Even Joseph Chamberlain eventually backed away from his earlier pronouncements on the subject, saying in December 1898 that Great Britain no longer hoped for a "permanent or general alliance," but only mutual consultations in the future and a concert of British and American policy where both governments agreed that it was necessary. Britons had to be content with the belief, widely accepted in the euphoric months of 1898, that the Americans would come to their aid if, at some time in the near future, the British nation found itself in extreme danger.[48] That some of them could believe such a thing at all testifies to the depth of the new-found British-American friendship.

Anglo-Saxonism played an important part in one other development in British-American relations in 1898: the warm support Britain gave to American annexation of Hawaii and the territories seized from Spain, especially the Philippines. "You will have noticed," James Bryce told Theodore Roosevelt, "that nearly everyone here applauds your imperialistic new departure."[49] This encouragement for American retention of the Philippines was largely a matter of sound policy for Britain, since Whitehall wanted to see the United States more deeply involved in Far Eastern affairs.[50] A study that takes into account the attitudes of the British public as well as the government, however, reveals that *Realpolitik* does not fully explain Britain's support for American expansion. As Geoffrey Seed discovered in surveying British journals of opinion, the most powerful incentive among the British populace toward support of American imperialism was the assumption of Anglo-American racial affinity. This assumption led Britons to predicate their support on three interconnected propositions: (1) It was racial instinct and destiny that led the United States to imperialism, and American expansion was therefore inevitable. (2) It was the duty of Americans, as members of a superior race, to aid in civilizing the world and keeping the peace. (3) American expansion would help protect Anglo-Saxon civilization and was a step toward Anglo-Saxon domination of the world.[51]

The first proposition, that it was the destiny of the race to expand its power and influence, was put most succinctly by George Sydenham Clarke, who asserted in August 1898 that "the inherited instincts of the race" were "forcing the American people onward and outward." Race energy and race aptitudes—the same forces, according to Clarke, that had played an instrumental part in the creation of the British Empire—were propelling the United States on its expansionist course. Clarke's words were echoed by a number of other eminent Englishmen who informed their readers that the elemental cause of the Spanish-American War was the inherent Anglo-Saxon hunger for land and power. Charles Beresford declared that those persons who opposed the policy of annexation "forget that the whole history of the Anglo-Saxon rise and development is to be found in this extension of boundaries." The United States surely would assume sovereignty in all the conquered lands.[52]

Undoubtedly the foremost spokesman for the concept of imperialism as the Anglo-Saxon's duty was Rudyard Kipling, whose famous poem "The White Man's Burden" was printed in the London *Times* and *McClure's* in the same month the Senate ratified the peace treaty with Spain.[53] Kipling was probably thinking mainly of the "Anglo-Saxon's burden" when he penned the oft-quoted words about the "White Man's Burden"; certainly many people at the time interpreted the poem in the Anglo-Saxon sense.[54] Joseph Chamberlain was cheered by the sight of Americans "entering the lists and sharing the task which might have proved too heavy for us alone." Chamberlain believed that the pursuit of a common mission would gradually draw together the British and American peoples and lead the two governments to a close relationship. Other British writers and public men proclaimed the good fortune of the Filipinos in coming under Anglo-Saxon rule. Of all the advanced races, they said, only the Anglo-Saxons took seriously their duty to uplift and enlighten their semicivilized charges. Americans would be better rulers and teachers than any other people except the British.[55]

The belief that American imperialism was a step toward Anglo-Saxon world domination was based on the assumption that an imperial policy would lead naturally to the desired alliance with Great Britain. Englishmen also supported American expansion in the belief that a greater role for the United States in international affairs would serve to safeguard Anglo-Saxon civilization. Cecil Spring Rice epitomized this kind of thinking. In a letter to Henry Cabot Lodge in July 1898, Spring Rice said that he had "no sympathy whatever with the people who believe that English institutions, literature, language and greatness are courtiers at the throne of London." On the contrary, he said, these things were "common possessions" of all Anglo-Saxons, "to be defended, as they were won, in common." Haunted for years by the possibility of the Germans or Russians overrunning the British Empire, Spring Rice saw the new departure in American foreign relations as an indication that he need be less fearful in the future. On hearing of the American decision to retain the Philippines, he wrote to Theodore Roosevelt that the news made him feel "as if a nightmare was over. It means possibly that our race and civilisation is [sic] safe."[56]

The evidence thus suggests that much more than *Realpolitik* was involved in Great Britain's support for American annexation of the islands seized from Spain. Arguments based on the assumption of Anglo-American racial affinity and superiority were present in nearly every public discussion of the matter, and no doubt strongly influenced the British view of American imperialism. Of course, in justifying and extolling American expansion on racial grounds, the British were drawing on many of the same arguments as imperialists in the United States, who often declared that it was the divinely ordained mission of Americans, as representatives of a superior race, to extend their benevolent influence to the dark regions of the earth. "I believe," wrote Captain Mahan, "that the United States has duties to the world outside, as well as to herself—that in a general way the extension of 'Anglo-Saxon' control is a distinct benefit to the world." Albert Beveridge of Indiana, one of the most outspoken imperialists in the United States Senate, believed that the Anglo-Saxon inheritance of Americans rendered expansion both desirable and inevitable. After all, he told an Indianapolis audience, "we are of the ruling race of the world... ours is the blood of government; ours the hearts of dominion; ours the brain and genius of administration."[57] Proponents of expansion like Mahan and Beveridge could not help but contrast Britain's warm support with the spiteful attitude of other powers—Germany in particular—which coveted Spain's former island empire for themselves. And people in both the United States and Great Britain must have felt the bond between them strengthened by the shared belief that they, as Anglo-Saxons, had an imperial duty and destiny.

Thus it is clear that Anglo-Saxonism had considerable importance in bringing about a marked improvement in British-American relations in 1898. The assumed racial affinity of the two peoples accounted for much, if not most, of the sympathy Britons expressed for the American cause before and during the war with Spain, and for the spirited manner in which they greeted America's expansionist policy at the war's end. The American people returned British sentiment in kind, expressing time and again, in words sincere if at times exaggerated, their high regard for the British nation and devotion to the ideal of racial brotherhood. During the frenetic months of 1898, even the idea of a military alliance with Great Britain could get a hearing in the press, if not in the conference rooms of Washington. Theodore Roosevelt, himself highly distrustful of the British prior to the war with Spain, recognized in 1898 that a massive shift had occurred in American attitudes toward Great Britain. Because of British sympathy for the United States, Anglo-American relations were better now than at any time since Lexington and Concord.

Roosevelt told his English friends that every effort should be made to keep them that way: "for their interests are really fundamentally the same, and they are far more closely akin, not merely in blood, but in feeling and principle, than either is akin to any other people in the world." While recognizing that the emotional mutual admiration of 1898 would soon fade away, Roosevelt hoped that a residue of goodwill would remain to nourish the maturing Anglo-American rapprochement in the months and years to come.[58] As we shall see in succeeding chapters, his wish was fulfilled.

7

Anglo-Saxonism and the American Response to the Boer War

On 11 October 1899, Great Britain's long quarrel with the Boers in South Africa erupted into open warfare, as Boer forces struck southeast into Natal and west into Bechuanaland. For the next several months, the British position was dismal. The ill-prepared and poorly officered British troops in South Africa suffered a series of humiliating defeats. The Boers cut the Cape-Rhodesia rail line, laid siege to the garrisons at Kimberley, Mafeking, and Ladysmith, and invaded Cape Colony. Britain rushed reinforcements to South Africa, but until February 1900, all the fighting was in the territory of the British colonies.

A much more serious threat than the early Boer successes, however, was the explosion of anti-British feeling on the Continent. Most Europeans lauded the Boers as heroic freedom-fighters. Russia, ever watchful to extend its influence at the expense of Britain, sought a coalition with France and Germany to take advantage of the British preoccupation with South Africa.[1] Some people in Britain, remembering that a colonial war and European intervention had brought down the first British Empire, feared that history might repeat itself.

The Boer War provided a stiff test for the gradually developing rapprochement between Great Britain and the United States. The two countries might easily have slipped back into the old resentment and distrust. Most Americans sympathized almost instinctively with the Boers in their uneven contest with the mighty British Empire. They blamed the British for the war and condemned them as bullies and gold-hungry land-grabbers. Arthur Lee, who, like most Britons, had cheered American victories only a year and a half before, sadly observed in January 1900: "The gratitude for our support during the Spanish difficulty seems sadly evanescent in certain quarters."[2] Congress and the public were overwhelmingly pro-Boer, and this gave hope to Boer agents in their repeated attempts to secure American assistance in mediating an end to the war that would secure full independence for the two Boer republics.

Yet, remarkably, the policy of the United States government throughout the war was one of unabashed sympathy with Great Britain.[3] Ambassador Julian Pauncefote, writing to Lord Salisbury in mid-January 1900, reported: "The warmth & friendliness of manner shown towards me by the President & all his cabinet is very marked, & evidently intended to show their desire to maintain & promote the entente cordiale & the 'unwritten Treaty' which undoubtedly exists in spite of the outcry about the word 'alliance.'"[4] During the war, American diplomats looked after British interests and the welfare of British prisoners of war in the Transvaal and the Orange Free State. American bankers floated loans that paid roughly twenty percent of Britain's war costs. The government allowed the export of all manner of military supplies, an arrangement of considerable benefit to Britain, which controlled the seas. On the occasions when Americans tried to ship goods to the Boers, Washington's protests over alleged British violations of neutral rights were decidedly low-key. Most importantly, the United States government gave Boer envoys very cool receptions, and refused to pursue the idea of mediation. In fact, in March of 1900, Secretary of State John Hay purposely forestalled an anticipated mediation effort by the Continental powers by giving Salisbury an opportunity to reject it in advance. "For the present we seem to have spiked their guns," Hay told Henry White.[5]

Technically, all these American actions (and non-actions) were within the bounds then established in international law to govern the conduct of neutrals.[6] However, the practical result of the McKinley administration's behavior was a policy so favorable to Great Britain that Secretary Hay repeatedly had to deny charges that a "secret alliance" existed between the two countries. Basing his conclusion on the pro-British sympathies of key figures in the American government, and on the unfortunate results of American policy as far as the Boers were concerned, the scholar who gave the most attention to American diplomacy and the South African war flatly accused the United States of "assuring the annihilation of the Boer republics."[7]

Historians have offered a wide variety of explanations for the pro-British policy of the United States government: repayment for British benevolence in 1898; the personal bias of John Hay; the desire to use the friendship to extort British concessions in negotiations for a new Central American canal treaty and for a treaty on the Alaska boundary; the profitable wartime trade, and expectations of a much larger postwar South African trade if Britain was victorious; a healthy respect for British power and an appreciation of the value to the United States of continued British friendship; recognition that the Boers had oppressed British settlers (the "Uitlanders") and black Africans in their republics, and thus helped bring the war on themselves; the propaganda efforts of pro-British American missionaries in South Africa; concern lest a British disaster tilt the world balance of power against the United States; and unwillingness to condemn a British colonial war while Americans were fighting one of their own in the Philippines.[8]

At one time or another, all these considerations may have influenced the thinking of American policy-makers and the pro-British minority that provided important public support for the government's course of action. But there was another consideration that was seldom absent from American discussion of the war, and certainly exercised considerable influence on American policy: Anglo-Saxonism. Many Americans, both in and out of government, believed that a British victory in South Africa was essential to the prestige and influence of the Anglo-Saxon race; that it would be a good thing for Anglo-Saxons, for the Boers, and for the world at large if the British controlled the agricultural and mineral riches of South Africa; and that the Boers, while wonderfully brave, were a crude and inert people and an impediment to the advance of "civilization" as represented by Anglo-Saxon Britain. It will be the purpose of this chapter to explore the Anglo-Saxonist beliefs of articulate Americans, especially powerful and influential individuals like John Hay, Theodore Roosevelt, and Alfred Thayer Mahan, and to assess the impact of Anglo-Saxonism on American policy during the Boer War.

Just six days after the Boers initiated hostilities, Cecil Spring Rice, then attached to the British legation at Tehran, sat down to write an unhappy letter to Theodore Roosevelt. "If I were not an Englishman," he wrote, "I should certainly sympathize with the Boers—and we can't possibly complain of people doing it. But viewed impartially it would be a better thing that S. Africa should be Anglo-Saxon than Dutch[,] and I have learnt that from you [,] Dutchman as you are."[9]

Spring Rice was at least partly justified in naming Roosevelt as the source of his "impartial" view of the Boer War. As early as 1896, while still a police commissioner in New York City, Roosevelt had predicted serious trouble in South Africa and voiced an opinion on what the outcome should be. He told Henry White that he had great admiration for the Boers, but felt it was "to the interest of civilization that the English-speaking race should be dominant in South Africa, exactly as it is for the interest of civilization that the United States themselves, the greatest branch of the English-speaking race, should be dominant in the Western Hemisphere."[10] In the opinion of Roosevelt and those who thought like him, any extension of Anglo-Saxon rule was by definition a gain for humanity. It was this assumption that shaped Roosevelt's response to the outbreak of the Boer War. Replying to Spring Rice's letter, he said that the Boers had "many fine traits," an arguable cause, and a sympathetic audience in the United States. But in the end, the Boers would have to accept British rule, since "it would be for the advantage of mankind to have English spoken south of the Zambesi."[11]

John Hay, the most thoroughly partisan supporter of Britain in the American government, shared Roosevelt's opinion that the British, as the representatives of a superior race, were fighting the battle of civilization and progress in South Africa. Hay's beliefs were of particular significance because President McKinley left the formulation of American policy toward the war almost entirely in the hands of his secretary of state.[12] While ambassador at London prior to coming to the State Department, Hay had made the acquaintance of Cecil Rhodes and heard him describe his dream of extending British rule throughout South Africa. Hay was won over immediately to Rhodes's ideas.[13] His actions during the Boer War make clear his determination that the Boers, for whom he had only aristocratic contempt, should not stand in the way of Anglo-Saxon expansion. Shortly before the war broke out, Hay told Henry White that he hoped the British would "make quick work" of the Boers. Six months later, Hay told White he was convinced "that the fight of England in South Africa is the fight of civilization and progress." He was convinced, too, that "most men of sense" in the United States shared his view.[14]

Perhaps not "most men of sense" agreed with Hay, but a substantial number of them did. Harvard engineering professor and former naval officer I. N. Hollis told a meeting of Canadian and American civil engineers that the British cause was "the cause of the Anglo-Saxon race, which stands to me as the great bulwark of civilization and individual freedom." James Ford Rhodes, one of America's most honored historians, agreed. George F. Becker, a respected geologist and an expert on the South African gold fields, announced that the British were "fighting to obtain for British subjects in the Transvaal . . . liberty to be civilized after the manner of Anglo-Saxons."[15] Whitelaw Reid, editor of the nation's leading Republican journal, the *New York Tribune*, committed his considerable talents to convincing Americans that a British victory would be "best for the security of personal rights, for the ordered liberty and the advancing civilization of the world."[16] Reid's efforts early in the war drew a pleased response from Alfred Thayer Mahan, who thanked the editor "for keeping before our public that there is a British as well as a Boer side to the Transvaal controversy." Mahan feared that unsavory elements in the American populace (primarily Irishmen, Germans, and Democrats) would take advantage of widespread sympathy for the Boers to try to disrupt the Anglo-American understanding. Mahan thought it would be a calamity if they succeeded. He told Henry Cabot Lodge that he, personally, had no sympathy at all for the Boers. He believed they had provoked the war by attempting to impose the supremacy of "the Dutch race" in South Africa. "This the British, both at home & abroad, were determined not to have."[17]

Most of Britain's supporters in the United States pointedly differentiated British and Boer racial characteristics. (The notable exception was Theodore Roosevelt, who, as a Dutchman himself, had to believe that the Boers "down at bottom have the great basic virtues of the Teutonic races.")[18] Those who could not justify labeling the Boers as innate racial inferiors still found it easy to accuse them of backwardness and cultural inferiority. Their stubborn resistance to the modernizing tendencies introduced into South Africa by British settlers proved that they were "out of touch with the civilization of the modern world," said the *New York Times*. Most other organs of the New York press pictured the Boers—with some degree of accuracy—as a people who had scarcely advanced beyond the seventeenth century. Their social structure was patriarchal and oppressive; their economy was pastoral and stagnant; their religion had not changed since the days of John Calvin; and they treated black Africans as little better than slaves. "In this Transvaal war," said one New Yorker in a letter to E. L. Godkin, editor of the *Nation*, "Britain stands for freedom and civilization; the Boer 'Republic' represents the barbarism and the despotism that are a survival of the dark ages." South Africa badly needed civilizing by Anglo-Saxons.[19]

Some supporters of the British cause went much further in denouncing Boer backwardness. President Benjamin Ide Wheeler of the University of California declared that "the claim of local barbarism based on squatter sovereignty is likely to be recognised neither for the American Indian and Zulu, nor for Mormon or Boer." A writer in the *Arena* depicted the Boers as ignorant, dogmatic, slovenly, and unsociable, and went on to describe the war as essentially a "race war" between industrious and progressive Anglo-Saxons and "a race in direct and arid opposition to the advancement of civilization." By resisting progress, the Boers had forfeited any right to political independence.[20]

Believing as they did that civilization and the interests of the entire Anglo-Saxon race were wrapped up in the British war effort, American supporters of Britain were horrified at the terrible defeats inflicted on the British forces in December 1899. During the period known as "Black Week" (10–15 December)—the most disastrous week for British arms in the nineteenth century—an ill-conceived frontal assault by British infantry at Magersfontein resulted in a frightful slaughter; General Sir William Gatacre, advancing with a second British column, was routed at Stormberg; and the hapless General Sir Redvers Buller, leading a relief force towards the encircled garrison at Ladysmith, was repulsed at the Tugela River with heavy losses.

John Hay was appalled at these developments, particularly since the Boer victories greatly increased pro-Boer sympathy in the United States. "A smashing victory would quiet everything considerably," he wrote Ambassador Joseph Choate in London, "but I gravely fear the effect of another British defeat." Hay was also concerned that the English branch of the race had "lost all skill in fighting" and was becoming decadent. If this were so, he said, it was "a portentous fact," since British power "on the whole made for peace and civilization."[21]

Other members of the foreign policy elite in the United States were equally dismayed at the events of December. Henry Cabot Lodge, one of the most outspoken Republicans on the Senate Foreign Relations Committee and an implacable defender of the administration's policy, laid the blame for the British defeats on "the fact that they have been whipping hill tribes and Dervishes so long that they have forgotten how white men fight." He feared that the Continental powers would now intervene with the purpose of destroying the British Empire, a development that "no rational American" could see as anything but a catastrophe.[22]

Alfred Thayer Mahan and Theodore Roosevelt also dreaded European intervention in the conflict while Britain was down. Such intervention and British defeat, they agreed, would be a terrible blow to the Anglo-Saxon race and all it stood for. Mahan hurried off a letter to his English friend James R. Thursfield, saying, "I cannot express with what deep sorrow and anxiety your checks affect me.... But I cannot believe God will permit so beneficent a government to be permanently disabled."[23] Roosevelt, like John Hay, worried that "the lack of fighting edge in the British soldier" meant that the British had grown decadent. He admired the Boers for their military prowess, but "the frenzy of England's continental critics" in the wake of Black Week strengthened his conviction that the interests of the entire English-speaking race were threatened. "I should very strongly favor this country taking a hand in the game if the European continent selected this opportunity to try to smash the British Empire," he said. "Real liberty and real progress are bound up with the prosperity of the English-speaking peoples."[24]

Hay, Lodge, Mahan, and Roosevelt were in the minority in the United States in deploring Britain's ill fortune, but quite a few of their countrymen agreed with them. The New York *Mail and Express* said that "if Anglo-Saxon power and resourcefulness" had been on trial during the Spanish-American War, "they are today on trial to a greater degree." *Harper's Weekly* cautioned Americans not to "lose sight of the stupendous fact that British prestige is in mortal danger; nor can we fail, if we have a proper pride of race, or a decent sense of gratitude, or a consciousness of what the English have accomplished in the homes of the savage races, to mourn over these disasters." Godkin's *Nation* published a letter from a retired American journalist presently living in London, deploring the apparent fact that "probably not one in ten of our people sees far enough into the future of civilization to understand that the prevalent influence of England rather than that of any other of the European Powers... would be for the benefit of the race at large.... They cannot, or will not, see that England, everywhere she goes, is planting industrial and human interests which are growing and ripening not only for our race, but for all races of men." Whitelaw Reid told readers of the *Tribune* that they should hope for a quick recovery of British fortunes and the defeat of the Boers, so that Anglo-Saxon civilization might "more and more prevail throughout the earth."[25] Mark Twain, who was in England, wrote home to William Dean Howells that even though he had believed for some time that British actions in South Africa were "in every way shameful and excuseless," he could not now condemn the British cause:

> Every day I write (in my head) bitter magazine articles about it, but I have to stop with that. For England must not fall; it would mean an inundation of Russian and German political degradations which would envelop the globe and steep it in a sort of Middle-Age night and slavery which would last till Christ comes again. Even wrong—and she is wrong—England must be upheld. He is an enemy of the human race who shall speak against her now.[26]

The European intervention that some Americans feared never materialized, however, and during the weeks following the disastrous defeats of December, tens of thousands of British reinforcements poured into South Africa from Great Britain, India, and the dominions. In February 1900, the war entered a new phase, with overwhelmingly superior British forces (about 180,000 men compared to fewer than 50,000 Boer troops) taking the offensive. Under Lords Kitchener and Roberts, two of the Empire's best generals, they moved relentlessly northward, relieving the besieged garrisons and proceeding to invade the two Boer republics. "The champions of civilization have underrated the physical prowess of their neighbors, and they are now paying the penalty of their mistake," said a writer in the *North American Review* shortly after the surrender of the Boer General Cronjé at Paardeberg and the relief of Ladysmith. "But their ultimate triumph cannot be doubted." Observing the determination of the British to bring the Boers to heel, the Boston *Transcript* found evidence of the "racial capability" of the Anglo-Saxons. Although the British Army had suffered terrible defeats early in the war, after each defeat it had come up "in grim, set purpose to conquer." The paper concluded that "a more mercurial race might have given up its task, but the dogged courage of tenacity peculiar to the Anglo-Saxon asserted itself after every repulse, and finally won."[27]

With the British on the offensive and the Boers in full retreat, a new element became evident in American discussion of the war. Supporters of the British, taking the collapse of the Boers as proof positive of Boer "inferiority," began to talk of the war as a Darwinian struggle in which the "fit" Anglo-Saxon race would inevitably crush out the independence of the "unfit" Boers. "It is sad to witness a human race succumbing to the principle of the survival of the fittest," wrote one observer shortly after the British conquest and annexation of the Orange Free State; "but how much sadder would it not be to see the superior race succumb to the inferior?" According to Edwin Maxey, an authority on constitutional law, the Boers had not adapted to the liberal social and political environment of the twentieth century; and hence, like an animal species that failed to adapt to a new environment, they were doomed to defeat and possible extinction. Still another interested American, Professor Washburn Hopkins of Yale, declared that the evolutionary principles being manifested in South Africa constituted a "higher morality" than the international morality appealed to by Boer sympathizers:

> Is there not here a counterpart in the moral world to the inflexible severity of physical laws, whereby the maintenance of the race is upheld at the sacrifice of individuals? In the end, as far as man is concerned, the survival of the fittest is the success of the most civilized, or of those who potentially at least represent humanity's progress.... Therefore Spain bends to America, for ours is the right of way by the higher law of racial superiority.

"So, whether just or unjust, by the foot-rule of man's code," Hopkins concluded, "England's battle in Africa is in effect a moral struggle in behalf of the human race."[28]

Captain Mahan was one of those who perceived in the British advance the triumph of a race inherently superior to its opponent. Mahan was determined to do what he could to counteract the pro-Boer sentiments of the majority of Americans, and hence he conscientiously used his publicizing gifts to influence what he called "the class that thinks understandingly and most shapes that formless thing we call public opinion."[29] Mahan reacted angrily in late January 1900 to a statement by Senator George F. Hoar of Massachusetts, comparing the struggle of the Boers to the defense of Thermopylae by Leonidas and his three hundred Spartans. Mahan published a reply in the *Independent* in which he asserted that the Boers and the Spartans had only one thing in common—both were governed by corrupt and oppressive oligarchies. He then went on to argue that the Boers suffered from unfitness for modern conditions; the events of the recent past proved once and for all that the continued existence of the Boer republics was inconsistent with the general welfare of humanity and civilization. South Africa, Mahan concluded, must henceforth be subject to English traditions of liberty and law—traditions that had again proved their inherent fitness to survive.[30]

While Anglo-Saxonists like Mahan tried to explain and justify the new turn of events in South Africa through the use of Darwinian terminology, several prominent persons in England sought to bring their case before the American public by writing articles for the generally pro-British *North American Review*. In nearly every instance, they appealed for support on grounds of the supposed racial affinity of Britons and Americans and the superiority of Anglo-Saxon culture. The Marquis of Lorne, pointing out that "the nations that have no Anglo-Saxon stock . . . are all against us," asserted that Great Britain was "compelled" to pursue a policy of domination in South Africa; otherwise, the Uitlanders in the Boer republics would be denied the free institutions and superior civilization that were their birthrights as Anglo-Saxons. Similarly, Mary Endicott Chamberlain, the American wife of the secretary for the colonies, reminded her countrymen that the Anglo-Saxon race bore "the responsibility for the civilization and welfare of the vast populations which turn to the English-speaking people for protection and good government." Although Mrs. Chamberlain did not mention them specifically, she probably had in mind, among others, the black peoples of South Africa who had suffered at the hands of the Boers. Yet another observer in England believed most Americans realized "that it was better for the world at large that England should succeed." And later in the year 1900, Lord Charles Beresford assured readers of the *Review* that once the Boers had given up the struggle and been introduced to the advantages of Anglo-Saxon education and civil freedom, they would become "in their turn sturdy defenders of the Anglo-Saxon tradition, were the whole force of the Old World oligarchies to endeavor to stifle the progressive Anglo-Saxon race."[31]

John Hay did not have to be prodded with such appeals to rejoice at the steady advance of the British armies in South Africa. The Dutch minister, Baron Gevers, was greatly surprised one day, shortly after the British took the offensive, when he visited Secretary Hay and was greeted with the words, "At last we have had a success." When Gevers asked Hay in what field the United States had scored a success, the embarrassed secretary of state had to admit that he was referring to the British success in South Africa.[32] In mid-March, Hay wrote to Henry White that he hoped the British would soon finish the job of subduing the Boers. He felt confident, he said, that once the war ended and the Boer republics were absorbed into the British Empire, American public opinion would soon "settle down to the conviction that this was the only issue compatible with the honor of Great Britain or with our own future interests."³³ Two months later, Secretary Hay infuriated and bewildered a three-man Boer delegation that had come to Washington to seek a mediated settlement before the British could complete the defeat of the Boer armies. The three had been extravagantly feted on their arrival in New York City and escorted to Washington by a group of Democratic congressmen. Hay, however, was unimpressed. He granted them only a very brief, formal interview, during which he read them a prepared statement declaring that the policy of the United States toward the South African war was, and would continue to be, "impartial neutrality." To make things perfectly clear to the Boer envoys, the British ambassador, Lord Pauncefote, was ushered into Hay's office as they were being escorted out. Hay's conduct so angered the Boers that they spent several weeks thereafter touring the United States, denouncing the McKinley administration.³⁴

Theodore Roosevelt greeted the British advance with a combination of regret and hope. He regretted that "the representatives of two such splendid races" should still be killing each other; but he hoped that the British would now bring the war to a successful conclusion and get on with the task of establishing "a great English-speaking commonwealth south of the Zambesi."³⁵

Roosevelt's opinion of the Boers was higher than ever during the period of the British offensive. Always an admirer of military skill and courage, he declared that the early Boer successes on the battlefield proved conclusively that despite their "uncouthness and surface unattractiveness," the Boers possessed "at bottom the same qualities that the English and Scotch, Scandinavians, Netherlanders and Germans all have."³⁶ He had also concluded that both sides to the conflict, Briton and Boer, were, from their different standpoints, in the right. The Boers were perfectly justified in fighting for total political independence from the British Empire. The British, on the other hand, had a perfect right to demand equal treatment for British settlers in the Boer republics and to try to insure the security of their South African colonies and of the Cape route by bringing the Boers into line. Roosevelt was made melancholy by the thought that two superior peoples, each of them with a good cause, should have to fight one another.³⁷

His opinion held firm, however, that the advance of civilization depended on a British victory. He thought both sides would benefit from such a result. A British-controlled South Africa would lead to a fusion of the British and Dutch populations, such as had occurred 250 years earlier between his own Dutch ancestors and the English in the colony of New York. The Boers would fall heir to the "freedom and order and material and moral prosperity" that characterized the civilization of the English-speaking peoples. And the English-speaking race as a whole would benefit from the infusion of Boer blood and the addition of South Africa to its worldwide domain. Finally, Roosevelt believed that British domination of South Africa and the fusion of the British and Boer peoples would help insure that "the twentieth century will still be the century of the men who speak English." The civilization of the world would gain enormously from the continued supremacy of the English-speaking race.[38]

Unfortunately, Roosevelt's hope for a quick conclusion to the war, "to avoid bloodshed and leave as little rancor as may be behind," was not fully realized.[39] British forces entered Pretoria in June of 1900, and less than two months later the last Transvaal army was defeated in the eastern part of the republic. President Paul Kruger fled to Holland, and Lord Roberts formally annexed the Transvaal to the Crown. For almost two years after the annexation of the Transvaal, however, mobile units of Boer commandos carried on a protracted and painful guerrilla war in South Africa.

The Boers' refusal to surrender after their evident defeat meant that the administration's South African policy was bound to be an issue in the upcoming American political campaign. William Jennings Bryan, the acknowledged leader of the Democratic party, had begun appealing to pro-Boer sentiment among the voters as early as January 1900, attacking the British on the one hand and the policy of McKinley and Hay on the other. Most of the Democratic state conventions that met in the spring to elect delegates to the national convention adopted resolutions in support of the Boers. And as expected, when the Democrats assembled at Kansas City in July to put together a platform and nominate Bryan, they made much of the Boers' continuing struggle for independence. Applause greeted every mention of the Boers, and the platform adopted by the convention not only extended the party's sympathy to "the heroic burghers," but denounced "the ill-concealed Republican alliance with England."[40]

Many prominent Republicans were concerned lest the war issue damage McKinley's reelection prospects, and a number of Republican convention delegates announced their intention to work for a pro-Boer plank in their own party's platform. Secretary Hay, disgusted at the continuing uproar over the issue and at Bryan's pronouncements in favor of the Boers, wrote to Henry Adams on 15 June, just four days before the Republican convention was due to meet at Philadelphia: "I have the greatest admiration for the Boers' smartness, but it is their bravery that our idiotic public is snivelling over. If they were only as brave as they are slim, the war would have ended long ago by their extermination. . . . Your friend Bryan, ass that he is, says that the Boer War is an issue in our campaign—I suppose because the British are 16 to 1."[41]

On the very day that the Republican convention was gaveled to order, Joseph Chamberlain delivered a speech in London that was clearly meant to be heard in Washington and Philadelphia. Addressing the Women's Liberal Unionist Association, Chamberlain said that Britain expected Europe to be hostile to its efforts in South Africa. "But," he continued, "there are quarters whence even a note of disapproval would be a matter of serious concern." Two years before, when the United States was at war with Spain, the British had not entered into "quizzical disquisitions or technical discussions, but recognized that they [the Americans] were carrying out as Anglo-Saxons a great work of civilization and humanity." Now Great Britain was engaged in a similar task in South Africa, Chamberlain said, and the British people asked the people of the United States to see their actions in the same light; "and we believe that in the long run we shall gain the final seal of their approval."[42]

Chamberlain's words probably strengthened the determination of administration forces at the Republican convention not to allow a pro-Boer plank into the platform. After a difficult fight, they succeeded in getting the convention to adopt an ambiguous plank that commended the President for past efforts on behalf of peace; reaffirmed the principle of nonintervention in European controversies; and expressed an earnest hope that in South Africa, "a way may soon be found, honorable alike to both contending parties, to terminate the strife between them."[43]

As it turned out, the Boer issue probably had very little effect on the outcome of the election, primarily because most of the American public had accepted a British victory as inevitable. Bryan made some gains in areas of the country with large German populations, but McKinley, stressing national prosperity, was easily reelected. Furthermore, of the fourteen senators who stood for reelection in 1900 after supporting pro-Boer resolutions in the Senate, nine were defeated. Clearly, by the fall of 1900, most voters had lost interest in the war.[44]

The pressures of the reelection campaign thus failed to deflect the McKinley administration from its pro-British course in South Africa. Nor did the administration allow its position on the South African conflict to be altered by the difficulties surrounding the American effort to reach agreement with Great Britain on the terms of a new isthmian canal treaty to replace the old Clayton-Bulwer convention of 1850. The British refused to ratify the first attempt to reach such an agreement, the abortive Hay-Pauncefote treaty of 1900, after the United States Senate so amended the treaty as to alter its provisions almost entirely. In the second Hay-Pauncefote treaty, signed in November of 1901, Great Britain finally acquiesced to American demands for the right to fortify and defend the canal, and to act as the sole guarantor of its neutrality. If anything, however, the acquiescence was a willing one: hard pressed in South Africa and elsewhere, the British were eager to retain American friendship, and they knew that in conceding American predominance in Central America and the Caribbean—areas where British interests were not vital—they were only granting proper recognition to what had become a fact of international life. Moreover, Whitehall was not seriously opposed to leaving the defense of the status quo in that part of the world to the United States, especially since such an action would release British naval units for duties closer to home. In truth, as Lord Pauncefote declared soon after the second treaty was signed, the British government "surrendered no right worth keeping," while it displayed toward the United States a "generous & friendly" attitude that would "do much to keep up our good relations." In granting the United States all that it asked, the British almost certainly gained more than they relinquished.[45]

With the resolution of the difficult isthmian issue late in 1901, those two ardent Anglo-Saxonists, John Hay and Theodore Roosevelt (who became president in September of 1901 following McKinley's assassination), were free to maintain their friendly policy toward Britain and the British war effort in South Africa. Roosevelt clung to his hope for a great English-speaking commonwealth south of the Zambesi, and Hay continued to be motivated by his conviction that Britain's cause was the cause of all Anglo-Saxons. Hay's actions continued to reflect his bias. He made known to the exiled President Kruger that he would be unwelcome in the United States, and he made it very clear that the United States "could not possibly" use its good offices to bring the two parties to the conference table. In February 1902, he answered widespread complaints about the concentration camps the British had established in South Africa by asserting: "The Boer women and children are in the Concentration Camps simply because their husbands and brothers want them there, and as to the war with all its hideous incidents and barbarities, it will stop the instant [the Boer Generals] Botha and deWet wish it to stop."[46]

The war did stop about three months later, on 31 May 1902, when British and Boer representatives signed the Peace of Vereeniging. The Boers accepted British sovereignty, and the British in turn gave guarantees that the Boers would enjoy self-government in the not-too-distant future. President Roosevelt welcomed the end of the war with a final wish that the people of South Africa might become "a very valuable addition to the English-speaking stock throughout the world."[47] As for John Hay, he was proud of his efforts on behalf of the British cause. In 1903, the mayor of Dunedin, New Zealand sent him a number of gifts and testimonials that had originally been intended for Hay's son, Adelbert, who had served as United States consul at Pretoria in 1900 and had performed valuable services there for British and dominion (including New Zealander) prisoners of war. Adelbert had been accidentally killed in a fall shortly after his return to the United States, and hence the tokens of appreciation from New

Zealand were sent to his father. In his reply to the mayor of Dunedin, Hay said he was grateful that in the short span of life allotted to his son, "he was able to do something to testify to the sentiments of sympathy and friendship which unite all branches of the English-speaking race, however widely separated they may be."[48] It was just such sentiments that had helped to motivate John Hay's policy toward the Boer War for over two and a half years.

○ ○ ○

There can be little doubt that the Anglo-Saxonist convictions of John Hay and those who thought like him were a major determinant of American policy during the Boer War. Hay's actions were obviously influenced by his faith in the superior virtues of Anglo-Saxon civilization. Theodore Roosevelt based his support for the British primarily on racial considerations. Alfred Thayer Mahan, whose opinions on foreign policy matters carried considerable weight in the United States, devoted himself throughout the war to counteracting public sympathy for the Boers and promoting what he termed "the cause of the English speaking peoples & their common tradition."[49]

Nor were Hay, Roosevelt, and Mahan alone in citing Anglo-Saxon race sentiment as the justification for a pro-British policy. A substantial number of influential and articulate Americans, frequently citing Anglo-Saxon superiority and Anglo-American racial affinity, threw their support behind a policy that gave material support and moral comfort to Great Britain. The support of these people was a very important development, for it meant that the pro-Boer sympathies of the majority were tempered by what Roosevelt called "a very strong friendly feeling toward England."[50] This friendly feeling in turn helped make the government's policy politically feasible in the face of hostile majority opinion.

The Anglo-American rapprochement thus survived a stiff test during the Boer War. Had important members of the United States foreign policy community been less devoted to Anglo-Saxonism, they might have been more attentive to the opinions of the Boers' supporters and more benevolent toward the Boer cause—and correspondingly more contentious toward the embattled British. Such a course could have revived old antagonisms and wrecked the growing British-American understanding. As it was, however, Anglo-Saxonism prevailed. "One has only to imagine the tornado of invective that would have whirled over the country had the war broken out five years ago to gauge how far America has travelled from the point of view that made the Venezuelan outburst possible," said a British observer in 1900, recalling the boundary dispute that had momentarily aroused such passions in the United States.[51] The people of Great Britain, while unhappy at the support for the Boers evident in American public opinion, much appreciated the expressions of friendship by the pro-British minority and the decidedly friendly attitude of the United States government. The war in South Africa brought no serious deterioration in Anglo-American relations.

8

Dealing with the Russians in the Far East: The Slavic Threat to Anglo-Saxon Supremacy

On a June day in 1859, a small party of American sailors under Commodore Josiah Tattnall stood by aboard a chartered steamer to observe two British gunboats trying to force their way past the Chinese forts on the Pei-ho River. The Chinese forts were very strong, and it was soon evident, as the two sides exchanged fire, that the British were being worsted. Commodore Tattnall, who was supposed to be a neutral observer, could not tolerate the punishment the British were taking. Exclaiming "Blood is thicker than water," he ordered his men to join in the fray and assist the British in making ready the guns and moving up reserves. Tattnall's conduct was later approved by the secretary of the Navy.[1]

Forty years later, those favoring Anglo-American cooperation in the Far East appealed again to the blood ties between the two nations. This time, however, the opponent was not the decrepit Chinese Empire, but the Great Powers that were carving out spheres of influence in China and threatening to close the door on British and American trade and influence.

In the period 1898-1904, informed people in Great Britain and the United States generally viewed Russia as the chief threat to their Far Eastern interests. There was good reason for them to do so. Until the Russo-Japanese War, they considered Russia the strongest military power in the Far East. Moreover, St. Petersburg's policy was overtly aimed at excluding other powers from large areas of northern China. The Czar's government was determined on winning hegemony north of the Great Wall, and even hoped to annex outright the provinces of Manchuria. This combination of military power with expansionist intentions made the

Russians the most dangerous opponents of British and American hopes for equal trading opportunities throughout Chinese territory.[2]

Until Japan forcibly called a halt to St. Petersburg's expansionist policy, the Russian advance in North China was steady, and the cause of great consternation in London and Washington. In 1898 the Russians coerced the Chinese into leasing Port Arthur, which commanded the sea approaches to Peking. The next year, they fortified Dalny, and won a promise from the Chinese that if foreigners should ever be asked to build a rail line to Peking from north of the Great Wall, the Russians would be given preference. In 1900, using the pretext of the Boxer Rebellion, the Czar's government poured 50,000 troops into Manchuria and announced that they would not be withdrawn until China agreed to grant additional exclusive privileges to Russia in Manchuria. Foiled in this aim by the combined opposition of the other powers, Russia signed an agreement with China in April 1902 calling for a three-stage evacuation of the troops. A year later, however, St. Petersburg went back on the agreement, and, instead of withdrawing its occupying forces, made new and very extensive demands on China. In 1903 the most expansionist elements in the Russian government won over the Czar completely to their way of thinking, and proceeded to invite war with Japan by threatening the Japanese position in the Korean peninsula. In December 1903, Russia rejected Tokyo's final proposal for an agreement protecting Korea. Two months later, the Japanese attacked the Russian Pacific squadron at Port Arthur.

As these disturbing events unfolded, Englishmen and Americans were greatly concerned over the menace to their trade with China. The British were particularly disturbed, since their economic stake in China was enormous. About one-sixth of all British exports in 1900 went to China. British ships carried three-fourths of China's foreign trade and one-half of its coastwise trade. Moreover, British capitalists had several hundred million pounds sterling invested in China. Clearly, any threat to the Chinese "open door" was a serious threat to British prosperity.[3]

The immediate American interest in the China market was relatively insignificant, but hopes for future trade caused Americans to take a great interest in Far Eastern developments. Although

United States exports to China in the period seldom rose above one percent of the country's total export trade, Americans spoke glowingly of the potential for trade in the future. "I know of few things that in the process of the years are more important than this growing Chinese trade is to the United States," said Henry Cabot Lodge. Americans had particular cause for concern over the Russian advance, because most American exports to China went to Manchuria, the region most directly imperiled.[4]

Thus, even though their immediate economic stakes in China were grossly disproportionate, there was reason for Britons and Americans to believe that they shared an interest in keeping China open to trade. In January 1898, the *New York Times* wished Great Britain success in preventing the partition of China, saying "Our interests in the East are the same as hers." Two months later, the London *Times* announced that most Americans seemed to believe that "in the Far East, England and the United States have vast interests in common." Lord Charles Beresford, one of the foremost proponents of Anglo-American cooperation in the Far East, assumed that America's commercial interests were "identical with those of Great Britain."[5]

While there is no doubt that the threat to their trade was uppermost in the minds of Englishmen and Americans, other considerations tended to increase their sense of a common interest in opposing Russian expansion. One was a shared concern with the geopolitical consequences of St. Petersburg's policy; Britons and Americans were especially fearful that the steady augmentation of Czarist power in East Asia might induce Japan and Germany to seek an understanding with Russia. Another consideration that entered into British and American thinking was Anglo-Saxonism. Anglo-Saxonist theory suggested that Great Britain and the United States had a common interest in China that went beyond economic or geopolitical concerns. As we have seen in previous chapters, the idea of a Darwinian struggle for supremacy between the Anglo-Saxon and Slavic races was very prevalent at this time. We have seen, too, that at least some of the public support for an "Anglo-Saxon alliance" during and after the Spanish-American War was inspired by a perceived Russian threat to Anglo-Saxondom. Concern for the welfare of the race inevitably entered into the thoughts of Britons and Americans as they found themselves confronted with steady Russian encroachments on the markets and resources of China. As David Mills, Canada's minister of justice, spelled out the problem for Americans in 1898: "This, then, is not a question between England and Russia, but it is a question between Saxon and Slav. The danger is a danger not to one state, but to the race to which we all belong."[6] Anglo-Saxonists like Mills tended to see the rivalry for economic and strategic advantage in the Far East in terms of the ongoing struggle for supremacy between the Anglo-Saxon and Slavic races. Seen in this context, the economic and strategic concerns of the English-speaking powers commingled with, but were generally secondary to, the larger racial issue: Was Anglo-Saxon or Slavic civilization to dominate the world in the generations to come? This racial interpretation of events in the Far East provided an important rationale for Anglo-American cooperation there. And while the cooperation that many people hoped for never took place, the overall Anglo-American understanding was deepened by the perception of a common racial enemy in the Russians, and a common racial—as well as economic and strategic—interest in opposing their moves into northern China. In this way, Anglo-Saxonism contributed again to the growing rapprochement between Great Britain and the United States.

Britain's first proposal for Anglo-American cooperation in the Far East came in March of 1898, three months after naval units of the Russian Far Eastern squadron dropped anchor at Port Arthur. Ambassador Julian Pauncefote inquired whether the United States would join with Great Britain in opposing actions that tended to restrict equal trading opportunities in China. The United States, about to go to war with Spain and devoted, besides, to its traditional policy of nonentanglement, declined Britain's overtures. Ten months later, in January 1899, the British proposed Anglo-American "conjoint action" to block enlargement of the territorial concession of France—Russia's ally—at Shanghai. Again, the McKinley administration rejected the British proposal.[7]

Washington's discouraging replies to Britain's first proposals, however, could not dampen the hopes of the foremost British advocate of Anglo-American cooperation in the Far East, Colonial Secretary Joseph Chamberlain. Apparently, it was a memorandum from Chamberlain to Acting Foreign Secretary Arthur Balfour, on 3 February 1898, that had brought about Whitehall's initial approach to the United States.[8] Chamberlain was appalled at the steady progress of Russia in China. Not only did he see a threat to Britain's vital trading interests, but he feared that if the Russians were not stopped, they would overrun much of China, and "a time might come when hundreds of thousands of Chinamen and Tartars armed with Russian weapons and drilled and led by Russian officers would be added to the Russian army." If such a calamity occurred, Britain alone would be helpless to counteract it.[9] Yet, Chamberlain was convinced that if Great Britain were "assured of the friendship of the Anglo-Saxon race" in the Far East, the Russian advance could be thrown back. With Great Britain and America united, "there is no other combination that can make us afraid."[10]

Chamberlain hoped that the Russian threat in China might open up opportunities not only for an Anglo-Saxon combination, but for an alliance of the Anglo-Saxons with their Teutonic cousins in Germany. His memorandum to Balfour in February 1898, in which he had urged approaches to the United States, had proposed also an approach to the Germans. Three months later, in the famous speech at Birmingham in which he envisioned the British and American flags waving "together over an Anglo-Saxon alliance," Chamberlain again brought Germany into the picture. Reminding his audience of Russia's recent gains in China, he urged the British people, in the face of the Russian challenge, not to reject the idea of an alliance with Germany.[11]

Chamberlain held extensive conversations with German diplomats about an Anglo-German understanding during 1898-99, and late in 1899, he stunned Americans, Germans, and Britons by publicly proposing "a new Triple Alliance" among the three powers. The occasion was an address at Leicester on 30 November 1899, one day after the Kaiser had concluded a state visit to England. Chamberlain's words left nothing to the imagination:

> I may point out to you that at bottom the main character of the Teutonic race differs very slightly from the character of the Anglo-Saxon.... and if the union between England and America is a powerful factor in

the cause of peace, a new Triple Alliance between the Teutonic race and the two great branches of the Anglo-Saxon race, will be a still more potent influence in the future of the world.[12]

Chamberlain's bold public pronouncement at Leicester brought outbursts of indignation both at home and abroad. The German and American governments were embarrassed, especially as anti-British feeling in the two countries, because of the Boer War, was very strong. The *New York Times* said flatly that Chamberlain talked too much, and the Philadelphia *Press* observed that he had "added another to those haphazard utterances which spangle his speeches for ten years past." Sir Edward Grey, a leader of the Liberal Imperialists in Britain, called the Leicester speech "disastrous," and suggested that the colonial secretary "be kept out of foreign politics, or he will make everything impossible, even friendship with America." Obviously, Chamberlain had spoken much too bluntly.[13]

Nevertheless, there were many in Britain and the United States who shared his views. One of these was Archibald Colquhoun, whose popular 1898 work, *China in Transformation*, may have inspired Chamberlain's hope for an Anglo-Saxon-Teutonic alliance. Colquhoun was a British explorer, a former colonial adminstrator, a former special correspondent for the London *Times* in the Far East, and one of Britain's most respected authorities on Chinese and Pacific affairs. He was also a Russophobe who was convinced that the outcome of the Great-Power rivalry in the Far East would decide the future shape of world civilization. In the context of Anglo-American relations, his ideas are of particular interest because his books and articles on the Far East were widely read and often quoted in the United States as well as in Great Britain.[14]

In *China in Transformation*, Colquhoun argued that there existed "an obvious community of interest as well as community of sentiment" between "the English-speaking and Teutonic races" in China. He then went on to contend that the struggle for supremacy in China would ultimately take the shape of a struggle for world domination, pitting the Anglo-Saxons and the Teutons on one side against the Slavs and their Latin (French) allies on the other.[15]

Colquhoun's greatest fear was that the Russians would not be content with absorbing northern China, but would continue their expansionist policy until they had turned the entire country into a Russian dependency. In these circumstances, tens of millions of Chinese peasants would be subject to Russian rule, and thus available for enlistment in Russian industry and in Russian armies. If China's teeming masses were added to the already huge population of the Russian Empire, Colquhoun said, no power on earth could prevent the Czar from following in the footsteps of other conquerors out of Asia. The Russians would carry fire and sword over the earth. All Europe would soon fall to the Russo-Chinese hordes; the British Empire would collapse; the Pacific would become a Russian lake; and the semicivilization of the Slavs would supersede the civilization of the West in dominating the globe.[16]

In *China in Transformation*, Colquhoun stated that the best hope for averting this catastrophe was joint action by the two Anglo-Saxon powers and the Teutons.[17] In other works, however, especially as the hope for an Anglo-German understanding faded, he ignored the Teutons and concentrated his attentions on the need for an Anglo-Saxon *entente*. "May leaders arise who will guide both nations in the path of duty, of honor, and of prosperity," he wrote late in 1898, "and bring them to submit without murmur to the sacrifices which will enable the race to maintain the ascendancy it has so long held!"[18] It was a wish that was to be echoed in the months to come by many Anglo-Saxonists.

Another influential British advocate of Anglo-American cooperation in the Far East was Lord Charles Beresford. In 1898, Beresford was sent on a special mission to China by the Associated Chambers of Commerce of Great Britain. He spent three months touring the country, during which time he traveled the length of coastal China and penetrated as far inland as Hankow, six hundred miles up the Yangtze. He interviewed scores of Chinese officials and discussed Chinese affairs with a host of foreign diplomats and businessmen. Departing from Shanghai in January 1899, Beresford returned home via Japan and the United States, intending to mount efforts in both countries to influence business and governmental opinion in favor of defense of the open door. He was particularly eager to win American support. Three days before Beresford left Shanghai, the American consul general at Hong Kong wrote to Secretary of State Hay that the Englishman based "all his hopes of keeping the open door by enlisting the sympathies of America during his trip across the Continent."[19]

In the United States, Beresford addressed commercial organizations in San Francisco, Chicago, Buffalo, and New York. In Washington, he met President McKinley and was entertained by Secretary Hay. Shortly after his return to England, he published his conclusions about the Far East in a popular work entitled *The Break-up of China*, a book intended for study by interested Americans as well as Englishmen.[20]

In his speeches and writings, Beresford frequently adverted to the importance of China to the Anglo-Saxon race. "Investigations on the spot have convinced me that the maintenance of the Chinese Empire is essential to the honor as well as the interests of the Anglo-Saxon race," he wrote, "and I hope that when the British and American people are acquainted with the facts as a whole, they will be similarly convinced." It was Beresford's hope that he might contribute to the forging of a united Anglo-Saxondom to save China. "Are we going to let this opportunity slip of drawing the two Anglo-Saxon nations together for the cause of civilized progress, and the benefit of the world at large?" he asked rhetorically. While in San Francisco, he penned a brief article for the *Independent* in which he strongly implied the desirability of an Anglo-American alliance to block the partition of the Chinese Empire. In his later meetings with American businessmen and government officials, his constant theme was that "the problems connected with the future development of trade in China will be solved more easily if the powerful Anglo-Saxon races [*sic*] can come to some mutual understanding regarding them." Because of his travels and speeches and the popularity of his book and his articles on China, Beresford, like Archibald Colquhoun, came to be widely recognized in the period as a leading authority on East Asian affairs.[21]

Despite the warnings of these eminent Englishmen about the Russian threat, and their appeals for Anglo-Saxon collaboration, American governmental policy did not move in the direction of either forceful opposition to the Russians or cooperation with the British. John Hay's famous Open Door notes of 1899 and 1900 failed to differentiate in any way between Great Britain and the other powers involved in China; indeed, shortly before the first notes were sent, W. W. Rockhill, Hay's chief Far Eastern adviser, went so far as to declare that he considered England "as great an offender in China as is Russia itself."[22]

Nor did Hay's policy stand much chance of forestalling China's collapse. The British realized that Hay's notes only expressed pious hopes for the maintenance of Chinese territorial and administrative integrity, without any American commitment to act in defense of its policy objectives. Pious hopes could not stop Russia or any other power with designs on China. Hence, while Whitehall generally welcomed America's Open Door initiatives, it was disappointed both at the feebleness of Washington's action and at its unilateral character. From the standpoint of Anglo-American relations, the most that can be said for John Hay's Open Door policy is that it was widely interpreted in both countries as further evidence of the similarity of British and American goals in China; and consequently, it helped keep alive hopes for effective Anglo-American cooperation in the future.[23]

America's reluctance to adopt a policy more to the liking of the British can be explained partly in terms of the traditional United States policy of noncollaboration, and partly in terms of the relatively small American interest in the China trade. While a substantial number of Americans thought the China market held great promise for the future, few believed that the present American export trade was significant enough to warrant either a departure from noncollaboration or the risk of war with Russia. As Charles S. Campbell has pointed out, "No responsible government would resort to force to preserve what might possibly, one day or another, be of value but whose value in the present and in the foreseeable future was trifling."[24]

That is not to say, however, that there were not many Americans who embraced the idea of Anglo-American cooperation in China, and cited Anglo-Saxonist concepts in defense of their position. Only days after the armistice with Spain in August 1898, the Detroit *Free Press* declared that "England's policy of the 'open door' in the east is the one which will most benefit the world; and we, as Anglo-Saxons and as friends of commercial expansion, will sympathize with, and be deeply concerned in the success of Great Britain's struggle against the exclusive policy of Russia in China." Franklin H. Giddings, the noted Columbia University sociologist, went beyond the economic argument, repeating the familiar warnings that Russia was on the verge of consolidating all East Asia within its empire. Giddings urged that the United States ally itself with Great Britain in the "gigantic struggle" in China, or face the consequences in the future of a general Russian assault on "those things that we are accustomed to regard as the essentials of civilization." Giddings's opinion was similar to that of Professor Frederick Wells Williams of Yale, who also favored joint action by the United States and Great Britain to check Russian expansion. Writing in the spring of 1899, Williams declared: "Upon the highlands of Central Asia have been bred in the past the races which overran and dominated the civilized West, and whence those swarms were once raised other millions may spring up in the future to obey the call of the conqueror and spread devastation among those more cultured but less lusty peoples who represent our race."[25]

In an article in the *Cosmopolitan* in July 1900, Alexander Hume Ford, an American recently returned from the Far East, stated that, with the bulk of Britain's forces bogged down in South Africa, only military intervention by the United States could prevent Russian annexation of the greater part of China. Like other Anglo-Saxonist observers, Ford spread the alarming notion that if Russia were permitted to seize control of China, *"she will have a standing army greater than all the other combined forces of the world. . . . This is the stake Russia is playing for. Confident that the Anglo-Saxon race has seen the apex of its glory, the Slav believes he is to rise to the position of world-power with the twentieth century."* In his widely read and influential book, *World Politics at the End of the Nineteenth Century*, Paul S. Reinsch, the University of Wisconsin scholar who later (1913-19) served as America's minister at Peking, reinforced the Anglo-Saxonists' view of China as the scene of a decisive struggle for supremacy. "The very composition of the world civilization of the future is at stake upon the issue," Reinsch wrote.[26]

Among the most earnest advocates of Anglo-American cooperation in China was Brooks Adams, the brilliant, intense, and eccentric brother of one of Washington's best-known eccentrics, Henry Adams. Like Henry, Brooks Adams was closely acquainted with such key figures in American foreign policy as Theodore Roosevelt, Henry Cabot Lodge, and John Hay. From the mid-1890s onward, he frequently joined these men (and others, including Alfred Thayer Mahan and Cecil Spring Rice) for amiable discussion at his brother's popular Washington residence, a meeting place of the capital's elite society located at 1603 H Street—just across Lafayette Square from the White House and just around the corner from Hay's house on Sixteenth Street. Brooks had been a classmate of Lodge at Harvard, and was married to Lodge's sister-in-law. He was close enough to Roosevelt to serve as the latter's riding companion when Lodge loaned out his thoroughbreds for trots around Washington. All three men were warm admirers of Mahan and his ideas on naval power. When Adams published his first book, *The Law of Civilization and Decay*, in 1895, he asked Roosevelt to review it in the *Forum*. Roosevelt once accused Adams of being "a little unhinged," but there can be little doubt that the Rough Rider shared many of Adams's concerns about American foreign relations, and that he took a serious interest in some of Adams's ideas.[27]

In the months following the Spanish-American War, Brooks Adams established himself as one of the foremost American publicists of racial Darwinism and of the necessity for Anglo-Saxon cooperation to combat Slavic expansion. "From the humblest peasant to the mightiest empire," he said, "humanity is waging a ceaseless and pitiless struggle in which the unfit perish."[28] Adams had no doubt that in the contemporary world, the great competition for supremacy was between the Anglo-Saxons and the Continental powers of Russia, France, and Germany—the latter group dominated by Russia. He believed that the final showdown between these two groupings was about to take place in China. In August of 1898, Adams published a forcibly argued and widely noticed article in the *Forum* entitled "The Spanish War and the Equilibrium of the World." The message of the article was that, in the late nineteenth century, political and military power was dependent on economic power, on industrial potential and available capital; and that "the race for life" between the Anglo-Saxons and their rivals was to be decided largely by the outcome of the struggle for economic supremacy in China. As long as the Anglo-Saxons maintained free access to the markets and natural wealth of China, Adams indicated, their economic power would keep them in first place among the races. If, on the other hand, Great Britain lost its Far Eastern markets in the coming months to the Russian advance, the British would lose also their ability to purchase the industrial and agricultural surpluses of the United States. The loss of China would therefore spell economic disaster for the Anglo-Saxon race on both sides of the Atlantic, and might well be decisive in the world power struggle if the Russians in the meantime succeeded in winning the China trade for themselves. In summary, Adams stated his belief that in East Asia, "the moment seems at hand when two great competing systems will be left pitted against each other, and the struggle for survival will begin."[29]

Adams had a forthright solution for the problem of Russian aggression. Americans must recognize that "the risk of isolation promises to be more serious than the risk of an alliance," and join with Great Britain to protect the vital markets and resources of China. In the future, it would be up to the United States to take the lead in defending Anglo-Saxon interests in the world, for the British had lost their economic paramountcy, and as a result were suffering a steady deterioration of their international position. Already Britain stood as little more than "a fortified outpost of the Anglo-Saxon race," dependent on the United States for its food supply and for military aid in the event of an attack by a Continental coalition. Adams believed that the Royal Navy remained, however, one of Anglo-Saxondom's most powerful weapons, and that the economic well-being of the United States depended on the British market for American goods. Moreover, Britain was much more solidly ensconced in China than was the United States. All of these considerations led Adams to the conclusion that the United States should immediately join the British in defending the principles of the open door. Americans must come to see, before it was too late, that the prosperity, and therefore the power, of the entire Anglo-Saxon race was at stake in the Far East.[30]

In his published works, Adams pursued this theme right up

until the outbreak of the Russo-Japanese War, reiterating time and again, as he put it in the spring of 1899, that the economic and military supremacy of the twentieth century would fall to whoever controlled "the seat of empire" in China.[31] In 1900, in the wake of the Boxer Rebellion and the Russian invasion of Manchuria, he began to warn that Russian control of Manchuria and North China alone might present a very serious threat to the welfare of the United States. According to Adams, the Manchurian region contained the richest deposits of coal and iron in the world. Coal and iron were the two keys to industrial progress, and Adams feared the consequences if Russia gained free access to the mineral resources of China. Using cheap Chinese labor and German capital and administrative know-how, the Russians might win economic domination of the earth. "Hence Americans must accept the Chinese question as the great problem of the future, a problem from which there is no escape; and as the solution of these great struggles for supremacy often invokes an appeal to force, safety lies in being armed and organized against all emergencies."[32]

In an article written for the *Atlantic* just a few months before the Japanese attack on the Russian fleet in 1904, Adams repeated his views about the crucial importance of the Manchurian and northern Chinese mineral deposits. He said that Russia, with the tacit approval of Germany, was now determined to crush Japan and absorb once and for all the mineral-rich area in question. This was the moment of crisis, he declared, in which the two Anglo-Saxon powers must rally to the side of Japan to oppose Russia's designs. The United States must use force to block Russian ambitions, or face economic suffocation in the near future. "In these crucial moments," Adams concluded, "races either develop genius or sink into imbecility."[33]

Brooks Adams's ideas were well known to his friends in the American government, and doubtless contributed to their distrust of Russia and sympathetic regard for Great Britain in the Far East. John Hay learned of Brooks's theories in detail from Henry Adams, his close confidant for more than forty years and a man who was also extremely worried about Russia and impressed with his brother's speculations. During Hay's tenure at the State Department, he and Henry Adams made a habit of going out together late every afternoon for a brief walk through the streets of Washington, exchanging ideas and insights along the way. Among the subjects they frequently discussed were the situation in East Asia and Brooks Adams's theories concerning Russia's intentions.[34] Theodore Roosevelt, too, paid close attention to the speculations of Brooks Adams. "You have formulated the situation as I have never known of its being formulated," he told Brooks in 1903, in reference to the latter's writings about the Russian threat. Through his published essays and his personal contacts with Hay and Roosevelt, Brooks Adams helped to convince these American policy-makers that events in East Asia ought to be viewed in the context of a global struggle for supremacy between the Anglo-Saxon and his racial enemies.[35]

Alfred Thayer Mahan was another advocate of British-American cooperation in the Far East (and elsewhere) who had close contacts with Washington. Mahan was as concerned as Brooks Adams with the progress of Russian expansion in China, and as certain that only forceful action by Britain and the United States could bring it to a halt. About two weeks after John Hay dispatched the first of his Open Door notes, Mahan wrote to a friend in England to say: "In peace, Russia's aggressive advance moves over the inert Asiatics like a steam-roller; but the prospect of America and England, side by side, demanding that China be left open for trade, means either a change in her policy, or war."[36] Mahan, though not a war-monger, would not have flinched if the result had been the latter.

Mahan dealt most extensively with Far Eastern developments in his study *The Problem of Asia*, published in 1900. This book—a reprint of a series of articles Mahan had written for *Harper's* and the *North American Review* between March and November of 1900—was in part a political document aimed at helping William McKinley win reelection over the antiexpansionist William Jennings Bryan. Despite its political overtones, however, *The Problem of Asia* expressed Mahan's authentic opinions. It was written from the heart.[37]

As Mahan perceived developments in East Asia, they were leading inexorably toward war. Furthermore, the coming conflict was destined to be one "not of nationalities only, but of the larger groups which we know as races." A process of "natural selection" was about to take place in Asia, with the weaker racial groups being eliminated from the international struggle for existence, and the stronger races proceeding to the mastery of the world.[38]

Mahan believed that in the war to come, one of the contending parties would be made up of the Slavs and their Latin allies, the French. On the other side would be ranged—not in formal alliance, but in close cooperation—the three great "Teutonic" states, Germany, Great Britain, and the United States. Echoing earlier statements by the Englishmen Joseph Chamberlain and Archibald Colquhoun (from whom he probably borrowed some of his ideas), Mahan said that the three Teutonic countries were united not by interest only, but by "community of character and tradition, fostering community of ideals." Mahan expected Japan, because of its obvious interest in containing Russia, to adhere to the Teutonic group, but to play only a secondary role in the great war. Essentially, the conflict would be one between Slavs and Teutons, with Russia's great armies pitted against the vastly superior navies of Britain, the United States, and Germany. It would be a classic historical struggle between land power and sea power. "The Teuton, under the three great national heads, possesses the sea, from which the Slav is almost debarred. The Teuton is inferior in land power, for... he is geographically far removed from Asia, with which a great part of the Slavonic tenure is coterminous."[39]

Mahan's plan of action, to insure the success of the Teutons in the coming conflict, was an immediate move of their naval forces into the valley of the Yangtze—presently Britain's major sphere of influence in China. Because the Yangtze was navigable for some six hundred miles, deep into the heart of Asia, naval power on the river could effectively bar farther southward expansion by the Slavs. "This valley," Mahan wrote, "is the decisive field where commerce . . . can most certainly receive the support of the military arm of sea power, which . . . is the main reliance of the Teutonic peoples."[40]

Given his view of the enormous significance of the international rivalry in the Far East, it is little wonder that Captain Mahan despaired at Washington's reluctance to become more deeply involved there. When, in the late summer of 1900,

McKinley gave instructions for the complete withdrawal of the American troops involved in the relief of Peking, Mahan was filled with consternation. He sent a protest to the president, pointing out that St. Petersburg was showing no disposition to withdraw Russian troops from China. Russia was "playing her own game" there, he said, and "playing it with the unscrupulous craft of the Asiatic." The United States ought to have the foresight to counter Russia's aggressive intentions.[41]

Mahan did his best to see that his powerful political friends were apprised of his views. He mailed a copy of *The Problem of Asia* to Henry Cabot Lodge, who at the time was trying to win the chairmanship of the Senate Foreign Relations Committee.[42] Lodge read the book with care and informed the captain that he had found it very interesting; he agreed especially with Mahan's opinion regarding the Anglo-American community of interest in China.[43] A few days after Theodore Roosevelt was sworn in as vice president, Mahan wrote him an impassioned letter, repeating some of the arguments set forth in *The Problem of Asia*, and urging that the United States take action to insure that "European *thought*, as well as European commerce" was allowed to penetrate into all parts of China. Roosevelt, who had read Mahan's book "with the greatest interest," replied that "in the main" he agreed with Mahan's ideas. Specifically, Roosevelt thought "that the United States and England should so far as possible work together in China, and that their co-operation and the effective use of sea power on behalf of civilization and progress which this co-operation would mean in the valley of the Yangtze Kiang, is of the utmost importance for the future of Asia, and therefore of the world." Roosevelt was a practical politician as well as a partisan of Anglo-Saxonism, however, and he recognized that the American public was unlikely in the foreseeable future to lend its support to determined American action in East Asia. "I do not have to tell you," he wrote Mahan, " . . . that while something can be done by public men in leading the people, they cannot lead them further than public opinion has prepared the way. They can lead them somewhat further; but not very much. Now, as yet our public opinion is dull on the question of China."[44]

Roosevelt's words to Mahan are of particular significance because, as Howard K. Beale has pointed out, Roosevelt's conduct of Far Eastern diplomacy during the first three or four years of his presidency owed much to the ideas of Captain Mahan. Like Mahan, Roosevelt saw the struggle for supremacy in East Asia as more than a contest for trade or strategic advantage: it was part of a world struggle between competing races and civilizations.

> Russian interests were now challenging in the Far East Anglo-American interests that Roosevelt had by this time persuaded himself were the interests of "civilization." Hence Russian expansion . . . had become an obstacle to the "push" of another civilizing power. Whether Roosevelt was dominated more by a concept of superiority of English-speaking to Russian culture or by national self-interest, Russia nonetheless had to be stopped.[45]

As will be seen, Roosevelt was willing to join with Great Britain, Japan, or whatever other powers might offer their support to a policy aimed at containing Russian expansion. However, American public opinion never came around to Roosevelt's point of view, and his hopes met with continual frustration.

At least part of the reason for Roosevelt's frustration was the declining influence of Anglo-Saxonism in the United States. A survey of journals of opinion after 1900 shows a steady decline of public interest in such subjects as racial Darwinism and the reputed racial ties between Great Britain and the United States. Of course, men like Brooks Adams, Alfred Thayer Mahan, and Theodore Roosevelt remained as keen as ever on the racial rationale for Anglo-American friendship and cooperation in world affairs. But after 1900 they tended to be, at least as far as East Asian developments were concerned, voices crying in the wilderness. Most Americans were not interested in Anglo-Saxon solidarity if it threatened to involve them in an Asiatic war against a formidable foe like Russia.

John Hay shared Roosevelt's frustration at the apathy of the American public. Hay was a ceaseless proponent of Anglo-American cooperation in world affairs. In June of 1898, while he was still ambassador at London, Hay had addressed a personal appeal to President McKinley, asking for reconsideration of Washington's rejection of the first British proposal for Anglo-American collaboration in defense of the open door. McKinley would not reconsider, but Hay remained hopeful. When he was named to succeed William R. Day at the State Department in August 1898, much of the American press interpreted the appointment as signaling concerted British-American action in China in the near future.[46]

During Hay's seven years as secretary of state, the United States avoided cooperation with any other power in the Far East, and pursued the distinctly American policy set forth in the Open Door notes. In Hay's case, however, the abjuring of cooperative action was not a preference, but a regrettable necessity. As he wrote in September 1900, "If it were not for our domestic politics, we could and should join with England, whose interests are identical with ours, and make our ideas prevail." Hay's ideal throughout his tenure at the State Department was joint Anglo-American action in defense of their common interests in China.[47]

Hay's Far Eastern policy, Kenton J. Clymer has written, was based on both his concern for the future of American trade and "his broad vision of a world dominated by Anglo-Saxon civilization and his fear of the alternative." Henry Adams, of course, familiarized Hay with Brooks Adams's theories regarding the situation in China, and others of Hay's friends wrote to him of the disastrous consequences for the race if it were found wanting in China. The secretary of state was impressed with the racial interpretation of events in the Far East and fearful that Russian dominance of North China would bring not only the demise of American commercial interests, but, ultimately, the expulsion of Anglo-Saxon civilization from East Asia. Privately, he yearned for the chance to link American policy with the British. Anticipating the collapse of China in the early summer of 1900, and seeing an understanding with Great Britain as the only way of forestalling it, he wrote a despairing letter to ex-Secretary of State John W. Foster: "On the one side there is a great danger, on the other a great opportunity.... It is enough to turn the hair grey not to be able to avoid the one and embrace the other."[48]

The British were fully aware of the friendly attitude of Theodore Roosevelt and John Hay, and this may have helped inspire another attempt by them to secure American cooperation in the Far East. The occasion was Russia's flagrant violation, in April 1903, of its agreement with China to evacuate its forces from Manchuria. Rather than removing the troops, Russia demanded that China sign a new treaty—the so-called "convention of the seven points"—which would have converted Manchuria into a virtual Russian province. Under the terms of this convention, no new treaty ports could have been opened in Manchuria; no new foreign consulates would have been allowed; and no foreigners other than Russians would have been employed in Manchurian public service posts.[49]

The convention of the seven points brought the Far Eastern crisis to the flashpoint. Russia's aggressive intentions were clear. And Japan, at least, appeared ready to fight. The Japanese began military preparations; concurrently, they asked Britain to reinforce its Far Eastern squadron.

London was alarmed. In January 1902, the British had entered into an alliance with Japan, committing them to go to the aid of the Japanese if they became involved in war with more than one power in the Far East.[50] Yet few British diplomats or military officers considered little Japan to be a strong ally. The consensus of opinion was that if Britain were dragged into a Far Eastern conflict, the British would have to do most of the fighting themselves. That was something London was not willing to do.[51]

Faced with the prospect of war, with Japan alone as an ally, the British decided on new approaches to the United States. On 28 April 1903, Foreign Secretary Lord Lansdowne instructed Ambassador Michael Herbert, Pauncefote's successor, to inform the State Department as follows:

> The Cabinet while objecting most strongly to the action of Russia would certainly hesitate and probably refuse to go to war either alone or with Japan only as an ally to prevent the absorption of Manchuria and Mongolia. But if . . . the United States government should decide to press their claims even to the extremity of hostile actions H.M.G. would take similar actions, although no previous arrangement or alliance had been made with the United States government.

The American response was disappointing, but not unexpected. On 1 May Ambassador Herbert reported to Lansdowne that there was no hope of the United States going to war over Manchuria.[52]

John Hay and Theodore Roosevelt would have preferred a more positive response to the British inquiry, however. On the very day that Lansdowne sent his instructions to Herbert, Hay had written to Roosevelt, hinting that he would like to see the United States, in the interest of countering Russia's latest move, become a party to the Anglo-Japanese alliance. He fully realized, however, that such a development was out of the question. "If our rights and interests in opposition to Russia in the far East [*sic*] were as clear as noonday," Hay wrote, "we could not get a treaty through the Senate the object of which was to check Russian aggression."[53]

Roosevelt, who was on a tour of the Western states at the time, shared Hay's concern at the steady progress of Russian expansion. A clue to his larger view of the stakes in China may be found in a speech he delivered at San Francisco on 13 May 1903, two weeks after the terms of the seven-point convention became known. Echoing earlier statements by his friend Brooks Adams, Roosevelt told his audience that for centuries the seat of world power had been moving ever westward. Now, as the nineteenth century gave way to the twentieth, it appeared that the Pacific basin was about to become "the first... point of importance" in the world. Roosevelt believed that in the next generation, the people who controlled the commerce and strongpoints of the Pacific might very well command the supremacy of the earth.[54]

Few Americans were willing to see the fate of Manchuria in this context, however, and Roosevelt knew it. In his reply to Hay's complaint about the inability of the administration to act against the Russians, Roosevelt had to admit: "As for China, I do not see that there is anything we can say, even by way of suggestion. The mendacity of the Russians is something appalling. The bad feature of the situation... is that as yet it seems that we cannot fight to keep Manchuria open."[55]

In the end, the Russians decided to retreat from the convention of the seven points. They were fearful that if they moved too far, they might arouse dormant American opinion and drive the United States into the Anglo-Japanese alliance. They also feared that Japan might be ready to seek a violent solution to the controversy. Hence, in lieu of "crowding their convention on China," as Hay put it, the Russians settled for the face-saving device of extracting from the Chinese satisfactory answers to a number of questions regarding Russian privileges in Manchuria.[56]

Nonetheless, tensions remained high in the Far East, and Russian-American relations continued to deteriorate. In an attempt to counter further Russian moves in Manchuria, the Roosevelt administration opened negotiations with the Chinese in 1903 for a new commercial treaty, opening more Manchurian cities to trade. (At present, only Newchwang and Port Arthur were open.) China, however, came under heavy Russian pressure not to give the Americans what they wanted. Though a treaty was eventually signed, in October 1903, the Russians—"the powers of evil," Hay called them—succeeded in forcing the hapless Chinese to limit concessions to the United States.[57]

Had the Russians known fully, during 1903, of the strains that were threatening the Anglo-American relationship, they might have been tempted to push still harder in the Far East. The cause of the strained relations was the Alaska boundary controversy, which involved claims made by Canada to large areas of the Alaska panhandle.[58] Great Britain, as the power responsible for the foreign relations of the Dominion, was obliged to back Canada's dubious contention that much of the Alaskan coastline was actually Canadian territory. To most Americans, however, including President Roosevelt, Canada had no more right to the disputed area "than we have to take part of Cornwall or Kent."[59] In an effort to resolve the controversy, Secretary of State Hay and Ambassador Herbert signed a treaty in January of 1903, providing for the establishment of a six-man tribunal—three to be appointed by the United States and three by Great Britain—to adjudicate the issue and determine once and for all the boundary between southeastern Alaska and the Canadian territories of British Columbia and the Yukon. Roosevelt, however, had agreed to the tribunal only reluctantly, and he had no intention of seeing it compromise any substantial part of the American claim; nor, for that matter, was he about to allow a 3-3 tie vote by the tribunal, which would have caused a breakdown and a continuation of the long-running controversy. In Roosevelt's opinion, Canada's contentions were outrageous, and were not to be tolerated any longer. Accordingly, instead of the three "impartial jurists" called for by the Hay-Herbert treaty, Roosevelt named as the American commissioners three men (one of them was Senator

Lodge, the other two Senator George Turner of Washington and Secretary of War Elihu Root) who were certain to take a hard line on the boundary issue. He then instructed the three Americans not even to consider compromise on the question of paramount concern to Canada, access to the sea somewhere along the ragged Alaskan coastline. Finally, during the summer of 1903, Roosevelt made it known to the British government, through unofficial channels, that very serious consequences would result if the tribunal failed to reach an agreement favorable to the United States. There were two Canadian members of the British delegation, and one Englishman—Lord Alverstone, the chief justice of England's Supreme Court. Alverstone, everyone knew, held the balance of the decision, and could frustrate a settlement by voting with the Canadians. If that should happen, Roosevelt warned the British, he would respond by taking the matter to Congress and asking for "authority to run the line as we claim it . . . without any further regard to the attitude of England and Canada."[60]

The bewildered British knew that Roosevelt was in earnest, and that the results of such an action could be disastrous for the Anglo-American friendship. Britain itself had no direct interest in the boundary controversy, and most members of the British political establishment doubted that Canada had much of a case; nevertheless, they had hoped to avoid alienating the Canadians by failure to give strong support to their claims. In the face of Roosevelt's threats, however, the British were forced to sacrifice Canada's interests in order to save their friendly relationship with the United States. In October of 1903, Lord Alverstone—acting as much on political as on legal grounds—voted with the three American commissioners to award nearly all of the disputed territory to the United States. Alverstone's decision, although it enraged the Canadians, brought an end to the dispute.

In the Alaska controversy, then, the nationalism of Theodore Roosevelt had overwhelmed his Anglo-Saxonism, and for a time at least the president's belligerence and unwillingness to compromise had threatened to disrupt the British-American rapprochement. Seen from a longer perspective, however, the chief significance of the Alaskan settlement of 1903 was that it removed the last remaining major area of contention between Great

Britain and the United States. British concessions in Alaska, like earlier British concessions in Central America, helped assure that the Anglo-American friendship would be a lasting one.[61]

While he pursued his hazardous course toward an Alaskan settlement in 1903, Theodore Roosevelt during the same period was becoming increasingly annoyed at Russian actions in the Far East. Russia's conduct, it seemed, lent considerable credence to the alarming speculations of Brooks Adams and Alfred Thayer Mahan. The president's letters during the summer of 1903 revealed a growing conviction that force was the only solution to the Russian problem. On 22 June, he wrote to Albert Shaw, the Anglo-Saxonist editor of the *American Review of Reviews*, that "the Manchurian business" seemed to be "taking an acute stage owing to the well-nigh incredible mendacity of the Russians." Russia "seems to be ingeniously endeavoring to force us" into aligning with England and Japan. On the same day, Roosevelt wrote to another well-known Anglo-Saxonist, Lyman Abbott, editor of the *Outlook*, that the United States was asking only "that Russia shall do what over and over again she has agreed to do and shall not prevent the Chinese from giving us the rights for which we have fought in connection with the open-door policy." A month later, Roosevelt wrote to Brooks Adams to offer an appraisal of the present state of American opinion:

> Of course I have to continually pay heed to the state of public opinion. As yet public opinion is not so awake that I can go to the extent I would like to go in this Manchurian business; but already I can go a great deal farther than would have been possible a few years ago, and I think that the public is understanding the situation more and more all the time.[62]

The fact of the matter is that at least as early as July 1903, Roosevelt was giving thought to the possibility of war with Russia. He wrote to John Hay on 18 July that he was determined not to give way in Manchuria, and that "year by year" he was "growing more confident that this country would back me in going to an extreme in the matter." Less than two weeks later, he made a still stronger statement to the secretary of state: "I am beginning to have scant patience with Adam Zâd.... And I wish, in Manchuria, to go to the very limit I think our people will stand.

If only we were sure neither France nor Germany would join in, I should not in the least mind going to 'extremes' with Russia!"[63]

Roosevelt was still fully aware, however, that the American people would be exceedingly reluctant to back him in "extremes." When the British inquired one more time, in the very month these bellicose letters were written, about the possibility of Anglo-American cooperation against the Russians, they received another refusal. And when Japan's ambassador asked Secretary Hay, in September 1903, whether the United States would support his country in the event of a Russo-Japanese conflict, Hay informed him that Japan should have no illusions about American policy. "I told him plainly," Hay reported to Roosevelt, "that we could not take part in any use of force in that region, unless our own interests were directly involved.... It was a hard thing to say."[64]

Roosevelt could not use force in opposition to Russia, but he could support Japan as the surest bulwark against further Russian expansion. On 4 January 1904, four days after the American ambassador at Tokyo informed Hay that a Russo-Japanese conflict was "now almost inevitable,"[65] the president invited a small circle of friends and advisers to a White House luncheon. George Kennan, perhaps American's most outspoken opponent of the Russian autocracy, was one of those in attendance. Later in the day, Kennan provided a detailed account of the get-together in a letter to Lyman Abbott. As Kennan told it, Roosevelt was very angry at Russia. He praised Tokyo for standing firm, and expressed a wish that American naval forces might join the Japanese in forcibly opposing the Russians. Looking at Kennan, he laughed and said: "If everybody regarded this thing as Mr. Kennan and I do, I know where our warships would be."[66] A week later, in response to a Japanese inquiry as to the American attitude in the event of a Russo-Japanese conflict, Roosevelt assured Tokyo that American policy would be benevolent toward Japan.[67]

Certainly part of Roosevelt's distinct bias in favor of the Japanese can be explained by the fact that he tended to see Japan—an ally of Great Britain and a friend of the United States—as the champion of "Anglo-Saxon" interests in the Far East.[68] In Roosevelt's racial world view, the Japanese had long occupied a unique position. They were the one "non-Aryan and non-

Christian" people who could compete successfully with the West in both the economic and military spheres, and Roosevelt had the utmost respect for their achievements.[69] He particularly admired their military strength. "What extraordinary soldiers those little Japs are!" he exclaimed in the fall of 1900, after hearing reports of the discipline and efficiency of the Japanese troops during the allied advance on Peking.[70] Roosevelt was equally impressed with Japanese industrial development, and predicted in 1905 that within a dozen years Japan would be "the leading industrial nation of the Pacific." In general, Roosevelt saw the Japanese as a "great civilized nation," different in many important respects from the major Western powers, but enlightened enough to have used them as a model. As far as international rivalry in the Far East was concerned, the Japanese represented many of the same principles as the Anglo-Saxon countries, and, unlike Britain and the United States, they were willing to fight to block further Russian expansion. This combination of factors made Japan a valuable friend of British and American interests.[71]

If Japan stood as the exponent of Anglo-Saxon interests in the Far East, Russia remained, in Roosevelt's view, Anglo-Saxondom's most implacable and dangerous enemy. As the Russo-Japanese conflict approached, the possible consequences for the Anglo-Saxon race of continued Russian expansion was seldom absent from Roosevelt's calculations. Just six days before the Japanese attack on the Russian squadron at Port Arthur, Roosevelt wrote to Cecil Spring Rice to express his current feelings about the Russian threat. He was convinced, he said, that unless the Russians changed in some marked way, "they contain the chance of menace to the higher life of the world."[72] That "higher life," in Roosevelt's view, was best represented by the Anglo-Saxon race.

Japan's stunning successes in the war of 1904-5 abruptly ended any immediate Russian threat to British and American interests in the Far East. At the war's conclusion, there existed in that part of the world a rough balance of power between Russia and Japan that was to endure until the outbreak of the great European war in

1914. The "Slavic peril" was proved to be a myth, and with its demise an important stimulant to race-thinking in Great Britain and the United States was removed.

In the years between the Battle of Manila Bay and the Japanese attack on Port Arthur, however, Anglo-Saxon racism clearly helped to shape British and American perceptions of events in China. Men like Chamberlain, Colquhoun, Beresford, Brooks Adams, Mahan, Hay, and Roosevelt tended to interpret the Russian threat to British and American Far Eastern interests in terms of a clash of rival races and civilizations. These theoreticians and policy-makers viewed with alarm the steady advance of Slavic Russia, and often spoke of the need for Anglo-Saxon solidarity to meet the challenge. And while their hopes for a united Anglo-Saxon front were all frustrated in the end, their ideas contributed significantly to the rapprochement between Great Britain and the United States. The perception of a common racial enemy in the Far East, and of a common racial interest in addition to common economic and strategic interests, could not help but deepen the overall Anglo-American understanding.

Conclusion

The Decline of Anglo-Saxonism

Anglo-Saxonism's time as a major influence on British-American relations was brief. First emerging during the Venezuela boundary dispute as an intellectual conviction powerful enough to draw closer together the British and American peoples, Anglo-Saxonism reached the peak of its importance during the Spanish-American War. For a few years thereafter, the commitment of Britons and Americans to Anglo-Saxonism remained strong enough to affect materially the American response to the Boer War, and to help create the impression of a shared concern in the Far East.

After about 1904 or 1905, however, Anglo-Saxonism ceased to be an important factor in British-American relations. Public interest in Anglo-Saxonist ideas remained high for some time, and Anglo-Saxonist catchwords and phraseology continued to appear in public discussions of world affairs.[1] But with the outbreak of war in the Far East and the removal of Russia as an immediate threat to British and American interests, Anglo-Saxon racism ceased to affect significantly the development of Anglo-American relations.

The reasons for the decline of Anglo-Saxonism, as an influence on the British-American relationship, are nearly as complex as those that explain its rise, and we can only briefly summarize them here. A good part of the explanation is to be found in the gradual crumbling of the ideas on which Anglo-Saxonism was based. Those ideas, the most important of which were racial Darwinism and the germ theory of history, had been developed by British and American intellectuals over the course of two generations. Yet Anglo-Saxonism had hardly emerged as a full-blown doctrine in the 1890s before a new generation of intellectuals began to question the basic conceptions which created and sustained it. Social

Darwinism, the domestic equivalent of racial Darwinism, came under increasing attack even in what was probably its greatest stronghold, the United States. Before the first decade of the twentieth century had passed, Social Darwinism was largely replaced in the public mind by the reformist ideas of the Progressive era, which stressed environment rather than heredity as the principal determinant of human behavior, and sought to improve mankind through institutional change and governmental action rather than through the elimination of the weak by the strong. The undermining of social theories based upon Darwinism suggested to many thinking people that racial Darwinism was not a credible theory of international politics.

The Teutonic germ theory of history, also, was first questioned, then abandoned, by a new generation of intellectuals. The greatest English proponents of the theory—Stubbs, Green, and Freeman—were all dead by 1901, and, for the most part, the historians who followed them ceased to emphasize the ancient origins and historical continuity of English institutions. In the United States, the germ theory had always had its influential critics, and in 1893 it received its most serious challenge from Frederick Jackson Turner.[2] In his famous address of that year on the significance of the frontier in American history, Turner—ironically, a student of Herbert Baxter Adams, the great exponent of the germ theory— called on American historians to spend less time studying the European sources of American institutions and more time pondering the unique frontier environment that produced a new people and a new society. Turner's frontier thesis, appealing strongly to American nationalism, seriously weakened the influence of the Teutonic germ theory. A second original thinker in the historical profession, Charles A. Beard, was to deal another blow to the germ theory before the outbreak of the First World War, by emphasizing the economic origins of American ideas and institutions.

The internal contradictions and intellectual weakpoints of Anglo-Saxonism rendered it extremely vulnerable to such challenges. While many Britons and Americans could pretend for a time that they, as Anglo-Saxons, were racially superior to all other peoples, they could not hide from themselves forever the unpleasant fact that no such thing as the "Anglo-Saxon race" had ever existed. The British people, like all the other peoples of Europe, were descended from a multitude of tribes and nations: not Angles and Saxons only, but Scots, Welshmen, Irishmen, Danes, Normans, Flemings, Walloons, French Huguenots, and others. And if the ancestry of the British was complex, how much more complex was the ethnic heritage of the United States? Of course, it was absurd to speak of the British and Americans as comprising a distinct racial group.

At a time when Anglo-Saxonism was beginning to lose its status as a conventional wisdom, political and diplomatic developments combined to undercut its influence on Anglo-American diplomacy. American Anglophobia, latently powerful even at the height of the Anglo-Saxonist fervor in 1898, began to reassert itself during the Boer War, and helped dissipate the earlier good feeling. Frustrated in their hopes of securing effective American cooperation in the Far East and elsewhere, the British turned to other powers in search of allies. In 1902 they signed a treaty of alliance with Japan, and in 1904 they entered into the *Entente Cordiale* with France. Three years later, after the myth of the "Slavic peril" had been shattered by Russia's humiliation at the hands of the Japanese, the *Entente Cordiale* became the Triple Entente. World politics had changed. Obviously, the British could not speak too loudly of Anglo-Saxon superiority and the need for Anglo-Saxon solidarity, when they were bound up with Orientals, Latins, and Slavs.

While these developments were taking place, some of the most influential Anglo-Saxonists in the United States and Great Britain were disappearing from the diplomatic scene. Alfred Thayer Mahan had little influence on American foreign policy after 1903 or 1904, mainly because President Roosevelt consulted with him less as his presidency progressed. John Hay, following a long and debilitating illness, died in 1905. In Great Britain, Joseph Chamberlain resigned from the cabinet in the fall of 1903 to devote all his energies to the fight against free trade. Failing in the effort, he was struck down by an apoplectic stroke in 1906, and never returned to politics. Arthur Balfour, the other outstanding Anglo-Saxonist in the British government, became Prime Minister in 1902, but was turned out of office by the Liberal victory of 1905. With the declining influence or deaths of these men, their ideas about the role of race in Anglo-American relations ceased to have any significant impact on the conduct of Anglo-American diplomacy.

During the brief heyday of Anglo-Saxonism at the turn of the century, however, its racist assumptions provided much of the ideological underpinning of the British-American rapprochement. Indeed, as Charles S. Campbell has observed of Anglo-Saxon race patriotism, "Without it there would have been no such rapprochement as occurred around 1900."[3]

The transformation that took place in Anglo-American relations resulted from a complex interacting of power politics, diplomacy, and ideas. The ideas contained in Anglo-Saxonism were crucial to the whole process, for they were central to the way large numbers of the two peoples perceived one another: first, as blood relations between whom conflict was not only unnatural, but almost unthinkable; and second, as natural allies with a common civilizing mission. Anglo-Saxonism thus created intellectual and emotional ties that were conducive to the development of a vastly improved relationship between the two great English-speaking powers.

In three crucial episodes in British-American relations during the period, Anglo-Saxonism had a significant bearing on the outcome. During the Venezuela boundary dispute, racial sympathy contributed substantially to the revulsion Britons and Americans felt at the prospect of war. During the Spanish-American conflict, Anglo-Saxonism brought about a tremendous outpouring of mutual goodwill, and accounted in part for Britain's support of the United States. When the British themselves became involved in a difficult war a short time later in South Africa, the Anglo-Saxonism of an articulate and influential minority of the American public helped to make possible the McKinley administration's policy of benevolent neutrality. In addition to its role in these three episodes, Anglo-Saxonism also strengthened the rapprochement by leading large numbers of the two peoples to believe that their shared interest in opposing Russian expansion in the Far East was racial, as well as economic and strategic, in nature.

While Anglo-Saxonism faded as an important influence on British-American relations after about 1904 or 1905, the sense of partnership that it had helped to create did not disappear. In a letter to President Roosevelt in December of 1906, Sir Edward Grey, who had recently taken over the Foreign Office from Lord Lansdowne, referred to the lingering influence of race sentiment, and offered his own conclusions about the special character of the Anglo-American relationship.

> We are really well disposed (though there are perhaps too many sentimentalists), and there is a really friendly feeling towards the United States. Some people call it Anglo-Saxon feeling. But it is not really that as between us and you. Your Continent is making a new race and a new type, drawn from many sources, just as in old times the race of these Islands was evolved from many sources. So I do not dwell upon race feeling. But common language helps to draw us together, and religion also.... But, more than all this, I should say that some generations of freedom on both sides have evolved a type of man and mind that looks at things from a kindred point of view, and a majority that has hatred for what is not just or free.[4]

The moral and cultural bonds of which Grey spoke, and which many people had referred to in the past in connection with Anglo-Saxonism, were to help the friendship of Great Britain and the United States to endure for decades to come; and their friendship, despite some occasional differences between the two countries, was to have a decisive impact on world affairs in the first half of the twentieth century.

Notes

Introduction

1. James Bryce, "The Essential Unity of Britain and America," *Atlantic Monthly* 82 (July 1898): 28.
2. Carl Schurz, "The Anglo-American Friendship," ibid. (October 1898): 435.
3. Works dealing with the rapprochement include Lionel M. Gelber, *The Rise of Anglo-American Friendship* (London: Oxford University Press, 1938); Richard H. Heindel, *The American Impact on Great Britain, 1898–1914* (Philadelphia: University of Pennsylvania Press, 1940); Charles S. Campbell, *Anglo-American Understanding, 1898–1903* (Baltimore: Johns Hopkins Press, 1957); A. E. Campbell, *Great Britain and the United States, 1895–1903* (London: Longmans, Green and Co., 1960); R. G. Neale, *Great Britain and United States Expansion* (East Lansing, Mich.: Michigan State University Press, 1966); and Bradford Perkins, *The Great Rapprochement* (New York: Atheneum, 1968). Stressing Anglo-American conflict rather than harmony is Edward P. Crapol, *America for Americans* (Westport, Conn.: Greenwood Press, 1973); Crapol's study concludes, however, with the election of William McKinley in 1896, and thus does not really deal with the period of the rapprochement.

Chapter One

1. Stewart L. Murray, *The Peace of the Anglo-Saxons* (London: Watts & Co., 1905), pp. 94–95.
2. On Celticism and Gallicism in France, see Frank H. Hankins, *The Racial Basis of Civilization* (New York and London: Alfred A. Knopf, 1926), pp. 141–58. On Teutonism in Germany, ibid., pp. 51–100. On the Pan-German and Pan-Slav movements, Hannah Arendt, *The Origins of Totalitarianism* (New York: Harcourt, Brace and Co., 1951), chap. 8.
3. Jacques Barzun, *Race* (New York: Harcourt, Brace and Co., 1937), p. 10; Louis L. Snyder, *The Idea of Racialism* (New York: Van Nostrand Reinhold Co., 1962), pp. 25, 34. For a thought-provoking discussion of the rise of race-thinking in the West, see Arendt, *Origins of Totalitarianism*, chap. 6. On the linkage of racism and imperialism, see William L. Langer, *The Diplomacy of Imperialism, 1890–1902*, 2 vols. (New York and London: Alfred A. Knopf, 1935), vol. 1, chap. 3, passim.
4. Howard K. Beale, *Theodore Roosevelt and the Rise of America to World Power* (Baltimore: Johns Hopkins Press, 1956), p. 28; Snyder, *Idea of Racialism*, pp. 32–33.

5. M. F. Ashley Montagu, *Man's Most Dangerous Myth* (New York: Columbia University Press, 1942), pp. 4, 8. There are several good general works on the subjects of race and racism. See, besides the works of Montagu, Hankins, Barzun, and Snyder cited above, Ruth Benedict, *Race* (New York: Modern Age Books, 1940); and, more specialized, Thomas F. Gossestt, *Race* (Dallas: Southern Methodist University Press, 1963), and Léon Poliakov, *The Aryan Myth* (New York: Basic Books, 1974).
6. Snyder, *Idea of Racialism*, pp. 32–33. Rosebery quoted in Charles Waldstein, *The Expansion of Western Ideals and the World's Peace* (New York and London: John Lane, 1899), p. 17.
7. Washington Gladden, *England and America* (London: James Clarke & Co., 1898), p. 70.
8. Alfred Thayer Mahan, *Retrospect and Prospect* (Boston: Little, Brown, and Co., 1902), p. 108.
9. Barzun, *Race*, p. 5.
10. See Cynthia Fansler Behrman, "The Mythology of British Imperialism" (Ph.D. diss., Boston University, 1965), chap. 3. Behrman's interest is in traits considered by the British to be peculiar to themselves, but her findings apply equally well to the mythology of Anglo-Saxonism; with the confusion of race and nation, national traits were often thought of as racial in nature.
11. Franklin H. Giddings, *Democracy and Empire, with Studies of Their Psychological, Economic, and Moral Foundations* (New York and London: Macmillan, 1900), p. 305. See also Hannis Taylor, "England's Colonial Empire," *North American Review* 162 (June 1896): 683.
12. Aline Gorren, *Anglo-Saxons & Others* (New York: Charles Scribner's Sons, 1900), p. 107; George E. Boxall, *The Anglo-Saxon* (London: Grant Richards, 1902), pp. 170–75.
13. Gorren, *Anglo-Saxons & Others*, pp. 38–39.
14. Ibid., p. 107; Behrman, "Mythology of British Imperialism," chap. 3, passim; Benjamin Kidd, *Principles of Western Civilisation* (London and New York: Macmillan, 1902), p. 372; Taylor, "England's Colonial Empire," pp. 683–84; Walter Besant, "The Future of the Anglo-Saxon Race," *North American Review* 163 (August 1896): 130–32; Charles Beresford, "The Future of the Anglo-Saxon Race," ibid. 171 (December 1900): 804.
15. Behrman, "Mythology of British Imperialism," chap. 3, passim; Boxall, *Anglo-Saxon*, pp. 170–75; Charles Beresford, "The Anglo-American *Entente*," *Pall Mall Magazine* 18 (July 1899): 380.
16. Besant, "Future of Anglo-Saxon Race," pp. 130–31.
17. Ibid., p. 134.
18. See, for example, George B. Waldron, "Five Hundred Years of the Anglo-Saxon," *McClure's Magazine* 12 (December 1898): 185-88.
19. George Burton Adams, "A Century of Anglo-Saxon Expansion," *Atlantic Monthly* 79 (April 1897): 528.
20. Whitelaw Reid, "The English-Speaking Race," Response before the St. Andrew's Society of New York, 30 November 1900, and Address before the Massachusetts Club, Boston, 3 March 1900, drafts in Whitelaw Reid Papers, Manuscript Division, Library of Congress.
21. Henry Cabot Lodge, *A Frontier Town and Other Essays* (New York: Charles Scribner's Sons, 1906), p. 47.

22. Reid, "English-Speaking Race." See also Behrman, "Mythology of British Imperialism," p. 83.
23. J. Lawson Walton, "Imperialism," *Contemporary Review* 75 (March 1899): 307.
24. Caroline E. Playne, *The Pre-War Mind in Britain* (London: George Allen & Unwin, 1928), pp. 182–83; Archibald P. Thornton, *The Imperial Idea and Its Enemies* (London: Macmillan, 1959), pp. ix-x; Robert Rhodes James, *The British Revolution, 1880–1939* (New York: Alfred A. Knopf, 1977), pp. 24–25; Behrman, "Mythology of British Imperialism," chap. 5.
25. J. A. Cramb, *The Origins and Destiny of Imperial Britain and Nineteenth Century Europe* (New York: E. P. Dutton & Co., 1915), p. 239.
26. Edward Dicey, "The New American Imperialism," *Nineteenth Century* 44 (September 1898): 489.
27. See James K. Hosmer, *A Short History of Anglo-Saxon Freedom* (New York: Charles Scribner's Sons, 1890), p. 308; John R. Dos Passos, *The Anglo-Saxon Century and the Unification of the English-Speaking People* (New York and London: G. P. Putnam's Sons, 1903), pp. 3, 234; Charles A. Conant, "The United States as a World Power. II. Her Advantages in the Competition for Commercial Empire," *Forum* 29 (August 1900): 686.
28. *Congressional Record*, 56th Cong., 1st Sess., p. 711 (9 January 1900).
29. Cramb, *Origins and Destiny*, pp. 230–31.
30. Lyman Abbott, "The Rights of Man," *Outlook* 68 (June 1901): 487.
31. Josiah Strong, *Expansion under New World-Conditions* (New York: Baker and Taylor Co., 1900), p. 212.

Chapter Two

1. Reginald Horsman, "Origins of Racial Anglo-Saxonism in Great Britain before 1850," *Journal of the History of Ideas* 37 (July-September 1976): 387-410, especially 387-90; Léon Poliakov, *The Aryan Myth* (New York: Basic Books, 1974), pp. 47–49.
2. Horsman, "Origins of Anglo-Saxonism," pp. 389–90.
3. "The Course of Civilization," *United States Magazine and Democratic Review* 6 (September 1839): 211.
4. Frederic Bancroft, ed., *Speeches, Correspondence and Political Papers of Carl Schurz*, 6 vols. (New York and London: G. P. Putnam's Sons, 1913), 1:56–57. The German-born Schurz more often subsumed the Anglo-Saxons in the larger "Teutonic" or "Germanic" race.
5. Julius Pratt, "The Ideology of American Expansion," in *Essays in Honor of William E. Dodd by His Former Students at the University of Chicago*, ed. Avery Craven (Chicago: University of Chicago Press, 1935), pp. 344–45; Albert K. Weinberg, *Manifest Destiny* (Baltimore: Johns Hopkins Press, 1935), pp. 161, 178; David M. Pletcher, *The Diplomacy of Annexation* (Columbia, Mo.: University of Missouri Press, 1973), p. 579. Benton cited in Merle Curti, *The Growth of American Thought*, 3rd ed. (New York: Harper & Row, 1964), p. 646.
6. Joseph Arthur de Gobineau, *Essai sur l'inégalité des races humaines*, 4 vols. (Paris, 1853–55), translated by H. Hotz as *The Moral and Intellectual Diversity of Races . . .* (Philadelphia: J. B. Lippincott & Co., 1856). The translator admitted in

his introduction (p. 99) that he substituted words here and there, condensed freely, and omitted a number of sections.
7. The preceding paragraph draws heavily on the excellent analysis in John Higham, *Strangers in the Land*, rev. ed. (New York: Atheneum, 1963), pp. 9–11. See also Julius W. Pratt, *Expansionists of 1898* (Baltimore: Johns Hopkins Press, 1936), pp. 2–3; and George M. Frederickson, *The Black Image in the White Mind* (New York: Harper & Row, 1971), pp. 97–101.
8. Richard Hofstadter, *Social Darwinism in American Thought*, rev. ed. (Boston: Beacon Press, 1955), p. 171; Gertrude Himmelfarb, *Darwin and the Darwinian Revolution* (Garden City, N.Y.: Doubleday & Co., 1959), p. 393; Donald Fred Tingley, "The Rise of Racialistic Thinking in the United States in the Nineteenth Century" (Ph.D. diss., University of Illinois, 1952), p. 139.
9. Himmelfarb, *Darwin*, p. 394.
10. Charles Darwin, *The Descent of Man and Selection in Relation to Sex*, 2 vols. (London: J. Murray, 1871), 1:179. Darwin was quoting Zincke's *Last Winter in the United States* (London, 1868), p. 29.
11. Walter Bagehot, *Physics and Politics; or, Thoughts on the Application of the Principles of "Natural Selection" and "Inheritance" to Political Society* (London: C. Kegan Paul & Co., 1872), p. 43. For Bagehot's influence in the United States, see Hofstadter, *Social Darwinism*, p. 92.
12. Theodore Roosevelt, "Kidd's 'Social Evolution'," *North American Review* 161 (July 1895): 94, 109.
13. On Kidd, see Bernard Semmel, *Imperialism and Social Reform* (London: George Allen & Unwin, 1960), pp. 20-24; and Peter H. King, "The White Man's Burden" (Ph.D. diss., University of California at Los Angeles, 1958), pp. 200-208.
14. Benjamin Kidd, *Social Evolution*, 2nd ed. (New York and London: Macmillan, 1895), pp. 20, 205.
15. Ibid., p. 45.
16. Ibid., p. viii, and Kidd, *Principles of Western Civilisation* (London and New York: Macmillan, 1902), p. 395.
17. Kidd, *Social Evolution*, pp. 300-301.
18. Semmel, *Imperialism and Social Reform*, pp. 25-33.
19. Ibid., p. 30.
20. Karl Pearson, *National Life from the Standpoint of Science*, 2nd ed. (London: Cambridge University Press, 1905), pp. 36, 43.
21. Ibid., pp. 14-15.
22. Ibid., p. 26.
23. Josiah Strong, *Our Country* (New York: American Home Missionary Society, 1885), and *The New Era; or, The Coming Kingdom* (London: Hodder and Stoughton, 1893). The last figure is quoted by the publisher opposite the title page of Strong's 1901 book, *The Times and Young Men*. The other sales figures may be found facing the title page of *The New Era*.
24. Strong, *New Era*, pp. 11-12.
25. See William H. Berge, "The Impulse for Expansion" (Ph.D. diss., Vanderbilt University, 1969), p. 203.
26. Strong, *Our Country*, pp. 161, 165, 174, 178, and *New Era*, p. 69. Strong was a

fervent American nationalist. He thought the British Empire too scattered and sparsely populated to be of much help in Anglo-Saxonizing the world. The United States, enormous, compact, populous, and wealthy, was the true seat of Anglo-Saxondom. *Our Country*, pp. 165-66, and *New Era*, pp. 72-73.
27. Strong, *Our Country*, pp. 159-61; Berge, "Impulse for Expansion," pp. 196-97.
28. Strong, *Our Country*, pp. 174-75. Strong himself later quoted this passage in *The New Era*, p. 79.
29. In his book entitled *Expansion under New World-Conditions* (New York: Baker and Taylor Co., 1900), Strong fully endorsed American imperialism. In this work—which sold at least ten thousand copies—Strong called for retention of the Philippines; commended Alfred Thayer Mahan for his strong arguments in favor of American expansion in the Caribbean and the Pacific; pointed out the duty of Americans to join other advanced peoples in policing the world; supported an open-door policy in China; and portrayed the anti-imperialists as well-intentioned but misguided. It may be true, as Dorothea Muller has argued, that Strong "de-emphasized" the commercial and strategic goals pursued by many other advocates of American imperialism, and concentrated instead on the international responsibilities of a rich, powerful, and Christian people; Strong hardly ignored the economic and strategic advantages, however, and his statements about "responsibilities" were no less an argument for expansion. See Strong, *Expansion*, pp. 10, 133-34, 159-61, 196-97, 199-202, 204, 240-46, 254-58, 260-61, 274-75, 281-82, 287-95, 302; Dorothea Muller, "Josiah Strong and American Nationalism: A Reevaluation," *Journal of American History* 53 (December 1966): 497-500; and Frederick Merk, *Manifest Destiny and Mission in American History* (New York: Alfred A. Knopf, 1963), pp. 245-46.
30. Strong, *Our Country*, pp. 169, 175-78. See also Muller, "Strong," p. 494; and Merk, *Manifest Destiny*, p. 240.
31. Strong, *New Era*, pp. 69, 71, 80, and *Our Country*, pp. 178-79.
32. Charles Beresford, "The Future of the Anglo-Saxon Race," *North American Review* 171 (December 1900): 810.
33. Victor Bérard, *British Imperialism and Commercial Supremacy* (London: Longmans, Green, and Co., 1906), p. 279. Bérard was secretary of the *Revue de Paris*.
34. John Barrett, "The Problem of the Philippines," *North American Review* 167 (September 1898): 267.
35. Brooks Adams, "Economic Conditions for Future Defense," *Atlantic Monthly* 92 (November 1903): 648. See also ibid., p. 632, and Adams, "The Spanish War and the Equilibrium of the World," *Forum* 25 (August 1898): 650-51.
36. See, for example, Senator Beveridge's speech, *Congressional Record*, 56th Cong., 1st Sess., p. 711 (9 January 1900); and Wolf von Schierbrand, *America, Asia and the Pacific, with Special Reference to the Russo-Japanese War and Its Results* (New York: Henry Holt and Co., 1904), pp. 302-3, 311.
37. J. C. Guffin, "Evolution *vs.* Imperialism," *Arena* 23 (February 1900): 142.
38. Tingley, "Rise of Racialistic Thinking," pp. 2, 135-36, 174; Helen E. Knuth, "The Climax of American Anglo-Saxonism, 1898-1905" (Ph.D. diss., Northwestern University, 1958), pp. 26, 46, 48.

39. Jacques Barzun, *Race* (New York: Harcourt, Brace and Co., 1937), pp. 40–42.
40. Edward A. Freeman, *An Introduction to American Institutional History* (Baltimore: Johns Hopkins University Studies..., 1882), p. 30.
41. John Mitchell Kemble, *The Saxons in England*, 2 vols. (London: Longman, Brown, Green & Longmans, 1849). One scholar believes that Sharon Turner's *History of the Anglo-Saxons* (1799–1805) should be considered the first historical work of this school. L. P. Curtis, Jr., *Anglo-Saxons and Celts* (Bridgeport, Conn.: University of Bridgeport Conference on British Studies, 1968), p. 76.
42. Curtis, *Anglo-Saxons and Celts*, p. 82; G. P. Gooch, *History and Historians in the Nineteenth Century* (London: Longmans, Green, and Co., 1913), pp. 340–41, 344. See William Stubbs, *The Constitutional History of England in Its Origin and Development*, 3 vols. (Oxford: Clarendon, 1880), vol. 1, and *Lectures on Early English History*, ed. Arthur Hassall (London and New York: Longmans, Green, and Co., 1906).
43. J. R. Green, *A Short History of the English People* (London: Macmillan, 1875), p. 45; Adams to Francis Parkman, 21 December 1884, Harold D. Cater, ed., *Henry Adams and His Friends* (Boston: Houghton Mifflin Co., 1947), p. 133; Gooch, *History and Historians*, p. 355; Bradford Perkins, *The Great Rapprochement* (New York: Atheneum, 1968), p. 139.
44. Louis L. Snyder, *The Idea of Racialism* (New York: Van Nostrand Reinhold Co., 1962), p. 55; Gooch, *History and Historians*, pp. 347–48; Curtis, *Anglo-Saxons and Celts*, pp. 79–81; Edward N. Saveth, *American Historians and European Immigrants, 1875–1925* (New York: Columbia University Press, 1948), pp. 17–19. See Edward A. Freeman, *The Growth of the English Constitution from the Earliest Times* (London: Macmillan, 1872).
45. Freeman, *Introduction to Institutional History*, p. 23.
46. Edward A. Freeman, *Lectures to American Audiences* (Philadelphia: Porter & Coates, 1882), pp. 9–11, 54–55. On Freeman's trip to the United States, see W. R. W. Stephens, *The Life and Letters of Edward A. Freeman*, 2 vols. (London and New York: Macmillan, 1895), 2:177–84; and Herbert Baxter Adams, "Mr. Freeman's Visit to Baltimore," in Freeman, *Introduction to Institutional History*, pp. 5–12.
47. Edward A. Freeman, *Some Impressions of the United States* (New York: Henry Holt and Co., 1883), pp. 15–16, and *Greater Greece and Greater Britain; and, George Washington, the Expander of England* (London: Macmillan, 1886).
48. John Lothrop Motley, *The Rise of the Dutch Republic*, 3 vols. (New York: Harper & Brothers, 1855), 1:v–vi. Parkman quoted in Thomas F. Gossett, *Race* (Dallas: Southern Methodist University Press, 1963), p. 95.
49. Saveth, *American Historians*, pp. 10, 15, 21, 90.
50. Higham, *Strangers in the Land*, pp. 95–96, 139; Milton Berman, *John Fiske* (Cambridge, Mass.: Harvard University Press, 1961), pp. 218–19; Barbara Miller Solomon, *Ancestors and Immigrants* (Cambridge, Mass.: Harvard University Press, 1956).
51. Solomon, *Ancestors and Immigrants*, p. 63.
52. Herbert Baxter Adams, *The Germanic Origins of New England Towns* (Baltimore: Johns Hopkins University Studies..., 1882), and *Saxon Tithing-Men in America* (Baltimore: John Hopkins University Studies..., 1883).
53. Woodrow Wilson, "Bryce's American Commonwealth," *Political Science Quar-*

terly 4 (March 1889): 169. Wilson's devotion to Teutonism early in his career is discussed in Saveth, *American Historians*, pp. 137–40.

54. Saveth, *American Historians*, pp. 25–26, 90; James K. Hosmer, *A Short History of Anglo-Saxon Freedom* (New York: Charles Scribner's Sons, 1890).
55. "The Anglo-Saxon Courts of Law," in *Essays in Anglo-Saxon Law* (Boston: Little, Brown, and Co., 1876), pp. 1–54; Ernest Samuels, *Henry Adams: The Major Phase* (Cambridge, Mass.: Harvard University Press, 1964), p. 351. In later years, Adams abandoned the Teutonic theory altogether, ascribing his earlier involvement with it to the rashness of youth. Nevertheless, race remained for him one of the prime determinants of human history. Without race, he said, "history was a nursery tale." The three keys to the success of a nation were "geography, geology and race energy." Adams to Henry Osborn Taylor, 4 May 1901, Worthington C. Ford, ed., *Letters of Henry Adams (1892-1918)*, 2 vols. (Boston and New York: Houghton Mifflin Co., 1938), 2:332; Henry Adams, *The Education of Henry Adams* (Boston: Massachusetts Historical Society, 1918), pp. 411–12; Adams to Brooks Adams, 7 October 1900, Cater, ed., *Adams and His Friends*, p. 500.
56. Saveth, *American Historians*, p. 32; Berman, *Fiske*, pp. 139, 259, 268.
57. Solomon, *Ancestors and Immigrants*, p. 62; Fiske to Alfred Bowker, 20 October 1900, Ethel F. Fisk, ed., *The Letters of John Fiske* (New York: Macmillan, 1940), p. 689.
58. Berman, *Fiske*, pp. 86–88, 129–30; John Spencer Clark, *The Life and Letters of John Fiske*, 2 vols. (Boston and New York: Houghton Mifflin Co., 1917), 2:139–41, 165–66.
59. John Fiske, *American Political Ideas Viewed from the Standpoint of Universal History* (New York and London: Harper & Brothers, 1885), pp. 9–10; Berman, *Fiske*, pp. 127, 139; Clark, *Fiske*, 2:165.
60. Fiske, *American Political Ideas*, pp. 125, 127, 129–32, 143–52. See also Berman, *Fiske*, pp. 138–40; and Merk, *Manifest Destiny*, p. 239.
61. Berman, *Fiske*, pp. 219, 259–60. Berman estimates that an average of ten thousand copies of Fiske's books were sold in the United States each year between 1887 and Fiske's death in 1901; these were formidable sales figures for works of nonfiction.
62. Fiske, *American Political Ideas*, pp. 6–7; Freeman to Fiske, 9 August 1889, Fisk, ed., *Letters of Fiske*, p. 568. See also Freeman to Hannis Taylor, 8 November 1889, Stephens, *Freeman*, 2:410. Fiske thought Freeman "our greatest master in history, almost the greatest that ever lived!" Fiske to Abby Fiske, 24 March 1892, Fisk, ed., *Letters of Fiske*, p. 592.
63. Saveth, *American Historians*, p. 32.
64. William L. Langer, *The Diplomacy of Imperialism, 1890-1902*, 2 vols. (New York and London: Alfred A. Knopf, 1935), 1:71; Marquess of Crewe, *Lord Rosebery* (New York and London: Harper & Brothers, 1931), p. 251.
65. Charles W. Dilke, *Greater Britain*, 3rd ed. (London: Macmillan, 1869), pp. 572–73, 197–98.
66. J. R. Seeley, *The Expansion of England* (London and New York: Macmillan, 1883), pp. 8, 11–16.
67. James Anthony Froude, *Oceana; or, England and Her Colonies* (London: Longmans, Green, and Co., 1886), p. 2.
68. Probably the first Englishman to advocate a union of all the Anglo-Saxon countries, including Great Britain, the United States, Canada, Australia, and New Zealand,

was the historian and publicist Goldwin Smith. He began to do so in the 1860s, and continued his efforts until his death in 1910. See Goldwin Smith, "England and America," *Atlantic Monthly* 14 (December 1864): 748–69; and Elisabeth Wallace, "Goldwin Smith on England and America," *American Historical Review* 59 (July 1954): 884–94.
69. W. T. Stead, ed., *The Last Will and Testament of Cecil John Rhodes* . . . (London: "Review of Reviews" Office, 1902), pp. 99–102; Cynthia Fansler Behrman, "The Mythology of British Imperialism" (Ph.D. diss., Boston University, 1965), p. 21.
70. W. T. Stead, *The Americanisation of the World; or, The Trend of the Twentieth Century* (London: "Review of Reviews" Office, 1902), pp. 7, 5. See also Stead, "The Future of the English-Speaking World," *Cosmopolitan* 32 (January 1902): 341–46. When Stead went down with the *Titanic* in 1912, J. L. Garvin eulogized him with the words: "His grave is where he might have chosen it, midway between England and America." Frederic Whyte, *The Life of W. T. Stead*, 2 vols. (New York and Boston: Houghton Mifflin Co., 1925), 2:315.
71. Whyte, *Stead*, 2:206–7; Stead, ed., *Last Will of Rhodes*, pp. 58–59, 63, 73; Stead, "Future of English-Speaking World," p. 342.
72. Sarah G. Millin, *Cecil Rhodes* (New York and London: Harper & Brothers, 1933), p. 195.
73. See ibid., pp. 35–36; and Basil Williams, *Cecil Rhodes* (New York: Henry Holt & Co., 1921), pp. 50–51.
74. Stead, ed., *Last Will of Rhodes*, pp. 62–63. See also Millin, *Rhodes*, p. 51; and Williams, *Rhodes*, pp. 36–37.
75. Stead, ed., *Last Will of Rhodes*, p. 59.
76. James Milne, "The Federation of the English-Speaking People. A Talk with the Right Hon. Sir George Grey, K.C.B.," *Contemporary Review* 66 (August 1894): 201, 205–7, 194.
77. Andrew Carnegie, "Distant Possessions—the Parting of the Ways," *North American Review* 167 (August 1898): 240, and "Americanism *versus* Imperialism," ibid. 168 (January 1899): 6.
78. Joseph F. Wall, *Andrew Carnegie* (New York: Oxford University Press, 1970), pp. 429–42, 676–80.
79. Andrew Carnegie, "Does America Hate England?" *Contemporary Review* 72 (November 1897): 661; Carnegie to Balfour, 23 July 1903, Burton J. Hendrick, *The Life of Andrew Carnegie*, 2 vols. (Garden City, N.Y.: Doubleday, Doran & Co., 1932), 2:193. See also Carnegie to William McKinley, 27 April 1898, William McKinley Papers, Manuscript Divison, Library of Congress.
80. Andrew Carnegie, "Imperial Federation: An American View," *Nineteenth Century* 30 (September 1891): 502–3, and *Triumphant Democracy*, rev. ed. (New York: Charles Scribner's Sons, 1893), pp. 520–21, 523, 532–33, 547–48.
81. Mahan to James R. Thursfield, 7 June 1894, Robert Seager II and Doris D. Maguire, eds., *Letters and Papers of Alfred Thayer Mahan*, 3 vols. (Annapolis, Md.: Naval Institute Press, 1975), 2:283; Wall, *Carnegie*, pp. 677–78.
82. Carnegie, *Triumphant Democracy*, p. 524, and "Imperial Federation," p. 507.
83. Carnegie, *Triumphant Democracy*, p. 541. See Wall, *Carnegie*, p. 680; Hendrick, *Carnegie*, 1:442; and Edwyn Anthony, "Mr. Andrew Carnegie and the Re-Union of

the English-Speaking Race," *Westminster Review* 163 (June 1905): 636–42.
84. U.S. Bureau of the Census, *Historical Statistics of the United States, 1789–1945* (Washington: Government Printing Office, 1949), p. 33; Knuth, "Climax of Anglo-Saxonism," pp. 258–59.
85. See Solomon, *Ancestors and Immigrants*, chap. 9.
86. Hosmer, *Short History*, p. 325; John W. Burgess, *Political Science and Comparative Constitutional Law*, 2 vols. (Boston and London: Ginn & Co., 1890), 1:44–45; Edward A. Ross, "The Causes of Race Superiority," *Annals of the American Academy of Political and Social Science* 18 (July 1901): 88; Whitelaw Reid, *American and English Studies*, 2 vols. (New York: Charles Scribner's Sons, 1913), 1:50, 52–53, 57.
87. Higham, *Strangers in the Land*, pp. 102–3 and passim; Oscar Handlin, *The Uprooted* (New York: Grossett & Dunlap, 1951), p. 288. The most extensive treatment of the activities of the Immigration Restriction League is in Solomon, *Ancestors and Immigrants*, chaps. 5–7, 10.
88. Francis A. Walker, "Restriction of Immigration," *Atlantic Monthly* 77 (June 1896): 828; Paul F. Boller, *American Thought in Transition* (Chicago: Rand McNally & Co., 1969), p. 211; *Atlantic Monthly* 70 (July 1892): 57.
89. For an extensive treatment of Anglo-Saxonism in American literature, see Gossett, *Race*, chap. 9.
90. Snyder, *Idea of Racialism*, p. 60; Langer, *Diplomacy of Imperialism*, 1:83.
91. Edmond Gosse, "The Literature of Action," *North American Review* 168 (January 1899): 17; King, "White Man's Burden," p. 193. For interesting discussions of Kipling's idealistic imperialism, see Vasant A. Shahane, *Rudyard Kipling* (Carbondale, Ill.: Southern Illinois University Press, 1973), pp. 32–33, 36–39; and Angus Wilson, *The Strange Ride of Rudyard Kipling* (New York: Viking Press, 1978), p. 250.
92. King, "White Man's Burden," pp. 191, 192, 194–95.
93. Bérard, *British Imperialism*, p. 46. See also Henry R. Marshall, "Rudyard Kipling and Racial Instinct," *Century Magazine* 36 (July 1899): 375–77. For expressions of Kipling's distaste for American society, see his book *Somthing of Myself for My Friends Known and Unknown* (Garden City, N.Y.: Doubleday, Doran & Co., 1937), pp. 122–23, 128, 130–31, 141.
94. Gossett, *Race*, pp. 202, 205; Robert Barltrop, *Jack London* (London: Pluto Press, 1976), pp. 86–87; Andrew Sinclair, *Jack* (New York: Harper & Row, 1977), pp. 73–74.
95. Jack London, *A Daughter of the Snows* (Philadelphia: J. B. Lippincott, 1902), p. 77.
96. Jack London, *The Valley of the Moon* (New York: Macmillan, 1913), pp. 102–3. Interestingly, the heroine who made this observation was one "Saxon Brown." Her unusual first name "was supposed to symbolize the purity and strength and grace of the peoples who founded the English race." Richard O'Connor, *Jack London* (Boston and Toronto: Little, Brown and Co., 1964), p. 333. Although *The Valley of the Moon* was published later than the period under discussion, it typifies much of London's earlier writing.
97. Gossett, *Race*, pp. 202, 204; Franklin Walker, *Frank Norris* (New York: Russell &

Russell, 1963), pp. 67–68; Knuth, "Climax of Anglo-Saxonism," p. 80. See also Cynthia Eagle Russett, *Darwin in America* (San Francisco: W. H. Freeman and Co., 1976), pp. 182–83.
98. *Moran of the Lady Letty*, quoted in Larzer Ziff, *The American 1890s* (New York: Viking Press, 1966), p. 265.
99. Frank Norris, *The Octopus* (Garden City, N.Y.: Doubleday & Co., 1901), bk. 2, pp. 356–57. See also Norris, "The Frontier Gone at Last...," *World's Work* 3 (February 1902): 1728–31.
100. Walker, *Norris*, pp. 273–74; Alice P. Hackett, *70 Years of Best Sellers, 1895–1965* (New York: Bowker, 1967), p. 99; James D. Hart, *The Popular Book* (New York: Oxford University Press, 1950), p. 220; Perkins, *Great Rapprochement*, p. 132. Sales figures for all of Norris's novels may be found in Walker, *Norris*, p. 286n.
101. *The Son of the Wolf*, London's first book, was published in 1900 and was an immediate critical and popular success; the prestigious *Atlantic Monthly* received it with an affirmation that "the book produces in the reader a deeper faith in the manly virtues of our race." *Children of the Frost* (1902) was another critical success, while the first edition of 10,000 copies of *The Call of the Wild* (1903) sold out on the day it was released. *People of the Abyss*, also published in 1903, was applauded across the country. As for *The Sea-Wolf*, it created a sensation among the critics and the reading public alike; forty thousand copies were sold to bookstores even before its publication in 1904. *The Faith of Men*, a short-story collection which appeared in the same year, went through three editions almost immediately. And *The War of the Classes*, a collection of London's lectures and articles, came out in 1905 and also went through three editions. Barltrop, *London*, pp. 76, 90, 93, 100, 105–6, 109 (*Atlantic* quotation from p. 76); Hart, *Popular Book*, p. 215; Charles Child Walcutt, *Jack London*, University of Minnesota Pamphlets on American Writers, no. 57 (Minneapolis: University of Minnesota Press, 1966), pp. 11, 13.

Chapter Three

1. George Burton Adams, "The United States and the Anglo-Saxon Future," *Atlantic Monthly* 78 (July 1896): 44; Mahan to Clarke, 5 November 1892, Robert Seager II and Doris D. Maguire, eds., *Letters and Papers of Alfred Thayer Mahan*, 3 vols. (Annapolis, Md.: Naval Institute Press, 1975), 2:84 (hereafter cited as *Letters of Mahan*); David Mills, "Which Shall Dominate—Saxon or Slav?" *North American Review* 166 (June 1898): 738.
2. John R. Dos Passos, *The Anglo-Saxon Century and the Unification of the English-Speaking People* (New York and London: G. P. Putnam's Sons, 1903), p. 9.
3. George E. Boxall, *The Anglo-Saxon* (London: Grant Richards, 1902), pp. 72–77, passim; "The Success of the Anglo-Saxons," *Edinburgh Review* 187 (January 1898): 130; H. H. Powers, "The War as a Suggestion of Manifest Destiny," *Annals of the American Academy of Political and Social Science* 12 (September 1898): 185. See also Howard Mumford Jones, *The Age of Energy* (New York: Viking Press, 1971), p. 202.
4. "Success of Anglo-Saxons," p. 130.

NOTES

5. Brooks Adams, "The New Struggle for Life among Nations," *McClure's Magazine* 12 (April 1899): 558.
6. Roosevelt to Cecil Spring Rice, 29 May 1897, Elting E. Morison, ed., *The Letters of Theodore Roosevelt*, 8 vols. (Cambridge, Mass.: Harvard University Press, 1951–54), 1:620 (hereafter cited as *Letters of Roosevelt*); Franklin H. Giddings, *Democracy and Empire, with Studies of Their Psychological, Economic, and Moral Foundations* (New York and London: Macmillan, 1900), p. 243. See also Powers, "War as Suggestion," p. 186; George B. Waldron, "Five Hundred Years of the Anglo-Saxon," *McClure's Magazine* 12 (December 1898): 186–88; and Aline Gorren, *Anglo-Saxons & Others* (New York: Charles Scribner's Sons, 1900), p. 113.
7. Edmond Demolins, *Anglo-Saxon Superiority* (New York: R. F. Fenno & Co., 1899), p. xix. Highly favorable reviews appeared in the *Outlook* 59 (July 1898): 509–10; *Edinburgh Review* 187 (January 1898): 130–50; and the *Westminster Review* 152 (July 1899): 73–82. A favorable French review was printed in *Living Age* 215 (December 1897): 656–64.
8. See Archibald R. Colquhoun, *The Mastery of the Pacific* (New York and London: Macmillan, 1902), pp. 415–16; and Wolf von Schierbrand, *America, Asia and the Pacific, with Special Reference to the Russo-Japanese War and Its Results* (New York: Henry Holt and Co., 1904), p. 282.
9. See Archibald R. Colquhoun, *Greater America* (New York and London: Harper & Brothers, 1904), p. 405. Some of the less attractive qualities attributed to the Germans are mentioned in Cynthia Fansler Behrman, "The Mythology of British Imperialism" (Ph.D. diss., Boston University, 1965), p. 100.
10. Otto Eltzbacher, "German Colonial Ambitions and Anglo-Saxon Interests," *Fortnightly Review* 73 (March 1903): 487. See also Colquhoun, *Greater America*, p. 409; and Stewart L. Murray, *The Peace of the Anglo-Saxons* (London: Watts & Co., 1905), p. 113.
11. Tyler Dennett, *John Hay* (New York: Dodd, Mead & Co., 1933), p. 384.
12. Hay to Henry Cabot Lodge, 27 July 1898, A. L. P. Dennis, *Adventures in American Diplomacy, 1896–1906* (New York: E. P. Dutton & Co., 1928), p. 98.
13. Lodge to White, 9 February 1900, Henry Cabot Lodge Papers, Massachusetts Historical Society, Boston.
14. Roosevelt to George L. Meyer, 12 April 1901, *Letters of Roosevelt*, 3:52; Roosevelt to Lodge, 27 March 1901, Henry Cabot Lodge, ed., *Selections from the Correspondence of Theodore Roosevelt and Henry Cabot Lodge, 1884–1918*, 2 vols. (New York and London: Charles Scribner's Sons, 1925), 1:484–85; Hiram Maxim to Roosevelt, 29 October 1901, and Roosevelt to Cecil Spring Rice, 1 November 1905, Theodore Roosevelt Papers, Manuscript Division, Library of Congress.
15. For a notable British exception,' see 'A Biologist,' "A Biological View of Our Foreign Policy," *Saturday Review* 81 (February 1896): 118–20.
16. See Mills, "Which Shall Dominate?" p. 734; Charles W. Dilke, "The Future Relations of Great Britain and the United States," *Forum* 26 (January 1899): 528; Roosevelt to Spring Rice, 16 March 1901, Stephen Gwynn, ed., *The Letters and Friendships of Sir Cecil Spring Rice*, 2 vols. (Boston and New York: Houghton Mifflin Co., 1929), 1:344–45 (hereafter cited as *Letters of Spring Rice*); Mahan to Leopold J. Maxse, 7 March 1902, *Letters of Mahan*, 3:13.

17. A particularly striking example of this point of view is contained in Henry Adams, *The Education of Henry Adams* (Boston: Massachusetts Historical Society, 1918), pp. 438–40.
18. John A. S. Grenville, *Lord Salisbury and Foreign Policy* (London: Athlone Press of the University of London, 1964), p. 291. Recent studies of the century-long "Great Game" between Britain and Russia for predominance in Asia include Michael Edwardes, *Playing the Great Game* (London: Hamish Hamilton, 1975); and David Gillard, *The Struggle for Asia, 1828–1914* (London: Methuen & Co., 1977).
19. Grenville, *Salisbury and Foreign Policy*, pp. 292–93.
20. Spring Rice to Edith Roosevelt, 20 January 1904, *Letters of Spring Rice*, 1:377.
21. Josiah Strong, *Expansion under New World-Conditions* (New York: Baker and Taylor, Co., 1900), p. 189; Giddings, *Democracy and Empire*, p. 290; Edward Dicey, "The Rival Empires," *Nineteenth Century and After* 54 (December 1903): 886, 891, 892. See also Frederick Wells Williams, "The Real Menace of Russian Aggression," *Annals of the American Academy of Political and Social Science* (Supplement) 13 (May 1899): 195; Colquhoun, *Greater America*, p. 375; Charles A. Conant, *The United States in the Orient* (Boston and New York: Houghton Mifflin Co., 1900), pp. 180–81; Wolf von Schierbrand, *Russia* (New York and London: G. P. Putnam's Sons, 1904), pp. 6–7, 46.
22. James K. Hosmer, *A Short History of Anglo-Saxon Freedom* (New York: Charles Scribner's Sons, 1890), p. 358. On Slavic racial characteristics, see also Schierbrand, *Russia*, pp. 31, 42–43.
23. Giddings, *Democracy and Empire*, p. 288; Schierbrand, *America, Asia and the Pacific*, pp. 138–39; Albert J. Beveridge, *The Russian Advance* (New York and London: Harper & Brothers, 1903), p. 13; Brooks Adams, "Russia's Interest in China," *Atlantic Monthly* 86 (September 1900): 312.
24. Strong, *Expansion*, p. 190.
25. See Charles A. Gardiner, *The Proposed Anglo-American Alliance* (New York and London: G. P. Putnam's Sons, 1898), pp. 5, 28; Colquhoun, *Greater America*, pp. 375–76; Conant, *United States in the Orient*, p. 227; Giddings, *Democracy and Empire*, pp. 288–89; Albion W. Tourgée, "The Twentieth Century Peacemakers," *Contemporary Review* 75 (June 1899): 892; John F. Simmons, "'Imperialism' an Historical Development," *Overland Monthly* 42 (October 1903): 315; Dicey, "Rival Empires," p. 889; Williams, "Real Menace," pp. 184, 187; Spring Rice to Roosevelt, 9 August 1900, Roosevelt Papers.
26. Quoted in Frederic Whyte, *The Life of W. T. Stead*, 2 vols. (New York and Boston: Houghton Mifflin Co., 1925), 2:126–27.
27. Beveridge, *Russian Advance*, pp. 109, 368, 461. The quotation is on p. 109.
28. Roosevelt to Spring Rice, 5 August 1896, *Letters of Roosevelt*, 1:555. See also Strong, *Expansion*, pp. 192–93, 202–3.
29. Ernest Samuels, *Henry Adams: The Major Phase* (Cambridge, Mass.: Harvard University Press, 1964), p. 200.
30. Strong, *Expansion*, pp. 185–86. See also Conant, *United States in the Orient*, p. 60; Gardiner, *Proposed Alliance*, p. 2; Giddings, *Democracy and Empire*, pp. v, 289–90; Powers, "War as Suggestion," p. 186; Simmons, "'Imperialism'," pp. 314–15; Williams, "Real Menace," pp. 196–97.
31. Murray, *Peace of the Anglo-Saxons*, p. 111; Strong, *Expansion*, pp. 204–5.

Chapter Four

1. At one time or another, members of the foreign policy elite who were in regular contact with one another included also such men as Brooks and Henry Adams, Whitelaw Reid, Albert Shaw, and Lyman Abbott. The detailed study that this group merits has never been written. However, nearly all historical works dealing with American expansion at the turn of the century mention the close ties and considerable influence of the group. See, for example, Howard K. Beale, *Theodore Roosevelt and the Rise of America to World Power* (Baltimore: Johns Hopkins Press, 1956), pp. 20–23, 55, 461; H. Wayne Morgan, *America's Road to Empire* (New York: John Wiley and Sons, 1965), p. 15; and Charles S. Campbell, *The Transformation of American Foreign Relations, 1865-1900* (New York: Harper & Row, 1976), pp. 152–54.
2. Roosevelt to Cecil Spring Rice, 13 June 1904, Elting E. Morison, ed., *The Letters of Theodore Roosevelt*, 8 vols. (Cambridge, Mass.: Harvard University Press, 1951–54), 4:832 (hereafter cited as *Letters of Roosevelt*); Theodore Roosevelt, *Biological Analogies in History* (New York: Oxford University Press, 1910), p. 41. A comprehensive account of Roosevelt's thinking on the subject of race of Thomas G. Dyer, "Theodore Roosevelt and the Idea of Race" (Ph.D. diss., University of Georgia, 1975).
3. Roosevelt to David B. Schneder, 19 June 1905, *Letters of Roosevelt*, 4:1240; David H. Burton, *Theodore Roosevelt: Confident Imperialist* (Philadelphia: University of Pennsylvania Press, 1968), p. 148.
4. Roosevelt to Thomas Gaffney, 10 May 1901, *Letters of Roosevelt*, 3:76; Roosevelt to Edward Grey, 18 February 1906, ibid., 5:529; Roosevelt, *Biological Analogies*, p. 21; Dyer, "Roosevelt and Race," p. 34.
5. Roosevelt to Lady Gregory, 8 June 1903, Theodore Roosevelt Papers, Manuscript Division, Library of Congress; Roosevelt to William Archer, 31 August 1899, and to John St. Loe Strachey, 27 January 1900, *Letters of Roosevelt*, 2:1063–64, 1145; Roosevelt to Finley Peter Dunne, 23 November 1904, ibid., 4:1040–41; Theodore Roosevelt, *The Winning of the West*, 6 vols. (New York: G. P. Putnam's Sons, 1889–96), 1:29, 38–39.
6. Roosevelt, *Winning of the West*, 1:17; Roosevelt to Lowell, 4 December 1897, *Letters of Roosevelt*, 1:724; Roosevelt to Elmer H. Capen, 3 July 1901, ibid., 3:104.
7. Roosevelt, *Winning of the West*, 1:20–24, 46 (quotation from p. 22). On the pervasiveness of Teutonism in Roosevelt's historical works, see Dyer, "Roosevelt and Race," chap. 3.
8. Roosevelt, *Biological Analogies*, p. 7. See also ibid., pp. 4, 14–15. Burton, *Roosevelt*, p. 154, says that this lecture "can well stand as Theodore Roosevelt's definitive statement of the place of evolution in human history."
9. Theodore Roosevelt, *The Strenuous Life* (New York: Century Co., 1900), pp. 6, 20; Burton, *Roosevelt*, pp. 135–36, 156–57; John Morton Blum, *The Republican Roosevelt* (Cambridge, Mass.: Harvard University Press, 1954), p. 25; George E. Mowry, *The Era of Theodore Roosevelt and the Birth of Modern America, 1900–1912* (New York: Harper & Row, 1958), p. 144.
10. Roosevelt, *Biological Analogies*, pp. 34–35; Address at Pomona College, Claremont, Calif., 8 March 1903, Theodore Roosevelt, *California Addresses* (San Francisco:

California Promotion Committee, 1903), pp. 22–23. See also the essay "Character and Success," in Roosevelt, *Strenuous Life*, pp. 113–21.
11. Roosevelt to Arthur Lee, 25 November 1898, and to Gustaf von Götzen, 7 February 1899, *Letters of Roosevelt*, 2:890, 934.
12. Roosevelt to Spring Rice, 13 August 1897 and 16 March 1901, Stephen Gwynn, ed., *The Letters and Friendships of Sir Cecil Spring Rice*, 2 vols. (Boston and New York: Houghton Mifflin Co., 1929), 1:229–31, 344–45 (hereafter cited as *Letters of Spring Rice*); Beale, *Roosevelt*, pp. 390–91.
13. Roosevelt to Spring Rice, 16 March 1901, *Letters of Spring Rice*, 1:344–45.
14. Roosevelt to Spring Rice, 13 August 1897, ibid., pp. 231–32. See also same to same, 19 March 1904, ibid., pp. 397–98; same to same, 13 June 1900, Roosevelt Papers; same to same, 29 May 1897, *Letters of Roosevelt*, 1:620–21; same to same, 16 March 1901, and Roosevelt to George F. Becker, 8 July 1901, ibid., 3:15–16, 112.
15. Beale, *Roosevelt*, p. 81.
16. A valuable study of Roosevelt's relationship with these and other English friends is David H. Burton, *Theodore Roosevelt and His English Correspondents* (Philadelphia: American Philosophical Society, 1973).
17. Roosevelt to Anna Roosevelt, 4 July 1895, and to Francis C. Moore, 9 February 1898, *Letters of Roosevelt*, 1:464, 771; Rudyard Kipling, *Something of Myself for My Friends Known and Unknown* (Garden City, N.Y.: Doubleday, Doran & Co., 1937), p. 131.
18. Roosevelt to Spring Rice, 2 December 1899, *Letters of Spring Rice*, 1:307.
19. A. E. Campbell, *Great Britain and the United States, 1895–1903* (London: Longmans, Green and Co., 1960), p. 200.
20. Lodge to Balfour, 1 February 1896, Henry Cabot Lodge Papers, Massachusetts Historical Society, Boston.
21. Henry Adams, *The Education of Henry Adams* (Boston: Massachusetts Historical Society, 1918), p. 420.
22. Lodge's aristocratic leanings can be gauged by reading passages such as those in his *Early Memories* (New York: Charles Scribner's Sons, 1913), pp. 208–11, 217.
23. See John A. S. Grenville and George Berkeley Young, *Politics, Strategy, and American Diplomacy* (New Haven, Conn., and London: Yale University Press, 1966), pp. 206–8; and Edward P. Crapol, *America for Americans* (Westport, Conn.: Greenwood Press, 1973), p. 222.
24. Mahan to Lodge, 8 December 1900, Lodge Papers.
25. The dissertation was published in *Essays in Anglo-Saxon Law* (Boston: Little, Brown, and Co., 1876), pp. 55–119.
26. See, for example, *A Frontier Town and Other Essays* (New York: Charles Scribner's Sons, 1906), pp. 23, 43, 233. On Lodge as a Teutonist historian, see Edward N. Saveth, *American Historians and European Immigrants, 1875–1925* (New York: Columbia University Press, 1948), pp. 51–64.
27. *Congressional Record*, 56th Cong., 1st Sess., p. 2621 (7 March 1900).
28. Henry Cabot Lodge, "The Distribution of Ability in the United States," *Century Magazine* 20 (September 1891): 687–94. See also Lodge, "The Restriction of Immigration," *North American Review* 152 (January 1891): 27–36.
29. Le Bon's theories are well summarized in the translated selection "The Influence of Race in History," *Popular Science Monthly* 35 (August 1889): 495–503. See also

NOTES

John Higham, *Strangers in the Land*, rev. ed. (New York: Atheneum, 1963), p. 142. Roosevelt sent for two Le Bon volumes, and after reading them pronounced Le Bon "really a thinker." Roosevelt to Lodge, 23 March and 29 April 1896, Henry Cabot Lodge, ed., *Selections from the Correspondence of Theodore Roosevelt and Henry Cabot Lodge, 1884–1918*, 2 vols. (New York and London: Charles Scribner's Sons, 1925), 1:216, 218.

30. Lodge's speech of 16 March 1896 is one of the most important sources for his views on race. *Congressional Record*, 54th Cong., 1st Sess., pp. 2817–20. The speech is summarized in John A. Garraty, *Henry Cabot Lodge* (New York: Alfred A. Knopf, 1965), pp. 142–43.
31. On Lodge's fight for immigration restriction, see Higham, *Strangers in the Land*, pp. 96, 103–5; and Barbara Miller Solomon, *Ancestors and Immigrants* (Cambridge, Mass.: Harvard University Press, 1956), pp. 117–19, 124.
32. See Garraty, *Lodge*, pp. 203, 214–15, 222–23; and Grenville and Young, *Politics, Strategy, and American Diplomacy*, pp. 208, 214.
33. Tyler Dennett, *John Hay* (New York: Dodd, Mead & Co., 1933), p. 148; Kenton J. Clymer, *John Hay* (Ann Arbor, Mich.: University of Michigan Press, 1975), pp. 40, 44.
34. Dennett, *Hay*, pp. 147–49; Clymer, *Hay*, pp. 87–89.
35. Dennett, *Hay*, p. 181.
36. Hay to Clara Hay, 29 August 1898, John Hay Papers, Manuscript Division, Library of Congress. See also Hay to Sir John Clark, 30 August 1898, *Letters of John Hay and Extracts from His Diary*, 3 vols. (New York: Gordian Press, 1969), 3:131.
37. Hay to Balfour, 29 July 1902, Hay Papers.
38. Dennett, *Hay*, p. 218.
39. John Hay, *Addresses* (New York: Century Co., 1906), pp. 78–79.
40. Hay to White, 24 September 1899, William R. Thayer, *The Life and Letters of John Hay*, 2 vols. (Boston and New York: Houghton Mifflin Co., 1915), 2:221.
41. Alfred Thayer Mahan, *From Sail to Steam* (New York: Harper & Brothers, 1907), p. xii.
42. Mahan to Samuel A. Ashe, 11 March 1885, Robert Seager II and Doris D. Maguire, eds., *Letters and Papers of Alfred Thayer Mahan*, 3 vols. (Annapolis, Md.: Naval Institute Press, 1975), 1:593 (hereafter cited as *Letters of Mahan*). In his intense Anglophilia and Anglo-Saxonism, Mahan was somewhat representative of the naval officer corps. There was a strong sense of camaraderie between British and American naval officers throughout much of the nineteenth century. See Peter Karsten, *The Naval Aristocracy* (New York: Free Press, 1972), pp. 107–9, 112–16.
43. Roosevelt's high regard for Captain Mahan and his ideas is evident in his letters to Mahan, 3 May, 17 May, and 9 June 1897, and to Lodge, 26 August 1897, all in *Letters of Roosevelt*, 1:607–8, 611, 622–23, 659. See also W. D. Puleston, *Mahan* (New Haven, Conn.: Yale University Press, 1939), pp. 182–83, 185. For Mahan's influence on Lodge, see Grenville and Young, *Politics, Strategy, and American Diplomacy*, pp. 209, 221.
44. Mahan to Ella Evans Mahan, 1 June 1894, *Letters of Mahan*, 2: 277; Robert Seager II, *Alfred Thayer Mahan* (Annapolis, Md.: Naval Institute Press, 1977), pp. 258, 278–80, 291–99; Charles C. Taylor, *The Life of Admiral Mahan* (New York: George H. Doran Co., 1920), chap. 7. When Mahan was feted at St. James's Hall, a huge

banner, bearing the legend "BLOOD IS THICKER THAN WATER," adorned the orchestra stand. Karsten, *Naval Aristocracy*, p. 108.
45. Mahan to Ella Evans Mahan, 22 February 1894, and to J. B. Sterling, 31 May 1897, *Letters of Mahan*, 2:234, 512.
46. Mahan to James R. Thursfield, 10 January 1896, and to J. B. Sterling, 13 February 1896, ibid., pp. 441–42, 445.
47. Mahan to James R. Thursfield, 1 December 1897, ibid., p. 529. Mahan's influence is most thoroughly documented in William E. Livezey, *Mahan on Sea Power* (Norman, Okla.: University of Oklahoma Press, 1947).
48. See, for example, "The United States Looking Outward," *Atlantic Monthly* 66 (December 1890): 821; and "Possibilities of an Anglo-American Reunion," *North American Review* 159 (November 1894): 558.
49. Mahan, *The Problem of Asia and Its Effect upon International Policies* (Boston: Little, Brown, and Co., 1900), pp. 192–94, and "A Twentieth-Century Outlook," *Harper's New Monthly Magazine* 95 (September 1897): 531; "The English-Speaking Race: Summary of an Address to a McGill University Convocation," Montreal, 18 May 1900, *Letters of Mahan*, 3:604.
50. Mahan, "United States Looking Outward," pp. 823–24, "Possibilities of Reunion," pp. 551–60, "Twentieth-Century Outlook," p. 531, and "Hawaii and Our Future Sea-Power," *Forum* 15 (March 1893): 11.
51. See Salisbury to Sir Henry Drummond Wolff, 17 July 1899, quoted in Ernest R. May, *Imperial Democracy* (New York: Harcourt, Brace & World, 1961), p. 32; and Robert Rhodes James, *The British Revolution, 1880–1939* (New York: Alfred A. Knopf, 1977), p. 74.
52. The best study of Salisbury's foreign policy is John A. S. Grenville, *Lord Salisbury and Foreign Policy* (London: Athlone Press of the University of London, 1964).
53. Ibid., pp. 55–56; William L. Strauss, *Joseph Chamberlain and the Theory of Imperialism* (Washington, D.C.: American Council on Public Affairs, 1942), pp. 81–82. On the very serious differences between Salisbury and Chamberlain, both personal and political, see James, *British Revolution*, pp. 167–69.
54. Speech at Birmingham, 6 January 1902, reported in the *Times* (London), 7 January 1902.
55. See Strauss, *Chamberlain and Imperialism*, pp. 60, 79–80; and J. L. Garvin, *The Life of Joseph Chamberlain*, 3 vols. (London: Macmillan, 1932–34), 1:494; 3:21. Chamberlain's many speeches on imperialism are particularly enlightening. See, for example, the speech at the Imperial Institute, 11 November 1895, reported in the *Times* (London), 12 November 1895; and the speech before the Royal Colonial Institute, 31 March 1897, Charles W. Boyd, ed., *Mr. Chamberlain's Speeches*, 2 vols. (Boston and New York: Houghton Mifflin Co., 1914), 2:3.
56. Quoted in Garvin, *Chamberlain*, 2:334.
57. Joseph Chamberlain, "Recent Developments of Policy in the United States and Their Relation to an Anglo-American Alliance," *Scribner's Magazine* 24 (December 1898): 674–82.
58. Garvin, *Chamberlain*, 3:7–8; Kenneth Young, *Arthur James Balfour* (London: G. Bell and Sons, 1963), pp. 168–69.
59. Balfour to White, 12 December 1900, quoted in Denis Judd, *Balfour and the British Empire* (London: Macmillan, 1968), p. 100.

60. See ibid., pp. 313–15; Young, *Balfour*, pp. 172, 452–53; Lionel M. Gelber, *The Rise of Anglo-American Friendship* (London: Oxford University Press, 1938), p. 19; Edward S. Martin, *The Life of Joseph Hodges Choate as Gathered Chiefly from His Letters*, 2 vols. (London: Constable & Co., 1920), 2:291–93. Balfour told an American newspaper correspondent in May of 1898 that he would "certainly never abandon" his hope for an Anglo-American alliance, though the hope might not be realized in his lifetime. *Review of Reviews* 17 (June 1898): 603.
61. Quoted in Young, *Balfour*, p. 279.
62. On this document and its place in Balfour's thinking, see ibid., pp. 277–84. Young believes the document was intended for the information of Theodore Roosevelt, who visited England in 1909 on his post-presidential trip.
63. Roosevelt to Spring Rice, 13 August 1897, *Letters of Roosevelt*, 1:644. Roosevelt felt the same eight years later. Roosevelt to Spring Rice, 1 November 1905, Roosevelt Papers.
64. On the latter point, see Gelber, *Rise of Friendship*, pp. 177, 179, 210–11; and Roosevelt to Spring Rice, 27 December 1904, *Letters of Spring Rice*, 1:442–43, 446.
65. Adams to John Hay, 6 May 1905, Worthington C. Ford, ed., *Letters of Henry Adams (1892-1918)*, 2 vols. (Boston and New York: Houghton Mifflin Co., 1938), 2:448.
66. Spring Rice to R. Munro Ferguson, 29 March 1887, *Letters of Spring Rice*, 1:61.
67. Spring Rice to Henry Cabot Lodge, 25 March 1904, and to Roosevelt, n.d. [March 1904], ibid., pp. 407, 396–97. See also Spring Rice to Roosevelt, 3 November 1897, ibid., p. 235.
68. Spring Rice to Theodore Roosevelt, 14 September 1896, ibid., p. 211. See also Spring Rice to Stephen Spring Rice, 11 January 1896, ibid., p. 188.
69. Spring Rice to Roosevelt, 1 August 1897, ibid., p. 228; same to same, 9 August 1900, Roosevelt Papers; Spring Rice to Stephen Spring Rice, 30 October 1898, *Letters of Spring Rice*, 1:263.

Chapter Five

1. The literature on the Venezuela boundary dispute is extensive. See the bibliography in Charles S. Campbell, *The Transformation of American Foreign Relations, 1865–1900* (New York: Harper & Row, 1976), pp. 365–67.
2. Especially valuable on this point is Gerald G. Eggert, *Richard Olney* (University Park, Pa.: Pennsylvania State University Press, 1974), pp. 220–23.
3. *Congressional Record*, 54th Cong., 1st. Sess., pp. 240–47 (19 December 1895), 255–65 (20 December 1895). The British memorial is on p. 245.
4. *Literary Digest* 12 (January 1896): 277.
5. Roosevelt to Henry Cabot Lodge, 20 December 1895, Elting E. Morison, ed., *The Letters of Theodore Roosevelt*, 8 vols. (Cambridge, Mass.: Harvard University Press, 1951–54), 1:500. Roosevelt remained highly belligerent for months. See his letters to Lodge, 27 December 1895 and 29 April 1896, Henry Cabot Lodge, ed., *Selections from the Correspondence of Theodore Roosevelt and Henry Cabot Lodge, 1884–1918*, 2 vols. (New York and London: Charles Scribner's Sons, 1925), 1:204–5, 218–19.
6. Pauncefote to Salisbury, 20 December 1895, quoted in A. E. Campbell, *Great Brit-*

ain and the United States, 1895–1903 (London: Longmans, Green and Co., 1960), p. 16.
7. Bryce to Roosevelt, 1 January 1896, Theodore Roosevelt Papers, Manuscript Division, Library of Congress; Patricia D. Herzig, "British Public Opinion on the Venezuelan Crisis of 1895–1896 with the United States" (M.A. thesis, Stanford University, 1949), p. 42.
8. Ernest R. May, *Imperial Democracy* (New York: Harcourt, Brace & World, 1961), p. 49; Dexter Perkins, *The Monroe Doctrine, 1867–1907* (Baltimore: Johns Hopkins Press, 1937), pp. 201–2; *Times* (London), 21 December 1895; *New York World*, 24–25 December 1895; *Literary Digest* 12 (December 1895): 244. See also Joseph Chamberlain's account of his conversation with Sir William Harcourt, Chamberlain Diary, JC 8/1/5 (9 January 1896), Joseph Chamberlain Papers, Birmingham University Library. Harcourt reportedly told the colonial secretary that "he would have nothing to do with war with America," and "he was sure that the people were on his side."
9. *New York World*, 25 December 1895.
10. *Times* (London), 18 December 1895; *Public Opinion* 19 (December 1895): 844; Lester D. Langley, *Struggle for the American Mediterranean* (Athens, Ga.: University of Georgia Press, 1976), p. 159.
11. *Public Opinion* 19 (December 1895): 844; *Times* (London), 18 December 1895.
12. *Saturday Review* 80 (December 1895): 857.
13. Jennie A. Sloan, "Anglo-American Relations and the Venezuelan Boundary Dispute," *Hispanic American Historical Review* 18 (November 1938): 495; Chamberlain to Lord Selborne, 20 December 1895, Selborne Papers, Department of Western Manuscripts, Bodleian Library, Oxford (Selborne was Chamberlain's under-secretary at the Colonial Office); Bryce to Roosevelt, 1 January 1896, Roosevelt Papers; *Literary Digest* 12 (February 1896): 503. See also James Bryce, "British Feeling on the Venezuelan Question," *North American Review* 162 (February 1896): 147–48; and Robert Seager II, *Alfred Thayer Mahan* (Annapolis, Md.: Naval Institute Press, 1977), p. 351.
14. On the British response to the Kruger telegram, see William L. Langer, *The Diplomacy of Imperialism, 1890–1902*, 2 vols. (New York and London: Alfred A. Knopf, 1935), 1:240–46.
15. Edward Dicey, "Common Sense and Venezuela," *Nineteenth Century* 39 (January 1896): 9, 15; W. T. Stead, "To All English-Speaking Folk," *Review of Reviews* 13 (February 1896): 99; Bryce, "British Feeling," pp. 152–53; "American Dislike for England. From the Spectator," *Living Age* 208 (February 1896): 443–44.
16. *Times* (London), 16 January 1896; Blanche E. C. Dugdale, *Arthur James Balfour, First Earl of Balfour, K.G., O.M., F.R.S., Etc.*, 2 vols. (London: Hutchinson & Co., 1936), 1:225–27. For the background of this speech in British cabinet discussions, see Joseph Chamberlain's Diary, JC 8/1/5 (11 January 1896), Chamberlain Papers.
17. Lodge to Balfour, 1 February 1896, Henry Cabot Lodge Papers, Massachusetts Historical Society, Boston. Lodge's earlier bellicosity can be gauged by the gross historical distortions in his article "England, Venezuela, and the Monroe Doctrine," *North American Review* 160 (June 1895): 651–58. In this article, he purported to show (p. 653) "the steady course of British aggression against a weak power with the view of getting possession of one of the great river systems of South America [the Orinoco]."

NOTES 197

18. Chamberlain to Lord Selborne, 20 December 1895, Selborne Papers.
19. *Times* (London), 27 January 1896. On the Armenian situation, see John A. S. Grenville, *Lord Salisbury and Foreign Policy* (London: Athlone Press of the University of London, 1964), pp. 74–78.
20. *Times* (London), 4 February 1896.
21. *Public Opinion* 20 (January 1896): 9. Pauncefote had detected a hopeful shift in American opinion as early as 24 December. Pauncefote to Salisbury, 24 December 1895, quoted in R. B. Mowat, *The Life of Lord Pauncefote, First Ambassador to the United States* (Boston and New York: Houghton Mifflin Co., 1929), pp. 186–87.
22. Many prominent academicians, especially experts on international law like John Bassett Moore of Columbia and Theodore Woolsey of Yale, were opposed to Cleveland's action from the beginning, as were a number of important newspaper and periodical editors, including Godkin, Pulitzer, and Whitelaw Reid. The business community was appalled when panicky British investors began dumping American securities and withdrawing huge quantities of gold from the country. With stock market and agricultural commodity prices plummeting, the nation's business press, boards of trade, and chambers of commerce commenced excoriating the president for inviting war with America's most important trading partner. Finally, the clergy and the religious press, pacifistic by nature, jumped on the president for threatening war just a week before the celebration of the birthday of the Prince of Peace. These developments are discussed in Perkins, *Monroe Doctrine*, pp. 194–99; Campbell, *Transformation of Foreign Relations*, pp. 211–12; and May, *Imperial Democracy*, pp. 57–58.
23. *Public Opinion* 20 (January 1896): 8, 6.
24. Mahan to Thursfield, 10 January 1896, and to Bouverie F. Clark, 17 January 1896, Robert Seager II and Doris D. Maguire, eds., *Letters and Papers of Alfred Thayer Mahan*, 3 vols. (Annapolis, Md.: Naval Institute Press, 1975), 2:442, 444 (hereafter cited as *Letters of Mahan*).
25. *Congressional Record*, 54th Cong., 1st Sess., pp. 859–60 (22 January 1896).
26. Andrew Carnegie, "The Venezuelan Question," *North American Review* 162 (February 1896): 131, 141–42.
27. Edward Atkinson, "The Cost of an Anglo-American War," *Forum* 21 (March 1896): 74–88; Sidney Sherwood, "An Alliance with England the Basis of a Rational Foreign Policy," ibid., pp. 89–99.
28. George Burton Adams, "The United States and the Anglo-Saxon Future," *Atlantic Monthly* 78 (July 1896): 37, 44.
29. Olney's forebears were among the first settlers of Massachusetts and Rhode Island. Eggert, *Olney*, pp. 3–4.
30. Olney to Chamberlain, 28 September 1896, Richard Olney Papers, Manuscript Division, Library of Congress. Chamberlain's reply, same date, reaffirmed British reluctance to make war on an Anglo-Saxon country. Ibid. Chamberlain's visit to the United States is discussed in J. L. Garvin, *The Life of Joseph Chamberlain*, 3 vols. (London: Macmillan, 1932–34), 3: 163–64.
31. For terms of the agreement, see *Papers Relating to the Foreign Relations of the United States, 1896* (Washington, 1897), pp. 254–55.
32. The best study of the abortive arbitration treaty is still Nelson M. Blake, "The Olney-Pauncefote Treaty of 1897," *American Historical Review* 50 (January 1945): 228–43.

33. Frederic Whyte, *The Life of W. T. Stead*, 2 vols. (New York and Boston: Houghton Mifflin Co., 1925), 2:85–86.
34. The text of the memorial is in Stead, "To All English-Speaking Folk," p. 100.
35. Campbell, *Transformation of Foreign Relations*, p. 213.
36. *Hansard's Parliamentary Debates. Fourth Series*, vol. 37, col. 110 (11 February 1896).
37. "Anglo-American Reunion. International Response to the Appeal for Arbitration," *Review of Reviews* 13 (March 1896): 260–66; "The Anglo-American Union," ibid. (April 1896), pp. 364–65; Sloan, "Anglo-American Relations," p. 496.
38. *Nation* 62 (February 1896): 169; "Anglo-American Reunion," p. 260; Campbell, *Transformation of Foreign Relations*, p. 213, and *From Revolution to Rapprochement* (New York: John Wiley & Sons, 1974), pp. 183–84; Walter Besant, "The Future of the Anglo-Saxon Race," *North American Review* 163 (August 1896): 129–43, especially 142–43.
39. The treaty and correspondence are in *Foreign Relations, 1896*, pp. 222–40. The story of the negotiations is told well in Eggert, *Olney*, pp. 229, 234–36, 250–52.
40. More than two thousand petitions and memorials on the treaty were printed in *Senate Documents*, 55th Cong., 1st Sess., no. 63 (Serial 3561). The senators complaining about public pressure included George F. Hoar of Massachusetts, John Sherman of Ohio, William J. Sewell of New Jersey, and William M. Stewart of Nevada. *Congressional Record*, 54th Cong., 2nd Sess., pp. 1045–47 (22 January 1897).
41. *Literary Digest* 14 (January 1897): 358; Blake, "Olney-Pauncefote Treaty," p. 234; May, *Imperial Democracy*, pp. 62–63.
42. *Public Opinion* 22 (January 1897): 69–70; *Senate Documents*, 55th Cong., 1st Sess., no. 63, passim.
43. Mahan to J. B. Sterling, 27 April 1897, *Letters of Mahan*, 2:504. See also same to same, 13 February 1896, and Mahan to Seth Low, 12 March 1897, ibid., pp. 445–46, 498.
44. *Literary Digest* 14 (January 1897): 358; *Senate Documents*, 55th Cong., 1st Sess., no. 63, p. 106; *Public Opinion* 22 (January 1897): 70.
45. On Olney's efforts, see May, *Imperial Democracy*, pp. 60–61; and Olney to H. L. Nelson, 11 February 1897, Olney Papers.
46. The Senate amendments and the final vote are in *Journal of the Executive Proceedings of the Senate*, vol. 31, pt. 1, pp. 102–5. For the committee hearings on the treaty and the minority report opposing ratification even in the amended form, see *Senate Documents*, 56th Cong., 2nd Sess., no. 231, pt. 8 (Serial 4054), pp. 388–93, 410–25.
47. Pulitzer's *New York World* analyzed the regional nature of the vote. *Literary Digest* 15 (May 1897): 64. See also Blake, "Olney-Pauncefote Treaty," p. 242; and Campbell, *Transformation of Foreign Relations*, p. 220. For analyses of the factors involved in the treaty's defeat, see Blake, "Olney-Pauncefote Treaty," pp. 238–43; and W. Stull Holt, *Treaties Defeated by the Senate* (Baltimore: Johns Hopkins Press, 1933), pp. 154–62.
48. *Literary Digest* 15 (May 1897): 65; Pauncefote to Salisbury, 7 May 1897, quoted in Mowat, *Pauncefote*, p. 169. For comment in the British and American press, see the *Literary Digest* 15 (May 1897): 64–65; and *Public Opinion* 22 (May 1897): 581–82.
49. Olney to White, 8 May 1897, Olney Papers.

50. White to Olney, 23 September 1897, ibid.
51. Richard Olney, "International Isolation of the United States," *Atlantic Monthly* 81 (May 1898): 588; May, *Imperial Democracy*, p. 61.

Chapter Six

1. The only study to deal specifically with the events of 1898, Bertha Ann Reuter's *Anglo-American Relations during the Spanish-American War* (New York: Macmillan, 1924), is inadequate and badly outdated. The most complete recent account is R. G. Neale, *Great Britain and United States Expansion* (East Lansing, Mich.: Michigan State University Press, 1966). For other recent accounts of British-American relations and the Spanish-American War, see Charles S. Campbell, *Anglo-American Understanding 1898–1903* (Baltimore: Johns Hopkins Press, 1957); A. E. Campbell, *Great Britain and the United States, 1895–1903* (London: Longmans, Green and Co., 1960); John A. S. Grenville, *Lord Salisbury and Foreign Policy* (London: Athlone Press of the University of London, 1964); and Bradford Perkins, *The Great Rapprochement* (New York: Atheneum, 1968).
2. "Spain and the United States," *Spectator* 80 (March 1898): 397.
3. See *Public Opinion* 24 (February 1898): 199.
4. *Daily Chronicle* quoted in Campbell, *Anglo-American Understanding*, p. 28. *Papers Relating to the Foreign Relations of the United States, 1898* (Washington, 1901), pp. 1057–62; Mahan to J. B. Sterling, 4 March 1898, and to William R. Henderson, 7 March 1898, Robert Seager II and Doris D. Maguire, eds., *Letters and Papers of Alfred Thayer Mahan*, 3 vols. (Annapolis, Md.: Naval Institute Press, 1975), 2:545, 546 (hereafter cited as *Letters of Mahan*).
5. *Hansard's Parliamentary Debates. Fourth Series*, vol. 54, col. 1526 (hereafter cited as *Hansard's*).
6. Joseph E. Wisan, *The Cuban Crisis as Reflected in the New York Press (1895–1898)* (New York: Columbia University Press, 1934), pp. 406–7.
7. *Times* (London), 28 and 29 March 1898.
8. Hay to McKinley, 4 April 1898, John Hay Papers, Manuscript Division, Library of Congress. Hay repeated the possibility of British naval assistance in a letter to Henry Cabot Lodge the next day. Ibid. There is no evidence that Hay's assertion was correct, however, and much evidence to the contrary. Anyway, Earl Grey was not in the government. See Campbell, *Anglo-American Understanding*, p. 30n.
9. Representative William C. Arnold, *Congressional Record*, 55th Cong., 2nd Sess., p. 3193.
10. Lodge to Anna Lodge, 8 and 13 October 1895, Henry Cabot Lodge Papers, Massachusetts Historical Society, Boston. See also same to same, 9 October 1895, ibid.; and Lodge to Edith Roosevelt, 23 October 1895, Henry Cabot Lodge, ed., *Selections from the Correspondence of Theodore Roosevelt and Henry Cabot Lodge, 1884–1918*, 2 vols. (New York and London: Charles Scribner's Sons, 1925), 1:194.
11. *Congressional Record*, 55th Cong., 2nd Sess., p. 3193 (24 March 1898). On the American image of the Spaniard, see Ernest R. May, *Imperial Democracy* (New York: Harcourt, Brace & World, 1961), p. 69; Helen E. Knuth, "The Climax of American Anglo-Saxonism, 1898–1905" (Ph.D. diss., Northwestern University,

1958), p. 88; and especially Gerald F. Linderman, *The Mirror of War* (Ann Arbor, Mich.: University of Michigan Press, 1974), pp. 114–27.

12. Campbell, *Britain and the United States*, pp. 147–49; Spring Rice to Roosevelt, 3 November 1897, Stephen Gwynn, ed., *The Letters and Friendships of Sir Cecil Spring Rice*, 2 vols. (Boston and New York: Houghton Mifflin Co., 1929), 1:234–35 (hereafter cited as *Letters of Spring Rice*). See also the revealing comments of the London *Telegraph*, *Literary Digest* 16 (April 1898): 512.

13. Harry Thurston Peck, *Twenty Years of the Republic, 1885–1905* (New York: Dodd, Mead & Co., 1919), p. 557. When Dewey sailed from Hong Kong upon news of the outbreak of war, he received a rousing sendoff from patients on a British hospital ship.

14. "The Causes of the War," *Spectator* 80 (April 1898): 564. *Daily Chronicle* in *Literary Digest* 16 (April 1898): 512. *Daily Mail* in *Public Opinion* 24 (May 1898): 548–49. *Le Temps* in *Literary Digest* 16 (May 1898): 652. See also ibid., p. 562; "England's Attitude and the War," *Spectator* 80 (April 1898): 566; and Andrew Carnegie to McKinley, from Cannes, 27 April 1898: "Without exception the British are our friends.... I know the British so well as to be able to assure you that no possible move upon the political stage would be so wildly welcomed as one which would draw close together the two branches of our English-speaking race." William McKinley Papers, Manuscript Division, Library of Congress.

15. Hay to Lodge, 25 May 1898, Lodge Papers.

16. Balfour in Henry White to Lodge, 3 June 1898, ibid. Grey speech at Colchester, reported in the *Times* (London), 23 April 1898. Asquith quoted in Israel Tarkow-Naamani, "The Abandonment of 'Splendid Isolation'" (Ph.D. diss., Indiana University, 1945), p. 159. The *Review of Reviews* 17 (June 1898): 603–8, features expressions of support for Anglo-American cooperation by many of Britain's leading political figures, as well as leaders of the intellectual, religious, scientific, and artistic communities.

17. "The Capture of Manilla [sic]," *Spectator* 80 (May 1898): 654; White to Lodge, 3 June 1898, Lodge Papers; Washington Gladden, *Recollections* (Boston and New York: Houghton Mifflin Co., 1909), pp. 357–58. See also Sidney Low, "The Change in English Sentiment toward the United States," *Forum* 26 (November 1898): 370.

18. Spring Rice to Hay, 7 May 1898, *Letters of Spring Rice*, 1:248; Charles Beresford, "The Anglo-American *Entente*," *Pall Mall Magazine* 18 (July 1899): 382. British writers pursuing this theme in American periodicals included Benjamin Kidd, "The United States and the Control of the Tropics," *Atlantic Monthly* 82 (December 1898): 722–24; and George Sydenham Clarke, "Imperial Responsibilities a National Gain," *North American Review* 168 (February 1899): 134–35.

19. Pauncefote to Salisbury, 26 May 1898, quoted in Campbell, *Anglo-American Understanding*, p. 49.

20. Lodge to Hay, 21 April 1898, Lodge Papers. Other Lodge letters in a similar vein are those to Henry White, 12 August 1898, ibid., and to Cecil Spring Rice, 12 August 1898, *Letters of Spring Rice*, 1:250.

21. Mahan to George Sydenham Clarke, 24 May 1898, *Letters of Mahan*, 2:556, and Mahan, *Lessons of the War with Spain and Other Articles* (Boston: Little, Brown, and Co., 1899), p. 232; Hay to Lodge, 25 May 1898, Lodge Papers. See also Hay

address at Mansion House, London, 21 April 1898. John Hay, *Addresses* (New York: Century Co., 1906), pp. 78–79.
22. Roosevelt to Spring Rice, 11 August 1898, *Letters of Spring Rice*, 1:293. On his way to Cuba with the Rough Riders, Roosevelt prepared for battle by reading Edmond Demolins's popular study, *Anglo-Saxon Superiority*. Thomas G. Dyer, "Theodore Roosevelt and the Idea of Race" (Ph.D. diss., University of Georgia, 1975), p. 16.
23. James H. Bridge, "The Collapse of Spain and the Rise of the Anglo-Saxons," *Overland Monthly*, 2nd ser. 32 (July 1898): 89. See also the *American Monthly Review of Reviews* 18 (July 1898): 84. In 1909, French E. Chadwick, a retired rear admiral who had served in the war as chief of staff to Admiral Sampson, published his classic study, *The Relations of the United States and Spain, Diplomacy*. Tracing Spanish-American relations from the American Revolution to the declaration of war in 1898, Chadwick argued that the chief cause of Spanish-American tensions and conflict since the birth of the United States had been "the absolute racial unlikeness" (p. 4) of the two peoples. The war of 1898, which he believed was due mainly to "a want of political aptitude" (p. 11) on the part of the Latin people of Spain, "was the final act in the struggle for supremacy between Anglo-Saxons and men of the Latin race in North America.... It was the end of a race struggle which had lasted full three hundred years." (p. 587)
24. *Public Opinion* 24 (May 1898): 550, 616; Louis Martin Sears, "French Opinion and the Spanish-American War," *Hispanic American Historical Review* 7 (February 1927): 25–44, especially 34; Richard H. Heindel, *The American Impact on Great Britain, 1898–1914* (Philadelphia: University of Pennsylvania Press, 1940), p. 77n.; May, *Imperial Democracy*, p. 185.
25. Henry Cabot Lodge, *The War with Spain* (New York and London: Harper & Brothers, 1899), p. 2; Lodge speech of 13 April 1898, *Congressional Record*, 55th Cong., 2nd Sess., p. 3783.
26. Heindel, *American Impact on Britain*, p. 37; *Review of Reviews* 17 (June 1898): 599–600, 612–13. Stead believed the Fourth of July "has every claim to be regarded as one of the sacred days in the calendar of the English-speaking race." Ibid., p. 599.
27. *Times* (London), 14 July 1898; *Public Opinion* 25 (July 1898): 75; *An American Response to Expressions of English Sympathy* (New York: Printed for the Anglo-American Committee, 1899).
28. *American Response to English Sympathy*.
29. Campbell, *Anglo-American Understanding*, pp. 25–26.
30. James to Henry Rutgers Marshall, 8 February 1899, Henry James, ed., *The Letters of William James*, 2 vols. (Boston: Little, Brown, and Co., 1920), 2:88. *Chronicle* in *Literary Digest* 16 (May 1898): 636. For reports of Irish and German protests, see *Literary Digest* 18 (May 1899): 510–12.
31. Finley Peter Dunne, *Mr. Dooley: Now and Forever* (Stanford, Calif.: Academic Reprints, 1954), pp. 43–44.
32. Neale, *Britain and Expansion*, pp. 15–32, 50–69.
33. See, for example, John Redpath Dougall, "An Anglo-Saxon Alliance," *Contemporary Review* 48 (November 1885): 693–706; George Sydenham Clarke, "A Naval Union with Great Britain," *North American Review* 158 (March 1894): 353–65; and Arthur Silva White, "An Anglo-American Alliance," ibid. (April 1894), pp. 484–93.

34. Campbell, *Anglo-American Understanding*, p. 48.
35. For Chamberlain's concern about the Russians, see the *Spectator* 80 (May 1898): 717. Hay's influence on Chamberlain was reported in Hay to Lodge, 25 May 1898, and confirmed in Henry White to Lodge, 3 June 1898, Lodge Papers.
36. *Times* (London), 14 May 1898.
37. See ibid., 16 May 1898, for a survey of European opinion.
38. *Spectator* quoted ibid. See *Public Opinion* 24 (May 1898): 615–16; and *Literary Digest* 16 (June 1898): 774–75.
39. *Hansard's*, vol. 58, col. 1438 (10 June 1898); Tarkow-Naamani, "Abandonment of Isolation," p. 162. See also the *Review of Reviews* 18 (June 1898): 601.
40. *Hansard's*, vol. 58, cols. 1437–38 (10 June 1898); Hay to Lodge, 25 May 1898, Lodge Papers.
41. *Literary Digest* 16 (May 1898): 635. For surveys of American press opinion, see ibid., pp. 635–37; *Public Opinion* 24 (May 1898): 643–45; and the *Times* (London), 16 May 1898. Whitelaw Reid's *New York Tribune*, 26 May 1898, offered a very strong endorsement of an alliance. One soap company tried to capitalize on alliance sentiment by running an advertisement in *Harper's Weekly* announcing: "Pears' Soap AND AN ANGLO-AMERICAN ALLIANCE WOULD IMPROVE THE COMPLEXION OF THE UNIVERSE."
42. Lyman Abbott, "The Basis of an Anglo-American Understanding," *North American Review* 166 (May 1898): 519–21; James K. Hosmer, "The American Evolution: Dependence, Independence, Interdependence," *Atlantic Monthly* 82 (July 1898): 32, 35–36; B. O. Flower, "The Proposed Federation of the Anglo-Saxon Nations," *Arena* 20 (August 1898): 223–38. The periodical articles discussing the possibility of an alliance are so numerous that it would be difficult to list them all. Particularly interesting examples are: "Anglo-Saxon Unity," *Overland Monthly*, 2nd ser. 31 (June 1898): 571–73; "American Greetings and Tributes to Britain," *American Monthly Review of Reviews* 18 (July 1898): 71–73; Frank E. Anderson, "America and the European Concert," *Arena* 20 (October 1898): 433–44; Carl Schurz, "The Anglo-American Friendship," *Atlantic Monthly* 82 (October 1898): 433–40. See also Charles A. Gardiner, *The Proposed Anglo-American Alliance* (New York and London: G. P. Putnam's Sons, 1898).
43. Albion W. Tourgée, "The Twentieth Century Peacemakers," *Contemporary Review* 75 (June 1899): 903. See James Bryce, "The Essential Unity of Britain and America," *Atlantic Monthly* 82 (July 1898): 22–29; A. V. Dicey, "England and America," ibid. (October 1898), pp. 441–45; Beresford, "Anglo-American Entente," pp. 379–83; Charles W. Dilke, "An Anglo-American Alliance," *Pall Mall Magazine* 16 (September 1898): 37–38; George Sydenham Clarke, "England and America," *Nineteenth Century* 44 (August 1898): 186–95; Low, "Change in English Sentiment," pp. 370–73. See also Walter Charles Copeland, "An Anglo-American Alliance," *Westminster Review* 150 (August 1898): 168–70; "The Anglo-American Alliance," *Spectator* 80 (May 1898): 718–19; "Alliances," ibid. 81 (December 1898): 897–98; "Great Fact of 1898," ibid., p. 972.
44. "England would no longer be 'isolated,' and the old mother and her big boy, without the necessity in all probability of striking a blow, would dominate the world as Gibraltar dominates the straits, by the mere fact of its commanding position and latent

power." Cushman K. Davis (chairman of the Senate Foreign Relations Committee) to William Severance, 5 May 1898, Davis Papers, Minnesota Historical Society, St. Paul.
45. Richard Temple, "An Anglo-American *versus* a European Combination," *North American Review* 167 (September 1898): 306–17.
46. Louis Tracy, *The Final War* (New York and London: G. P. Putnam's Sons, 1896); Benjamin Rush Davenport, *Anglo-Saxons, Onward!* (Cleveland: Hubbell Publishing Co., 1898). The Tracy book went through four new editions during the first half of 1898. The American reporter Julian Ralph said in February 1899 that "to-day no subject is more the vogue and no literature is more abundant" in England than that envisioning an Anglo-American war-making alliance. Ralph, "Anglo-Saxon Affinities," *Harper's New Monthly Magazine* 98 (February 1899): 385.
47. Oscar S. Straus, *Under Four Administrations, from Cleveland to Taft* (Boston and New York: Houghton Mifflin Co., 1922), p. 149. Straus was special American envoy at Constantinople, investigating the Near Eastern situation, when he met Rosebery.
48. *Edinburgh Review* quoted in Geoffrey Seed, "British Reactions to American Imperialism Reflected in Journals of Opinion, 1898–1900," *Political Science Quarterly* 73 (June 1958): 270. *Hansard's*, vol. 58, col. 1335 (10 June 1898); Joseph Chamberlain, "Recent Developments of Policy in the United States and Their Relation to an Anglo-American Alliance," *Scribner's Magazine* 24 (December 1898): 676. See also John Hay to Henry White, 24 September 1899, Hay Papers; and Howard K. Beale, *Theodore Roosevelt and the Rise of America to World Power* (Baltimore: Johns Hopkins Press, 1956), pp. 151–52.
49. Bryce to Roosevelt, 12 September 1898, Theodore Roosevelt Papers, Manuscript Division, Library of Congress.
50. Neale, *Britain and Expansion*, p. 132; Campbell, *Anglo-American Understanding*, p. 41. Lord Salisbury freely admitted that he expected America's new departure to "conduce to the interests of Great Britain," and Henry White reported that Britain's main desire was to see the United States committed to an active policy in the Far East. Salisbury speech at Lord Mayor's banquet, reported in the *Times* (London), 10 October 1898; White to Lodge, 3 June 1898, Lodge Papers.
51. Seed, "British Reactions," pp. 257–58, 261–62, and passim.
52. Clarke, "England and America," p. 194; Beresford, "Anglo-American *Entente*," p. 382. See also Edward Dicey, "The New American Imperialism," *Nineteenth Century* 44 (September 1898): 491, 499, 501.
53. *Times* (London), 4 February 1899; *McClure's Magazine* 12 (February 1899): 290–91.
54. Whitelaw Reid equated the two concepts in a *New York Tribune* editorial, 15 February 1899. Lady Randolph Churchill's *Anglo-Saxon Review* 1 (June 1899): 245, said that Kipling really had in mind the Anglo-Saxon populations of England, the colonies, and the United States. Seed, "British Reactions," p. 261, states that "white man's burden" was often a euphemism for "Anglo-Saxon's burden."
55. Chamberlain speech at Birmingham, reported in the *Times* (London), 30 January 1899. See Chamberlain, "Recent Developments of Policy," p. 682; Tourgée, "Twentieth Century Peacemakers," p. 897; "The Fate of the Philippines," *Spectator* 80 (May 1898): 645–46. See also Geoffrey Seed, "British Views of American Policy in the Philippines Reflected in Journals of Opinion, 1898–1907," *Journal of*

American Studies 2 (1968): 49–50. For a wonderful American parody of such attitudes, see Mortimer O. Wilcox, "Forerunners of Empire," *McClure's Magazine* 12 (December 1898): 189–92.
56. Spring Rice to Lodge, 8 July 1898, and to Roosevelt, 15 November 1898, *Letters of Spring Rice*, 1:249, 269–70.
57. Mahan to [?], 29 May 1898, *Letters of Mahan*, 2:557–58; Claude G. Bowers, *Beveridge and the Progressive Era* (Boston: Houghton Mifflin Co., 1932), p. 74. See also Beveridge's Senate speech of 9 January 1900, *Congressional Record*, 56th Cong., 1st Sess., p. 711.
58. Roosevelt to Arthur Lee, 25 November 1898, Elting E. Morison, ed., *The Letters of Theodore Roosevelt*, 8 vols. (Cambridge, Mass.: Harvard University Press, 1951–54), 2:890 (hereafter cited as *Letters of Roosevelt*); Roosevelt to Spring Rice, 14 February 1899, *Letters of Spring Rice*, 1: 292–93. See also Roosevelt to Arthur Lee, 18 March 1901, *Letters of Roosevelt*, 3:20. Lee was British military observer and Roosevelt's tent-mate during the Cuban campaign.

Chapter Seven

1. The Foreign Office learned in October 1899 that Count Mikhail Muraviev, the Russian foreign minister, was sounding out the French and Germans about a coalition. On that occasion, Muraviev failed to win over French Foreign Minister Théophile Delcassé. In March of 1900, the Kaiser told the Prince of Wales that Muraviev had again approached France and Germany. France was willing this time if Germany would go along, but the Kaiser declined. On European diplomacy and the Boer War, see William L. Langer, *The Diplomacy of Imperialism, 1890–1902*, 2 vols. (New York and London: Alfred A. Knopf, 1935), vol. 2, chap. 20.
2. Lee to Theodore Roosevelt, 29 January 1900, Theodore Roosevelt Papers, Manuscript Division, Library of Congress.
3. The best scholarly account is John H. Ferguson, *American Diplomacy and the Boer War* (Philadelphia: University of Pennsylvania Press, 1939). Elizabeth Zeil, "The United States and the Boer War" (M.A. thesis, Columbia University, 1950), adds very little. Placing the conflict in a broader context is Thomas J. Noer, *Briton, Boer, and Yankee* (Kent, O.: Kent State University Press, 1978). On Anglo-American relations and the war, see also Charles S. Campbell, *Anglo-American Understanding, 1898–1903* (Baltimore: Johns Hopkins Press, 1957); and Bradford Perkins, *The Great Rapprochement* (New York: Atheneum, 1968), pp. 89–98.
4. Pauncefote to Salisbury, 19 January 1900, quoted in Campbell, *Anglo-American Understanding*, pp. 171–72. Joseph Chamberlain had created a stir in the United States when, in a speech at Leicester on 30 November 1899, he used the word "alliance" to describe the relationship between "the two great branches of the Anglo-Saxon race," Great Britain and the United States. The speech was printed in the *Times* (London), 1 December 1899. For an explanation of Chamberlain's unfortunate choice of words, see "'Entangling Alliances,'" *Spectator* 83 (December 1899): 865–66.
5. Hay to White, 18 March 1900, Henry White Papers, Manuscript Division, Library of

Congress. On this episode, see Ferguson, *American Diplomacy and the Boer War*, pp. 138–42; and Perkins, *Great Rapprochement*, p. 96.

6. America's willingness to aid British prisoners of war in no way compromised the nation's neutrality, especially since later in the war a similar service was extended to Boer prisoners in British hands. As to loans and the sale of military supplies, the United States throughout the war stood by the well-established principle that its citizens were free to purchase the securities of both sides to the conflict, and to sell war materials to all belligerents. However, because the Boers had little money or credit and no navy, only Great Britain benefited to any significant degree from the American position. And of course, the United States was under no legal obligation to press the British hard on mediation or on issues affecting neutral rights, or to treat Boer representatives in a manner more to their liking. For an extended discussion of American neutrality, see Ferguson, *American Diplomacy and the Boer War*, pp. 48–49, 50–65, 79, 91, 94, 137–39.

7. Ibid., p. ix. This conclusion is supported by Noer, *Briton, Boer, and Yankee*, p. 68. Weeks before the war began, Ohio Democrats charged that the McKinley administration had concluded a secret alliance with Great Britain. Hay denied the charge in a letter to the chairman of the Ohio Republican party. Hay to Charles Dick, 11 September 1899, John Hay Papers, Manuscript Division, Library of Congress. On 19 February 1900, the House of Representatives asked Hay to confirm or deny the existence of a secret pact. Hay, in offering his denial, pointed out that a secret alliance was impossible under the American Constitution. See *House Documents*, 56th Cong., 1st Sess., no. 458 (Serial 3988), pp. 1–2. Rumors continued to circulate, however, and Hay had to deny the charge again in a letter to Senator James McMillan of Michigan, 3 July 1900. Hay Papers. Still, the Democratic platform of 1900 denounced "the ill-concealed Republican alliance with England."

8. Ferguson, *American Diplomacy and the Boer War*, pp. 122–23, 176, and passim; Zeil, "United States and the Boer War," passim; Noer, *Briton, Boer, and Yankee*, pp. 68, 70–71, 85–87; Cambell, *Anglo-American Understanding*, pp. 179–81; Perkins, *Great Rapprochement*, p. 93.

9. Spring Rice to Roosevelt, 17 October 1899, Roosevelt Papers.

10. Roosevelt to White, 30 March 1896, Elting E. Morison, ed., *The Letters of Theodore Roosevelt*, 8 vols. (Cambridge, Mass.: Harvard University Press, 1951–54), 1:523 (hereafter cited as *Letters of Roosevelt*).

11. Roosevelt to Spring Rice, 2 December 1899, Stephen Gwynn, ed., *The Letters and Friendships of Sir Cecil Spring Rice*, 2 vols. (Boston and New York: Houghton Mifflin Co., 1929), 1:305 (hereafter cited as *Letters of Spring Rice*). See also Howard K. Beale, *Theodore Roosevelt and the Rise of America to World Power* (Baltimore: Johns Hopkins Press, 1956), pp. 99–100; and Roosevelt to F. C. Selous, 7 February 1900: "I am ... a believer in the fact that it is for the good of the world that the English-speaking race in all its branches should hold as much of the world's surface as possible." *Letters of Roosevelt*, 2:1176–77.

12. This fact is itself the best evidence of McKinley's own pro-British sentiments. H. Wayne Morgan, *William McKinley and His America* (Syracuse, N.Y.: Syracuse University Press, 1963), pp. 460–61, points out one or two instances in which McKinley betrayed his partisanship. However, because of McKinley's habit of con-

cealing his inner thoughts, there is no indication in his personal papers of what may have motivated him to favor the British.
13. John Hays Hammond, *Autobiography*, 2 vols. (New York: Farrar and Rinehart, 1935), 2:446–47. Hammond was an American mining engineer who had served as one of Rhodes's undercover agents in Johannesburg and been jailed in the wake of the Jameson raid in 1896. He introduced Hay to Rhodes. See also Perkins, *Great Rapprochement*, p. 90; and Kenton J. Clymer, *John Hay* (Ann Arbor, Mich.: University of Michigan Press, 1975), p. 257. On Hay's extreme pro-British partisanship, see Ferguson, *American Diplomacy and the Boer War*, pp. 123, 175; and Tyler Dennett, *John Hay* (New York: Dodd, Mead & Co., 1933), p. 246.
14. Hay to White, 24 September 1899, William R. Thayer, *The Life and Letters of John Hay*, 2 vols. (Boston and New York: Houghton Mifflin Co., 1915), 2:221; same to same, 18 March 1900, White Papers. Hay's Anglo-Saxonist view of the war is described in Clymer, *Hay*, pp. 157–66.
15. Hollis speech at Boston reported in the *Times* (London), 3 March 1899; Rhodes letter in *New York Tribune*, 11 February 1900; George F. Becker, "Rights and Wrongs in South Africa," *Forum* 29 (March 1900): 36.
16. Address before the New York Chamber of Commerce, 21 November 1899, draft in Whitelaw Reid Papers, Manuscript Division, Library of Congress. The *Tribune*'s editorial policy, of course, reflected Reid's view. See, for example, the editorials of 29 November and 21 December 1899.
17. Mahan to Lodge, 8 December 1900, Henry Cabot Lodge Papers, Massachusetts Historical Society, Boston; Mahan to Reid, 20 October 1899, Royal Cortissoz, *The Life of Whitelaw Reid*, 2 vols. (London: Thornton Butterworth, 1921), 2:269–70. See also Mahan to James R. Thursfield, 28 October and 15 December 1899, and to James Ford Rhodes, 30 January 1900, Robert Seager II and Doris D. Maguire, eds., *Letters and Papers of Alfred Thayer Mahan*, 3 vols. (Annapolis, Md.: Naval Institute Press, 1975), 2:664–65, 674, 679–80 (hereafter cited as *Letters of Mahan*); Mahan, "The Merits of the Transvaal Dispute," *North American Review* 170 (March 1900): 325; and Robert Seager II, *Alfred Thayer Mahan* (Annapolis, Md.: Naval Institute Press, 1977), pp. 425–27.
18. Roosevelt to John St. Loe Strachey, 27 January 1900, *Letters of Roosevelt*, 2:1144.
19. *New York Times*, 8 September 1899. See also editorial, ibid., 5 September 1899; and Noer, *Briton, Boer, and Yankee*, pp. 64, 68. Zeil, "United States and the Boer War," pp. 18–19, 23, 25, quotes extensively from the New York press. Alfred Swan to Godkin, 21 May 1900, *Nation* 70 (May 1900): 396.
20. Wneeler quoted in H. H. Bowen, "American Public Opinion of the War," *Nineteenth Century* 47 (May 1900): 745. Johannes Hrolf Wisby, "The South African War of Races," *Arena* 23 (May 1900): 476, 479. See also Edward J. Hodgson, "An American View of the Boer War," *Nineteenth Century* 48 (August 1900): 279–82; Becker, "Rights and Wrongs in South Africa," p. 36; Henry Cust, "The Dutch in South Africa," *North American Review* 170 (February 1900): 198–211, passim; and George Lacy, "Some Boer Characteristics," ibid. (January 1900), pp. 43–53, passim. Andrew Carnegie published a rebuttal to the Boer-inferiority arguments, saying the Boers were as civilized as the British, and that the latter had committed a serious error in fomenting a "racial war" in South Africa. Carnegie, "The South African Question," ibid. 169 (December 1899): 798–804.
21. Hay to Choate, 3 January 1900, and to Henry Adams, 15 June 1900, Hay Papers.

22. Lodge to Theodore Roosevelt, 16 December 1899 and 2 February 1900, Henry Cabot Lodge, ed., *Selections from the Correspondence of Theodore Roosevelt and Henry Cabot Lodge, 1884–1918*, 2 vols. (New York and London: Charles Scribner's Sons, 1925), 1:429, 446. See also Henry White to Lodge, 9 February 1900, Lodge Papers. Noer, *Briton, Boer, and Yankee*, p. 79, briefly discusses Lodge's effective defense in the Senate of administration policy.
23. Mahan to Thursfield, 15 December 1899, *Letters of Mahan*, 2:674. See also Mahan's letter to the editor, *New York Times*, 22 January 1900.
24. Roosevelt to John R. Proctor, 23 December 1899, Roosevelt Papers. Roosevelt had earlier expressed his support for American intervention if Europe attacked Great Britain in a letter to Arthur Lee, 19 December 1899, quoted in David H. Burton, *Theodore Roosevelt and His English Correspondents* (Philadelphia: American Philosophical Society, 1973), p. 28. His concern about British decadence was expressed in a letter to Anna Roosevelt Cowles, 17 December 1899, Anna Roosevelt Cowles, ed., *Letters from Theodore Roosevelt to Anna Roosevelt Cowles, 1870–1918* (New York and London: Charles Scribner's Sons, 1924), p. 226 (hereafter cited as *Roosevelt-Cowles Letters*). On the latter point, see also Roosevelt to Spring Rice, 12 March 1900, *Letters of Spring Rice*, 1:317. His increased admiration for the Boers is evident in Roosevelt to Walter G. Cumming, 17 January 1900, *Letters of Roosevelt*, 2:1143. Roosevelt was also concerned that the collapse of the British Empire would lead to European adventurism in the New World and a military challenge to the Monroe Doctrine. See Roosevelt to Elihu Root, 29 January 1900, Elihu Root Papers, Manuscript Division, Library of Congress.
25. *Mail and Express*, 18 December 1899, quoted in Zeil, "United States and the Boer War," pp. 18–19. *Harper's* in *Literary Digest* 20 (January 1900): 2. W. J. Stillman to Godkin, 9 February 1900, *Nation* 70 (February 1900): 144. Editorial, *New York Tribune*, 21 December 1899.
26. Twain to Howells, 25 January 1900, Albert B. Paine, ed., *Mark Twain's Letters*, 2 vols. (New York and London: Harper & Brothers, 1917), 2:693.
27. Thomas C. Hutten, "The Doom of the Boer Oligarchies. A Netherlander's View of the South African Problem," *North American Review* 170 (March 1900): 331; *Public Opinion* 28 (March 1900): 299.
28. Wisby, "South African War of Races," p. 479; Edwin Maxey, "The Race Supremacy Question in South Africa," in Maxey, *Some Questions of Larger Politics* (New York: Abbey Press, 1901), pp. 23–24; Washburn Hopkins, "England and the Higher Morality," *Forum* 28 (January 1900): 569–70. See also *Literary Digest* 20 (January 1900): 42; Bowen, "American Opinion of the War," p. 744; and the editorials in the *New York Times*, 5 and 8 September 1899. Albert Shaw, the Anglo-Saxonist editor of the *American Review of Reviews*, had set forth a somewhat similar view of the Anglo-Boer controversy more than three years before the war began. See Shaw, "Empire-Building in South Africa," *Cosmopolitan* 20 (March 1896): 480.
29. Mahan to Seth Low, 28 March 1900, *Letters of Mahan*, 2:685. See also Mahan to Leopold J. Maxse (editor of the *National Review*), 9 December 1901, ibid., p. 736. In late 1900, Mahan published an account of the war which was based almost entirely on British sources and was very biased. Mahan, *The Story of the War in South Africa, 1899–1900* (London: Sampson Low, Marston and Co., 1900); Seager, *Mahan*, p. 427.
30. Alfred Thayer Mahan, "The Transvaal and the Philippines," *Independent* 52 (Feb-

ruary 1900): 289–91. See also Mahan to James R. Thursfield, 15 December 1899, *Letters of Mahan*, 2:674; and Mahan, "The Influence of the South African War upon the Prestige of the British Empire," *National Review* 38 (December 1900): 511. Senator Hoar's statement was contained in a letter read to a mass meeting at Boston on 17 January in support of the Boers. W. D. Puleston, *Mahan* (New Haven, Conn.: Yale University Press, 1939), p. 220.

31. Marquis of Lorne, "Realities of the South African War," *North American Review* 170 (March 1900): 304–8 (quotations from pp. 305, 304); Mary Endicott Chamberlain, "An Obligation of Empire," ibid. (April 1900), p. 503; Sydney Brooks, "America and the War," ibid. (March 1900), p. 346; Charles Beresford, "The Future of the Anglo-Saxon Race," ibid. 171 (December 1900): 804. For racial appeals from British and Canadian newspapers, see the *Literary Digest* 20 (February 1900): 222.
32. Memorandum of conversation between Count Quadt, the German chargé, and Baron Gevers, 9 November 1900, quoted in Dennett, *Hay*, p. 386.
33. Hay to White, 18 March 1900, White Papers.
34. For a complete account of the Boer mission, see Ferguson, *American Diplomacy and the Boer War*, pp. 143–56. Henry White had warned Hay back in December that the Boers were planning to send a mission to the United States to bring pressure on the administration. White to Hay, 28 December 1899, White Papers. On the Boer tactic, see Montagu White (chief Boer agent in the United States) to F. C. Selous, 6 March 1900, Roosevelt Papers.
35. Roosevelt to Walter G. Cumming, 27 January 1900, *Letters of Roosevelt*, 2:1143; Roosevelt to Spring Rice, 16 March 1901, *Letters of Spring Rice*, 1:344.
36. Roosevelt to John St. Loe Strachey, 27 January 1900, and to Cecil Spring Rice, same date, *Letters of Roosevelt*, 2:1144, 1146. In the Strachey letter, Roosevelt pointed out that many men in the Boer ranks had the same names as some of his own ancestors. He believed he was probably a distant relative of these men.
37. Roosevelt to Anna Roosevelt Cowles, 2 and 5 February 1900, *Roosevelt-Cowles Letters*, pp. 234, 235; David H. Burton, *Theodore Roosevelt: Confident Imperialist* (Philadelphia: University of Pennsylvania Press, 1968), p. 162.
38. Roosevelt to F. C. Selous, 7 February 1900, *Letters of Roosevelt*, 2:1176; Roosevelt to Spring Rice, 16 March 1901, *Letters of Spring Rice*, 1:345. Roosevelt also drew the hopeful comparison between New York's past and South Africa's future in letters to Spring Rice, 2 December 1899, and to Walter G. Cumming and John St. Loe Strachey, both dated 27 January 1900. Ibid., p. 305; *Letters of Roosevelt*, 2:1143, 1144. See also Roosevelt to A. J. Sage, 9 March 1900, and to F. C. Selous, 19 March 1900, ibid., pp. 1214–15, 1234–35.
39. Roosevelt to George F. Becker, 6 February 1900, Roosevelt Papers.
40. Donald B. Johnson and Kirk H. Porter, comps., *National Party Platforms, 1840–1972*, 5th ed. (Urbana, Ill.: University of Illinois Press, 1973), p. 115. Ferguson, *American Diplomacy and the Boer War*, pp. 192–98, offers a good treatment of the war as a campaign issue.
41. Hay to Adams, 15 June 1900, Hay Papers.
42. *New York Tribune*, 20 June 1900.
43. Johnson and Porter, comps., *Party Platforms*, p. 124.

44. Ferguson, *American Diplomacy and the Boer War*, pp. 197–98; Morgan, *McKinley*, pp. 501–2, 503, 507.
45. Pauncefote to Lord Lansdowne, 22 November 1901, quoted in Campbell, *Anglo-American Understanding*, p. 238. Campbell's is the best treatment of the treaty negotiations. See also A. E. Campbell, *Great Britain and the United States, 1895–1903* (London: Longmans, Green and Co., 1960); Lionel M. Gelber, *The Rise of Anglo-American Friendship* (London: Oxford University Press, 1938), pp. 102–3; H. C. Allen, *Great Britain and the United States* (London: Odhams Press, 1954), p. 603; and John A. S. Grenville, *Lord Salisbury and Foreign Policy* (London: Athlone Press of the University of London, 1964), pp. 388–89.
46. Hay to Stanford Newel (United States minister at the Hague), 3 December 1900, and to Henry Cabot Lodge, 19 February 1902, Hay Papers.
47. Roosevelt to John St. Loe Strachey, 18 July 1902, quoted in Burton, *Roosevelt and His English Correspondents*, p. 39.
48. Hay to R. Chisholm, 10 July 1903, Hay Papers. On Adelbert Hay's consulship, which was widely interpreted at the time as another sign of the pro-British attitude of the United States, see Ferguson, *American Diplomacy and the Boer War*, pp. 113–20.
49. Mahan to Leopold J. Maxse, 9 December 1901, *Letters of Mahan*, 2:736.
50. Roosevelt to Henry White, 23 November 1900, *Letters of Roosevelt*, 2:1437. For an entertaining account of the divisions in American opinion, see Byron Farwell, "Taking Sides in the Boer War," *American Heritage* 27 (April 1976): 21–25, 92–97.
51. Brooks, "America and the War," p. 347.

Chapter Eight

1. On this famous incident, see Tyler Dennett, *Americans in Eastern Asia* (New York: Macmillan, 1922), pp. 338–40, 343.
2. On Russian expansionist policy in the Far East in these years, see David J. Dallin, *The Rise of Russia in Asia* (New Haven, Conn.: Yale University Press, 1949), pp. 34–77; and Edward H. Zabriskie, *American-Russian Rivalry in the Far East* (Philadelphia: University of Pennsylvania Press, 1946), pp. 65–100, passim.
3. Charles S. Campbell, *Anglo-American Understanding, 1898–1903* (Baltimore: Johns Hopkins Press, 1957), p. 12.
4. Lodge to Theodore Roosevelt, 21 May 1903, Theodore Roosevelt Papers, Manuscript Division, Library of Congress; Campbell, *Anglo-American Understanding*, p. 13. The literature on American concern with the China market is immense. A good starting point is the bibliographical essay in Charles S. Campbell, *The Transformation of American Foreign Relations, 1865–1900* (New York: Harper & Row, 1976), p. 374.
5. *New York Times*, 4 January 1898; *Times* (London), 16 March 1898; Charles Beresford, *The Break-up of China* . . . (New York and London: Harper & Brothers, 1899), p. ix. See also Campbell, *Transformation of Foreign Relations*, p. 327.
6. David Mills, "Which Shall Dominate—Saxon or Slav?" *North American Review* 166 (June 1898): 739. See also A. Maurice Low, "Russia, England, and the United States," *Forum* 28 (October 1899): 180–81.

7. A Whitney Griswold, *The Far Eastern Policy of the United States* (New York: Harcourt, Brace and Co., 1938), pp. 45–46, 49–50. One prominent American who was disappointed at the failure of the United States to cooperate with Great Britain was Senator Cushman K. Davis, the powerful chairman of the Foreign Relations Committee. Davis believed that Americans should "take our place in the scientific division of the races" and "enter into treaty relations" with the British "by which the dominions and interests of each in the Pacific Ocean north of the equator should be guaranteed by the other." Davis to William Severance, 5 May 1898, Cushman K. Davis Papers, Minnesota Historical Society, St. Paul.
8. Chamberlain's memo suggested approaches to both the United States and Germany to see if they would join Great Britain in defense of the open door against Russia. If the Russians refused their terms, they were to be driven out of Port Arthur by force. The memo is reprinted in full in Blanche E. C. Dugdale, *Arthur James Balfour, First Earl of Balfour, K.G., O.M., F.R.S., Etc.*, 2 vols. (London: Hutchinson & Co., 1936), 1:252-53.
9. Memorandum by Count von Bülow, the German foreign minister, of a conversation with Chamberlain, 24 November 1899, E. T. S. Dugdale, ed., *German Diplomatic Documents, 1871–1914*, 4 vols. (New York and London: Harper & Brothers, 1928–31), 3:111. In his use of the word "Tartars," Chamberlain was probably thinking of the Mongolians.
10. Speech at Wakefield, reported in the *Times* (London), 9 December 1898. See also Chamberlain's speech at Manchester, ibid., 16 November 1898.
11. Ibid., 14 May 1898. On this speech, see chap. 6 above.
12. *Times* (London), 1 December 1899. See also J. L. Garvin, *The Life of Joseph Chamberlain*, 3 vols. (London: Macmillan, 1932–34), 3:504–6. On the Anglo-German negotiations of 1898–99, see William L. Langer, *The Diplomacy of Imperialism, 1890–1902*, 2 vols. (New York and London: Alfred A. Knopf, 1935), vol. 2, chaps. 15 and 20, passim.
13. *Literary Digest* 19 (December 1899): 701; Grey to R. B. Haldane, 4 December 1899, quoted in George M. Trevelyan, *Grey of Fallodon* (Boston: Houghton Mifflin Co., 1937), p. 88; Garvin, *Chamberlain*, 3:508–10; Samuel H. Jeyes, *Mr. Chamberlain* (London: Sands & Co., 1903), pp. 420–22. Secretary of State John Hay, a good friend of Chamberlain, asked Henry White to tell the colonial secretary that he thought the speech altogether "right and admirable"; however, he regretted the use of the word "alliance." Hay to White, 27 December 1899, John Hay Papers, Manuscript Division, Library of Congress.
14. On Colquhoun's popularity in the United States, see Helen E. Knuth, "The Climax of American Anglo-Saxonism, 1898–1905" (Ph.D. diss., Northwestern University, 1958), p. 244.
15. Colquhoun, *China in Transformation* (New York and London: Harper & Brothers, 1898), p. ix.
16. Ibid., pp. 351, 357–58, 379, 381–82. See also Colquhoun, "Eastward Expansion of the United States," *Harper's New Monthly Magazine* 97 (November 1898): 932–38, and *Greater America* (New York and London: Harper & Brothers, 1904), p. 375.
17. Colquhoun, *China in Transformation*, p. 381.
18. Colquhoun, "Eastward Expansion," pp. 932–38. The quotation is on p. 938. See

also Colquhoun, *Greater America*, p. 376, and *The Mastery of the Pacific* (New York and London: Macmillan, 1902), p. 430.

19. Rounsevelle Wildman to Hay, 6 January 1899, quoted in Tyler Dennett, *John Hay* (New York: Dodd, Mead & Co., 1933), p. 287. On Beresford's trip and its relationship to British governmental policy, see R. G. Neale, *Great Britain and United States Expansion* (East Lansing, Mich.: Michigan State University Press, 1966), pp. 173–97.
20. Griswold, *Far Eastern Policy*, pp. 48–49.
21. Beresford, *Break-up of China*, pp. iv, 446; "China and the Powers," *North American Review* 168 (May 1899): 538; and "An Anglo-American Alliance," *Independent* 51 (February 1899): 527. See also Beresford's later articles, "The Anglo-American Entente," *Pall Mall Magazine* 18 (July 1899): 379–83, and "The Future of the Anglo-Saxon Race," *North American Review* 171 (December 1900): 802–10. On Beresford's influence in the United States, see Knuth, "Climax of Anglo-Saxonism," p. 244; and Betty Weaver Talbert, "The Evolution of John Hay's China Policy" (Ph.D. diss., University of North Carolina at Chapel Hill, 1974), p. 166.
22. Rockhill to Hay, 28 August 1899, A. L. P. Dennis, *Adventures in American Diplomacy, 1896–1906* (New York: E. P. Dutton & Co., 1928), p. 186. The British, fearing that the open door was doomed, had been carving out their own sphere of influence in China for some time.
23. Campbell, *Anglo-American Understanding*, pp. 167–69, and *Transformation of Foreign Relations*, p. 329. For a slightly more positive view, see Talbert, "Hay's China Policy," p. 239.
24. Campbell, "Anglo-American Relations, 1897–1901," in *Threshold to American Internationalism*, ed. Paolo E. Coletta (New York: Exposition Press, 1970), pp. 236–37.
25. *Public Opinion* 25 (August 1898): 205; Franklin H. Giddings, *Democracy and Empire, with Studies of Their Psychological, Economic, and Moral Foundations* (New York and London: Macmillan, 1900), pp. 288–89; Frederick Wells Williams, "The Real Menace of Russian Aggression," *Annals of the American Academy of Political and Social Science* (Supplement) 13 (May 1899): 194.
26. Alexander Ford, "Is Russia to Control All of Asia?" *Cosmopolitan* 29 (July 1900): 264; Paul S. Reinsch, *World Politics at the End of the Nineteenth Century, as Influenced by the Oriental Situation* (London and New York: Macmillan, 1900), p. 85. It must be noted, however, that a number of Americans, including former First Assistant Secretary of State Josiah Quincy and Senator Albert Beveridge, held that Russia had a civilizing mission in North China and was doing a great service to the world by bringing law and order to that region. See Quincy, "China and Russia," *North American Review* 171 (October 1900): 528–42; and Beveridge, *The Russian Advance* (New York and London: Harper & Brothers, 1903), especially pp. 9, 15, 17, 19, 21–22, 31.
27. Arthur F. Beringause, *Brooks Adams* (New York: Alfred A. Knopf, 1955), pp. 49, 129, 132, 157–58, 160–61, 164–65, 198, 243–44, 249; Roosevelt to Spring Rice, 29 May 1897, Elting E. Morison, ed., *The Letters of Theodore Roosevelt*, 8 vols. (Cambridge, Mass.: Harvard University Press, 1951–54), 1:620 (hereafter cited as *Letters of Roosevelt*).

28. Brooks Adams, "Economic Conditions for Future Defense," *Atlantic Monthly* 92 (November 1903): 632.
29. *Forum* 25 (August 1898): 645–46, 649–51 (quotation from p. 650).
30. Ibid., pp. 651, 645. See also Adams, "The New Struggle for Life among Nations," *McClure's Magazine* 12 (April 1899): 558–64; Henry Adams to Brooks Adams, 21 October 1899, Harold D. Cater, ed., *Henry Adams and His Friends* (Boston: Houghton Mifflin Co., 1947), p. 484; and Brooks Adams to Lodge, 14 October 1900, Henry Cabot Lodge Papers, Massachusetts Historical Society, Boston.
31. Adams, "New Struggle for Life," p. 564.
32. Adams, "Russia's Interest in China," *Atlantic Monthly* 86 (September 1900): 310, 316–17 (quotation from p. 317). See also Adams, "John Hay," *McClure's Magazine* 19 (June 1902): 180–82, for Adams's somewhat sanguine assessment of the efficacy of Hay's Open Door notes.
33. Adams, "Economic Conditions," p. 648.
34. Beringause, *Adams*, p. 191; Dennett, *Hay*, p. 156; Ernest Samuels, *Henry Adams: The Major Phasse* (Cambridge, Mass.: Harvard University Press, 1964), pp. 193–94. Said Henry Adams of the discussion during his daily walks with Hay: "We diagnosed the whole menagerie. We killed and buried, in advance, half the world and the neighboring solar systems." Adams to Hay, 26 June 1900, Worthington C. Ford, ed., *Letters of Henry Adams (1892–1918)*, 2 vols. (Boston and New York: Houghton Mifflin Co., 1938), 2:289. The two men had been friends since their first meeting in February 1861, soon after Hay was named private secretary to Abraham Lincoln, and before Adams sailed for England as secretary to his diplomat father, Charles Francis Adams.
35. Roosevelt to Adams, 18 July 1903, Roosevelt Papers. See William A. Williams, "Brooks Adams and American Expansion," *New England Quarterly* 25 (June 1952): 217–32; Beringause, *Adams*, p. 244; and Howard K. Beale, *Theodore Roosevelt and the Rise of America to World Power* (Baltimore: Johns Hopkins Press, 1956), pp. 255–57, 259.
36. Mahan to Samuel A. Ashe, 23 September 1899, Robert Seager II and Doris D. Maguire, eds., *Letters and Papers of Alfred Thayer Mahan*, 3 vols. (Annapolis, Md.: Naval Institute Press, 1975), 2:658 (hereafter cited as *Letters of Mahan*). See also Mahan to Whitelaw Reid, 20 October 1899, Royal Cortissoz, *The Life of Whitelaw Reid*, 2 vols. (London: Thornton Butterworth, 1921), 2:269–70.
37. W. D. Puleston, *Mahan* (New Haven, Conn.: Yale University Press, 1939), p. 223. See also Robert Seager II, *Alfred Thayer Mahan* (Annapolis, Md.: Naval Institute Press, 1977), pp. 462–67.
38. Mahan, *The Problem of Asia and Its Effect upon International Policies* (Boston: Little, Brown, and Co., 1900), pp. 18, 46.
39. Ibid., pp. 104, 108–9, 115–16, 133 (quotations from pp. 133, 116).
40. Ibid., pp. 176–77.
41. Mahan to McKinley, 2 September 1900, *Letters of Mahan*, 2:693. See also William E. Livezey, *Mahan on Sea Power* (Norman, Okla.: University of Oklahoma Press, 1947), p. 197. It should be pointed out that in 1902, despairing of any significant Anglo-American cooperation in the Far East, Mahan concluded that the best policy for Great Britain to pursue was acquiescence in Russia's deep involvement in China.

This would relieve Russian pressure on the Persian Gulf, which Mahan considered the area of greatest strategic importance to Britain, because of its position at the center of the line of communication to India. See Mahan to Leopold J. Maxse, 21 February, 7 March, and 27 May 1902, all in *Letters of Mahan*, 3:12, 13, 27. See also Mahan's article "The Persian Gulf and International Relations," *National Review* 40 (September 1902): 27–45.

42. Lodge eventually lost the contest for the committee chairmanship (which had been opened up by the death of Cushman K. Davis in November of 1900) to Shelby M. Cullom of Illinois, who had more Senate seniority. But because Cullom thereafter devoted most of his time to other concerns, Lodge tended to be the dominant figure on the Foreign Relations Committee. See John A. Garraty, *Henry Cabot Lodge* (New York: Alfred A. Knopf, 1965), pp. 214–15.

43. Livezey, *Mahan on Sea Power*, p. 197; Mahan to Lodge, 8 December 1900, Lodge Papers. Lodge had been in favor of Anglo-American cooperation to preserve the open door at least since January of 1898. See his letter to Henry White, 31 January 1898, ibid.

44. Mahan to Roosevelt, 12 March 1901, *Letters of Mahan*, 2:707–8; Roosevelt to Mahan, 18 March 1901, *Letters of Roosevelt*, 3:23.

45. Beale, *Roosevelt*, p. 262. See also Cecil Spring Rice to Roosevelt, 9 August 1900, Roosevelt Papers; and Roosevelt to Hermann Speck von Sternberg, 12 July 1901, *Letters of Roosevelt*, 3:117. As early as 1896, Roosevelt had shown concern lest the Russians take control of northern China and drill the Chinese to serve in their army. Roosevelt to Spring Rice, 5 August 1896, ibid., 1:555.

46. Tyler Dennett, "The Open Door Policy as Intervention," *Annals of the American Academy of Political and Social Science* 168 (July 1933): 79; *Public Opinion* 25 (August 1898): 232–33.

47. Hay to Alvey A. Adee, 14 September 1900, Hay Papers. Betty Weaver Talbert argues plausibly that Hay's Open Door notes represented a calculated effort to serve British as well as American interests without drawing Senate opposition. "Hay's China Policy," pp. 182, 186, 219–20.

48. Kenton J. Clymer, *John Hay* (Ann Arbor, Mich.: University of Michigan Press, 1975), p. 149; Hay to Foster, 23 June 1900, Hay Papers. See also Talbert, "Hay's China Policy," pp. 51–52, 270, 317.

49. Zabriskie, *American-Russian Rivalry*, p. 87. For the substance of the Russian demands, see Conger to Hay, 23 April 1903, *Papers Relating to the Foreign Relations of the United States, 1903* (Washington, 1904), pp. 53–54.

50. On the negotiation of the Anglo-Japanese Alliance, see Langer, *Diplomacy of Imperialism*, vol. 2, chap. 23; and Ian H. Nish, *The Anglo-Japanese Alliance* (London: Athlone Press of the University of London, 1966). Most Americans were very pleased at the conclusion of the alliance. See Sydney Brooks, "America and the Alliance," *Fortnightly Review* 71 (April 1902): 555–64; and Roosevelt to Spring Rice, 1 November 1905, Roosevelt Papers.

51. George Monger, *The End of Isolation* (London: Thomas Nelson and Sons, 1963), pp. 26, 124.

52. Ibid., pp. 124–25.

53. Hay to Roosevelt, 28 April 1903, Hay Papers. See also same to same, 25 April 1903,

ibid.; and Hay to Henry White, 22 May 1903, William R. Thayer, *The Life and Letters of John Hay*, 2 vols. (Boston and New York: Houghton Mifflin Co., 1915), 2:369.
54. Theodore Roosevelt, *California Addresses* (San Francisco: California Promotion Committee, 1903), pp. 95–96.
55. Roosevelt to Hay, 22 May 1903, *Letters of Roosevelt*, 3:478. Henry Cabot Lodge had written to Roosevelt on 21 May that he would like to see the United States join England and Japan in at least a joint protest of the Russian action. Lodge favored a strong policy, "whether alone or jointly." Roosevelt Papers.
56. Hay to Roosevelt, 4 May 1903, Hay Papers; Talbert, "Hay's China Policy," pp. 449–51.
57. Raymond A. Esthus, *Theodore Roosevelt and Japan* (Seattle, Wash., and London: University of Washington Press, 1966), pp. 12–13; Hay to Helen Hay Whitney, 9 October 1903, *Letters of John Hay and Extracts from His Diary*, 3 vols. (New York: Gordian Press, 1969), 3:280. The text of the treaty, which was never ratified because the Russo-Japanese War intervened, is in *Foreign Relations, 1903*, pp. 91–119.
58. The best account of the Alaska issue is contained in Campbell, *Anglo-American Understanding*. Also very useful is Charles C. Tansill, *Canadian-American Relations, 1875–1911* (New Haven, Conn.: Yale University Press, 1943). For the particular roles of Roosevelt and Hay, see, respectively, Beale, *Roosevelt*, pp. 110–31, and Clymer, *Hay*, pp. 166–71, 190–97.
59. Roosevelt to Arthur Lee, 24 April 1901, *Letters of Roosevelt*, 3:66.
60. Roosevelt to Oliver Wendell Holmes, 25 June 1903, ibid., p. 530. Roosevelt authorized Holmes, who was in England at the time, to make this information known "privately and unofficially" to Joseph Chamberlain.
61. Campbell, *Anglo-American Understanding*, pp. 345, 347; Clymer, *Hay*, p. 196.
62. Roosevelt to Shaw, 22 June 1903, and to Abbott, same date, *Letters of Roosevelt*, 3:497, 501; Roosevelt to Adams, 18 July 1903, Roosevelt Papers.
63. Roosevelt to Hay, 18 and 29 July 1903, *Letters of Roosevelt*, 3:520, 532; Dennis, *Adventures in American Diplomacy*, p. 361. See also Hay's reply to Roosevelt, 22 July 1903, Hay Papers. "Make ye no truce with Adam-zàd—the Bear that walks like a man," Rudyard Kipling had written in his anti-Russian poem of 1898, "The Truce of the Bear." Roosevelt and Hay knew the poem well. Beale, *Roosevelt*, p. 198n.
64. Hay to Roosevelt, 3 September 1903, Hay Papers. On the British inquiry of July 1903, see Monger, *End of Isolation*, p. 131.
65. Griscom to Hay, 31 December 1903, *Foreign Relations, 1903*, p. 622.
66. Kennan to Abbott, 4 January 1904, quoted in Taylor Stults, "Imperial Russia through American Eyes, 1894–1904" (Ph.D. diss., University of Missouri, 1970), pp. 222–23.
67. Tyler Dennett, *Roosevelt and the Russo-Japanese War* (Garden City, N.Y.: Doubleday, Page & Co., 1925), p. 27.
68. The view of Japan as the agent of Anglo-Saxon civilization and the representative of Anglo-Saxon interests was quite common in Great Britain and the United States, both before and during the Russo-Japanese War. For examples in Great Britain, see Bertram L. Simpson, *Manchu and Muscovite* (London and New York: Macmillan, 1904), pp. 516, 530; and Stewart L. Murray, *The Peace of the Anglo-Saxons* (Lon-

don: Watts & Co., 1905), p. 101. For the American view, see Knuth, "Climax of Anglo-Saxonism, pp. 250–51.
69. Roosevelt to Spring Rice, 19 March 1904, *Letters of Roosevelt*, 4:760.
70. Roosevelt to Spring Rice, 19 November 1900, ibid., 2:1423. See also Roosevelt to Hermann Speck von Sternberg, 19 November 1900, ibid., p. 1428; and same to same, 8 March 1901, ibid., 3:6.
71. Roosevelt to Henry Cabot Lodge, 16 June 1905, ibid., 4:1231, 1230; Beale, *Roosevelt*, p. 265.
72. Roosevelt to Spring Rice, 2 February 1904, Stephen Gwynn, ed., *The Letters and Friendships of Sir Cecil Spring Rice*, 2 vols. (Boston and New York: Houghton Mifflin Co., 1929), 1:377. Roosevelt spoke again in this letter of the possibility of war, "if the Russians push us improperly or too evidently" (p. 378).

Conclusion

1. One indication of the continuing public interest in Anglo-Saxonism was the reissue by the Library of Congress, in 1906, of a bibliography of works on the topic. The list was first compiled in 1903 by the library's chief bibliographer, in response to numerous requests for information on the subject. The 1906 reissue, an expanded version of the original list, included titles of some 50 books and 150 periodical articles, but still made no claim to completeness. See U.S. Library of Congress, *Select List of References on Anglo-Saxon Interests* (Washington, 1906).
2. Early criticisms of the Teutonic hypothesis are discussed in Edward N. Saveth, *American Historians and European Immigrants, 1875–1925* (New York: Columbia University Press, 1948), pp. 26–31.
3. Charles S. Campbell, *From Revolution to Rapprochement* (New York: John Wiley & Sons, 1974), p. 204.
4. Grey to Roosevelt, 4 December 1906, Theodore Roosevelt Papers, Manuscript Division, Library of Congress.

Bibliography

Primary Sources

Private Papers

Joseph Chamberlain Papers. Birmingham University Library.
Cushman K. Davis Papers. Minnesota Historical Society, St. Paul.
John Hay Papers. Manuscript Division, Library of Congress.
Henry Cabot Lodge Papers. Massachusetts Historical Society, Boston.
William McKinley Papers. Manuscript Division, Library of Congress.
Richard Olney Papers. Manuscript Division, Library of Congress.
Papers of William Waldegrave Palmer, second Earl of Selborne. Department of Western Manuscripts, Bodleian Library, Oxford.
Whitelaw Reid Papers. Manuscript Division, Library of Congress.
Theodore Roosevelt Papers. Manuscript Division, Library of Congress.
Elihu Root Papers. Manuscript Division, Library of Congress.
Henry White Papers. Manuscript Division, Library of Congress.

Published Documents and Government Records

55th Congress, 1st Session, Senate Document No. 63 (Serial 3561).
56th Congress, 1st Session, House Document No. 458 (Serial 3988).
56th Congress, 2nd Session, Senate Document No. 231 (Serial 4054).
Congressional Record. Washington, D.C.
Dugdale, E. T S., ed. *German Diplomatic Documents, 1871–1914*. 4 vols. New York and London: Harper & Brothers, 1928–31.
Hansard's Parliamentary Debates. Fourth Series. London.
Johnson, Donald B., and Porter, Kirk H., comps. *National Party Platforms, 1840–1972*. 5th ed. Urbana, Ill.: University of Illinois Press, 1973.
Journal of the Executive Proceedings of the Senate. Washington, D.C.
U.S. Library of Congress. *Select List of References on Anglo-Saxon Interests*. Washington, D.C., 1906.

Papers Relating to the Foreign Relations of the United States ... Washington, D.C.

Published Papers and Correspondence

Bancroft, Frederic, ed. *Speeches, Correspondence and Political Papers of Carl Schurz*. 6 vols. New York and London: G. P. Putnam's Sons, 1913.

Cater, Harold D., ed. *Henry Adams and His Friends: A Collection of His Unpublished Letters*. Boston: Houghton Mifflin Co., 1947.

Cowles, Anna Roosevelt, ed. *Letters from Theodore Roosevelt to Anna Roosevelt Cowles, 1870–1918*. New York and London: Charles Scribner's Sons, 1924.

Fisk, Ethel F., ed. *The Letters of John Fiske*. New York: Macmillan, 1940.

Ford, Worthington C., ed. *Letters of Henry Adams (1892–1918)*. 2 vols. Boston and New York: Houghton Mifflin Co., 1938.

Gwynn, Stephen, ed. *The Letters and Friendships of Sir Cecil Spring Rice*. 2 vols. Boston and New York: Houghton Mifflin Co., 1929.

James, Henry, ed. *The Letters of William James*. 2 vols. Boston: Little, Brown, and Co., 1920.

Letters of John Hay and Extracts from His Diary. 3 vols. New York: Gordian Press, 1969.

Lodge, Henry Cabot, ed. *Selections from the Correspondence of Theodore Roosevelt and Henry Cabot Lodge, 1884–1918*. 2 vols. New York and London: Charles Scribner's Sons, 1925.

Morison, Elting E., ed. *The Letters of Theodore Roosevelt*. 8 vols. Cambridge, Mass.: Harvard University Press, 1951–54.

Paine, Albert B., ed. *Mark Twain's Letters*. 2 vols. New York and London: Harper & Brothers, 1917.

Seager, Robert II, and Maguire, Doris D., eds. *Letters and Papers of Alfred Thayer Mahan*. 3 vols. Annapolis, Md.: Naval Institute Press, 1975.

Contemporary Books and Pamphlets

Adams, Henry. *The Education of Henry Adams*. Boston: Massachusetts Historical Society, 1918.

Adams, Herbert Baxter. *The Germanic Origins of New England Towns*. Baltimore: Johns Hopkins University Studies ..., 1882.

———. *Saxon Tithing-Men in America*. Baltimore: Johns Hopkins University Studies ..., 1883.

An American Response to Expressions of English Sympathy. New York: Printed for the Anglo-American Committee, 1899.

Bagehot, Walter. *Physics and Politics; or, Thoughts on the Application of the Principles of "Natural Selection" and "Inheritance" to Political Society.* London: C. Kegan Paul & Co., 1872.

Bérard, Victor. *British Imperialism and Commercial Supremacy.* London: Longmans, Green, and Co., 1906.

Beresford, Charles. *The Break-up of China* . . . New York and London: Harper & Brothers, 1899.

Beveridge, Albert J. *The Russian Advance.* New York and London: Harper & Brothers, 1903.

Boxall, George E. *The Anglo-Saxon: A Study in Evolution.* London: Grant Richards, 1902.

Boyd, Charles W., ed. *Mr. Chamberlain's Speeches.* 2 vols. Boston and New York: Houghton Mifflin Co., 1914.

Burgess, John W. *Political Science and Comparative Constitutional Law.* 2 vols. Boston and London: Ginn & Co., 1890.

Carnegie, Andrew. *Triumphant Democracy: Sixty Years' March of the Republic.* Rev. ed. New York: Charles Scribner's Sons, 1893.

Chadwick, French E. *The Relations of the United States and Spain, Diplomacy.* New York: Charles Scribner's Sons, 1909.

Colquhoun, Archibald R. *China in Transformation.* New York and London: Harper & Brothers, 1898.

———. *Greater America.* New York and London: Harper & Brothers, 1904.

———. *The Mastery of the Pacific.* New York and London: Macmillan, 1902.

Conant, Charles A. *The United States in the Orient: The Nature of the Economic Problem.* Boston and New York: Houghton Mifflin Co., 1900.

Cramb, J. A. *The Origins and Destiny of Imperial Britain and Nineteenth Century Europe.* New York: E. P. Dutton & Co., 1915.

Darwin, Charles. *The Descent of Man and Selection in Relation to Sex.* 2 vols. London: J. Murray, 1871.

Davenport, Benjamin Rush. *Anglo-Saxons, Onward! A Romance of the Future.* Cleveland: Hubbell Publishing Co., 1898.

Demolins, Edmond. *Anglo-Saxon Superiority: To What It Is Due.* New York: R. F. Fenno & Co., 1899.

Dilke, Charles W. *Greater Britain: A Record of Travel in English-Speaking Countries during 1866 and 1867.* 3rd ed. London: Macmillan, 1869.

Dos Passos, John R. *The Anglo-Saxon Century and the Unification of the English-Speaking People*. New York and London: G. P. Putnam's Sons, 1903.

Dunne, Finley Peter. *Mr. Dooley: Now and Forever*. Stanford, Calif.: Academic Reprints, 1954.

Essays in Anglo-Saxon Law. Boston: Little, Brown, and Co., 1876.

Fiske, John. *American Political Ideas Viewed from the Standpoint of Universal History*. New York and London: Harper & Brothers, 1885.

Freeman, Edward A. *Greater Greece and Greater Britain; and, George Washington, the Expander of England*. London: Macmillan, 1886.

———. *The Growth of the English Constitution from the Earliest Times*. London: Macmillan, 1872.

———. *An Introduction to American Institutional History*. Baltimore: Johns Hopkins University Studies..., 1882.

———. *Lectures to American Audiences*. Philadelphia: Porter & Coates, 1882.

———. *Some Impressions of the United States*. New York: Henry Holt and Co., 1883.

Froude, James Anthony. *Oceana; or, England and Her Colonies*. London: Longmans, Green, and Co., 1886.

Gardiner, Charles A. *The Proposed Anglo-American Alliance*. New York and London: G. P. Putnam's Sons, 1898.

Giddings, Franklin H. *Democracy and Empire, with Studies of Their Psychological, Economic, and Moral Foundations*. New York and London: Macmillan, 1900.

Gladden, Washington. *England and America: Addresses Delivered in England during the Summer of 1898*. London: James Clarke & Co., 1898.

———. *Recollections*. Boston and New York: Houghton Mifflin Co., 1909.

Gobineau, Joseph Arthur. *The Moral and Intellectual Diversity of Races...* Translated by H. Hotz. Philadelphia: J. B. Lippincott & Co., 1856.

Gorren, Aline. *Anglo-Saxons & Others*. New York: Charles Scribner's Sons, 1900.

Green, J. R. *A Short History of the English People*. London: Macmillan, 1875.

Hammond, John Hays. *Autobiography*. 2 vols. New York: Farrar and Rinehart, 1935.

Hay, John. *Addresses*. New York: Century Co., 1906.

Hosmer, James K. *A Short History of Anglo-Saxon Freedom: The Polity of the English-Speaking Race, Outlined in Its Inception, Development, Diffusion, and Present Condition*. New York: Charles Scribner's Sons, 1890.

Kemble, John Mitchell. *The Saxons in England: A History of the English Commonwealth till the Period of the Norman Conquest*. 2 vols. London: Longman, Brown, Green & Longmans, 1849.

Kidd, Benjamin. *Principles of Western Civilisation*. London and New York: Macmillan, 1902.

———. *Social Evolution*. 2nd ed. New York and London: Macmillan, 1895.

Kipling, Rudyard. *Something of Myself for My Friends Known and Unknown*. Garden City, N.Y.: Doubleday, Doran & Co., 1937.

Lodge, Henry Cabot. *Early Memories*. New York: Charles Scribner's Sons, 1913.

———. *A Frontier Town and Other Essays*. New York: Charles Scribner's Sons, 1906.

———. *The War with Spain*. New York and London: Harper & Brothers, 1899.

London, Jack. *A Daughter of the Snows*. Philadelphia: J. B. Lippincott, 1902.

———. *The Valley of the Moon*. New York: Macmillan, 1913.

Mahan, Alfred Thayer. *From Sail to Steam: Recollections of Naval Life*. New York: Harper & Brothers, 1907.

———. *Lessons of the War with Spain and Other Articles*. Boston: Little, Brown, and Co., 1899.

———. *The Problem of Asia and Its Effect upon International Policies*. Boston: Little, Brown, and Co., 1900.

———. *Retrospect and Prospect: Studies in International Relations, Naval and Political*. Boston: Little, Brown, and Co., 1902.

———. *The Story of the War in South Africa, 1899–1900*. London: Sampson Low, Marston and Co., 1900.

Maxey, Edwin. *Some Questions of Larger Politics*. New York: Abbey Press, 1901.

Motley, John Lothrop. *The Rise of the Dutch Republic: A History*. 3 vols. New York: Harper & Brothers, 1855.

Murray, Stewart L. *The Peace of the Anglo-Saxons: To the Working Men and Their Representatives*. London: Watts & Co., 1905.

Norris, Frank. *The Octopus: A Story of California*. Garden City, N.Y.: Doubleday & Co., 1901.

Pearson, Karl. *National Life from the Standpoint of Science*. 2nd ed. London: Cambridge University Press, 1905.

Reid, Whitelaw. *American and English Studies*. 2 vols. New York: Charles Scribner's Sons, 1913.

Reinsch, Paul S. *World Politics at the End of the Nineteenth Century, as Influenced by the Oriental Situation*. London and New York: Macmillan, 1900.

Roosevelt, Theodore. *Biological Analogies in History*. New York: Oxford University Press, 1910.

———. *California Addresses*. San Francisco: California Promotion Committee, 1903.

———. *The Strenuous Life: Essays and Addresses*. New York: Century Co., 1900.

———. *The Winning of the West*. 6 vols. New York: G. P. Putnam's Sons, 1889-96.

Schierbrand, Wolf von. *America, Asia and the Pacific, with Special Reference to the Russo-Japanese War and Its Results*. New York: Henry Holt and Co., 1904.

———. *Russia: Her Strength and Her Weakness* ... New York and London: G. P. Putnam's Sons, 1904.

Seeley, J. R. *The Expansion of England: Two Courses of Lectures*. London and New York: Macmillan, 1883.

Simpson, Bertram L. *Manchu and Muscovite*. London and New York: Macmillan, 1904.

Stead, W. T. *The Americanisation of the World; or, The Trend of the Twentieth Century*. London: "Review of Reviews" Office, 1902.

———, ed. *The Last Will and Testament of Cecil John Rhodes* ... London: "Review of Reviews" Office, 1902.

Straus, Oscar S. *Under Four Administrations, from Cleveland to Taft*. Boston and New York: Houghton Mifflin Co., 1922.

Strong, Josiah. *Expansion under New World-Conditions*. New York: Baker and Taylor Co., 1900.

———. *The New Era; or, The Coming Kingdom*. London: Hodder and Stoughton, 1893.

———. *Our Country: Its Possible Future and Its Present Crisis*. New York: American Home Missionary Society, 1885.

Stubbs, William. *The Constitutional History of England in Its Origin and Development*. 3 vols. Oxford: Clarendon, 1880.

———. *Lectures on Early English History*. Edited by Arthur Hassall. London and New York: Longmans, Green, and Co., 1906.

Tracy, Louis. *The Final War*. New York and London: G. P. Putnam's Sons, 1896.

Waldstein, Charles. *The Expansion of Western Ideals and the World's Peace*. New York and London: John Lane, 1899.

Newspapers

New York Times. 1898–1900.

New York Tribune. 1898–1900.

New York World. 1895.

Times (London). 1895–1902.

The periodicals *Literary Digest* and *Public Opinion* contain summaries and excerpts of newspaper editorials and articles, and were used to add opinion from other newspapers.

Contemporary Periodicals

American Monthly Review of Reviews
Anglo-Saxon Review
Annals of the American Academy of Political and Social Science
Arena
Atlantic Monthly
Century Magazine
Contemporary Review
Cosmopolitan
Edinburgh Review
Fortnightly Review
Forum
Harper's New Monthly Magazine
Independent
Living Age
McClure's Magazine
Nation
National Review
Nineteenth Century and *Nineteenth Century and After*
North American Review
Outlook
Overland Monthly
Pall Mall Magazine

Political Science Quarterly
Popular Science Monthly
Review of Reviews
Saturday Review
Scribner's Magazine
Spectator
Westminster Review
World's Work

Secondary Sources

Unpublished Manuscripts

Behrman, Cynthia Fansler, "The Mythology of British Imperialism: 1880–1914." Ph.D. dissertation, Boston University, 1965.

Berge, William H. "The Impulse for Expansion: John W. Burgess, Alfred Thayer Mahan, Theodore Roosevelt, Josiah Strong and the Development of a Rationale." Ph.D. dissertation, Vanderbilt University, 1969.

Dyer, Thomas G. "Theodore Roosevelt and the Idea of Race." Ph.D. dissertation, University of Georgia, 1975.

Herzig, Patricia D. "British Public Opinion on the Venezuelan Crisis of 1895–1896 with the United States." M.A. thesis, Stanford University, 1949.

King, Peter H. "The White Man's Burden: British Imperialism and Its Lessons for America as Seen by American Publicists from the Venezuela Crisis to the Boer War." Ph.D. dissertation, University of California at Los Angeles, 1958.

Knuth, Helen E. "The Climax of American Anglo-Saxonism, 1898–1905." Ph.D. dissertation, Northwestern University, 1958.

Stults, Taylor. "Imperial Russia through American Eyes, 1894–1904: A Study in Public Opinion." Ph.D. dissertation, University of Missouri, 1970.

Talbert, Betty Weaver. "The Evolution of John Hay's China Policy." Ph.D. dissertation, University of North Carolina at Chapel Hill, 1974.

Tarkow-Naamani, Israel. "The Abandonment of 'Splendid Isolation': A Study of British Public Opinion and Diplomacy, 1895–1902." Ph.D. dissertation, Indiana University, 1945.

Tingley, Donald Fred. "The Rise of Racialistic Thinking in the United States in the Nineteenth Century." Ph.D. dissertation, University of Illinois, 1952.

Zeil, Elizabeth. "The United States and the Boer War." M.A. thesis, Columbia University, 1950.

Books and Pamphlets

Allen, H. C. *Great Britain and the United States: A History of Anglo-American Relations (1783–1952)*. London: Odhams Press, 1954.

Arendt, Hannah. *The Origins of Totalitarianism*. New York: Harcourt, Brace and Co., 1951.

Barltrop, Robert. *Jack London: The Man, the Writer, the Rebel*. London: Pluto Press, 1976.

Barzun, Jacques. *Race: A Study in Modern Superstition*. New York: Harcourt, Brace and Co., 1937.

Beale, Howard K. *Theodore Roosevelt and the Rise of America to World Power*. Baltimore: Johns Hopkins Press, 1956.

Benedict, Ruth. *Race: Science and Politics*. New York: Modern Age Books, 1940.

Beringause, Arthur F. *Brooks Adams: A Biography*. New York: Alfred A. Knopf, 1955.

Berman, Milton. *John Fiske: The Evolution of Popularizer*. Cambridge, Mass.: Harvard University Press, 1961.

Blum, John Morton. *The Republican Roosevelt*. Cambridge, Mass.: Harvard University Press, 1954.

Boller, Paul F., Jr. *American Thought in Transition: The Impact of Evolutionary Naturalism, 1865–1900*. Chicago: Rand McNally & Co., 1969.

Bowers, Claude G. *Beveridge and the Progressive Era*. Boston: Houghton Mifflin Co., 1932.

Burton, David H. *Theodore Roosevelt and His English Correspondents: A Special Relationship of Friends*. Philadelphia: American Philosophical Society, 1973.

———. *Theodore Roosevelt: Confident Imperialist*. Philadelphia: University of Pennsylvania Press, 1968.

Campbell, A. E. *Great Britain and the United States, 1895–1903*. London: Longmans, Green and Co., 1960.

Campbell, Charles S. *Anglo-American Understanding, 1898–1903*. Baltimore: Johns Hopkins Press, 1957.

———. *From Revolution to Rapprochement: The United States and Great Britain, 1783–1900*. New York: John Wiley & Sons, 1974.

———. *The Transformation of American Foreign Relations, 1865–1900*. New York: Harper & Row, 1976.

Clark, John Spencer. *The Life and Letters of John Fiske*. 2 vols. Boston and New York: Houghton Mifflin Co., 1917.

Clymer, Kenton J. *John Hay: The Gentleman as Diplomat*. Ann Arbor, Mich.: University of Michigan Press, 1975.

Cortissoz, Royal. *The Life of Whitelaw Reid*. 2 vols. London: Thornton Butterworth, 1921.

Crapol, Edward P. *America for Americans: Economic Nationalism and Anglophobia in the Late Nineteenth Century*. Westport, Conn.: Greenwood Press, 1973.

Crewe, Marquess of. *Lord Rosebery*. New York and London: Harper & Brothers, 1931.

Curti, Merle. *The Growth of American Thought*. 3rd ed. New York and London: Harper & Row, 1964.

Curtis, L. P., Jr. *Anglo-Saxons and Celts: A Study of Anti-Irish Prejudice in Victorian England*. Bridgeport, Conn.: University of Bridgeport Conference on British Studies, 1968.

Dallin, David J. *The Rise of Russia in Asia*. New Haven, Conn.: Yale University Press, 1949.

Dennett, Tyler. *Americans in Eastern Asia: A Critical Study of the Policy of the United States with Reference to China, Japan and Korea in the 19th Century*. New York: Macmillan, 1922.

———. *John Hay: From Poetry to Politics*. New York: Dodd, Mead & Co., 1933.

———. *Roosevelt and the Russo-Japanese War* . . . Garden City, N.Y.: Doubleday, Page & Co., 1925.

Dennis, A. L. P. *Adventures in American Diplomacy, 1896–1906*. New York: E. P. Dutton & Co., 1928.

Dugdale, Blanche E. C. *Arthur James Balfour, First Earl of Balfour, K.G., O.M., F.R.S., Etc*. 2 vols. London: Hutchinson & Co., 1936.

Edwardes, Michael. *Playing the Great Game: A Victorian Cold War*. London: Hamish Hamilton, 1975.

Eggert, Gerald G. *Richard Olney: Evolution of a Statesman*. University Park, Pa.: Pennsylvania State University Press, 1974.

Esthus, Raymond A. *Theodore Roosevelt and Japan*. Seattle, Wash., and London: University of Washington Press, 1966.

Ferguson, John H. *American Diplomacy and the Boer War*. Philadelphia: University of Pennsylvania Press, 1939.

Fredrickson, George M. *The Black Image in the White Mind: The Debate on Afro-American Character and Destiny, 1817–1914*. New York: Harper & Row, 1971.

Garraty, John A. *Henry Cabot Lodge: A Biography*. New York: Alfred A. Knopf, 1965.

Garvin, J. L. *The Life of Joseph Chamberlain*. 3 vols. London: Macmillan, 1932–34.

Gelber, Lionel M. *The Rise of Anglo-American Friendship: A Study in World Politics, 1898–1906*. London: Oxford University Press, 1938.

Gillard, David. *The Struggle for Asia, 1828–1914: A Study in British and Russian Imperialism*. London: Methuen & Co., 1977.

Gooch, G. P. *History and Historians in the Nineteenth Century*. London: Longmans, Green, and Co., 1913.

Gossett, Thomas F. *Race: The History of an Idea in America*. Dallas: Southern Methodist University Press, 1963.

Grenville, John A. S. *Lord Salisbury and Foreign Policy: The Close of the Nineteenth Century*. London: Athlone Press of the University of London, 1964.

———, and Young, George Berkeley. *Politics, Strategy, and American Diplomacy: Studies in Foreign Policy, 1873–1917*. New Haven, Conn., and London: Yale University Press, 1966.

Griswold, A. Whitney. *The Far Eastern Policy of the United States*. New York: Harcourt, Brace and Co., 1938.

Hackett, Alice P. *70 Years of Best Sellers, 1895–1965*. New York: Bowker, 1967.

Handlin, Oscar. *The Uprooted: The Epic Story of the Great Migrations that Made the American People*. New York: Grossett & Dunlap, 1951.

Hankins, Frank H. *The Racial Basis of Civilization: A Critique of the Nordic Doctrine*. New York and London: Alfred A. Knopf, 1926.

Hart, James D. *The Popular Book: A History of America's Literary Taste*. New York: Oxford University Press, 1950.

Heindel, Richard H. *The American Impact on Great Britain, 1898–1914: A Study of the United States in World History*. Philadelphia: University of Pennsylvania Press, 1940.

Hendrick, Burton J. *The Life of Andrew Carnegie*. 2 vols. Garden City, N.Y.: Doubleday, Doran & Co., 1932.

Higham, John. *Strangers in the Land: Patterns of American Nativism, 1860–1925*. Rev. ed. New York: Atheneum, 1963.

Himmelfarb, Gertrude. *Darwin and the Darwinian Revolution*. Garden City, N.Y.: Doubleday & Co., 1959.

Hofstadter, Richard. *Social Darwinism in American Thought*. Rev. ed. Boston: Beacon Press, 1955.

Holt, W. Stull, *Treaties Defeated by the Senate: A Study of the Struggle*

Between President and Senate over the Conduct of Foreign Relations. Baltimore: Johns Hopkins Press, 1933.

James, Robert Rhodes. *The British Revolution, 1880–1939*. New York: Alfred A. Knopf, 1977.

Jeyes, Samuel H. *Mr. Chamberlain: His Life and Public Career*. London: Sands & Co., 1903.

Jones, Howard Mumford. *The Age of Energy: Varieties of American Experience, 1865–1915*. New York: Viking Press, 1971.

Judd, Denis. *Balfour and the British Empire: A Study in Imperial Evolution, 1874–1932*. London: Macmillan, 1968.

Karsten, Peter. *The Naval Aristocracy: The Golden Age of Annapolis and the Emergence of Modern American Navalism*. New York: Free Press, 1972.

Langer, William L. *The Diplomacy of Imperialism, 1890–1902*. 2 vols. New York and London: Alfred A. Knopf, 1935.

Langley, Lester D. *Struggle for the American Mediterranean: United States-European Rivalry in the Gulf-Caribbean, 1776–1904*. Athens, Ga.: University of Georgia Press, 1976.

Linderman, Gerald F. *The Mirror of War: American Society and the Spanish-American War*. Ann Arbor, Mich.: University of Michigan Press, 1974.

Livezey, William E. *Mahan on Sea Power*. Norman, Okla.: University of Oklahoma Press, 1947.

Martin, Edward S. *The Life of Joseph Hodges Choate, as Gathered Chiefly from His Letters*. 2 vols. London: Constable & Co., 1920.

May, Ernest R. *Imperial Democracy: The Emergence of America as a Great Power*. New York: Harcourt, Brace & World, 1961.

Merk, Frederick. *Manifest Destiny and Mission in American History: A Reinterpretation*. New York: Alfred A. Knopf, 1963.

Millin, Sarah G. *Cecil Rhodes*. New York and London: Harper & Brothers, 1933.

Monger, George. *The End of Isolation: British Foreign Policy, 1900–1907*. London: Thomas Nelson and Sons, 1963.

Montagu, M. F. Ashley. *Man's Most Dangerous Myth: The Fallacy of Race*. New York: Columbia University Press, 1942.

Morgan, H. Wayne. *America's Road to Empire: The War with Spain and Overseas Expansion*. New York: John Wiley and Sons, 1965.

―――. *William McKinley and His America*. Syracuse, N.Y.: Syracuse University Press, 1963.

Mowat, R. B. *The Life of Lord Pauncefote, First Ambassador to the United States*. Boston and New York: Houghton Mifflin Co., 1929.

Mowry, George E. *The Era of Theodore Roosevelt and the Birth of Modern America, 1900–1912*. New York: Harper & Row, 1958.

Neale, R. G. *Great Britain and United States Expansion: 1898–1900*. East Lansing, Mich.: Michigan State University Press, 1966.

Nish, Ian H. *The Anglo-Japanese Alliance: The Diplomacy of Two Island Empires, 1894–1907*. London: Athlone Press of the University of London, 1966.

Noer, Thomas J. *Briton, Boer, and Yankee: The United States and South Africa, 1870–1914*. Kent, O.: Kent State University Press, 1978.

O'Connor, Richard. *Jack London: A Biography*. Boston and Toronto: Little, Brown and Co., 1964.

Peck, Harry Thurston. *Twenty Years of the Republic, 1885–1905*. New York: Dodd, Mead & Co., 1919.

Perkins, Bradford. *The Great Rapprochement: England and the United States, 1895–1914*. New York: Atheneum, 1968.

Perkins, Dexter. *The Monroe Doctrine, 1867–1907*. Baltimore: Johns Hopkins Press, 1937.

Playne, Caroline E. *The Pre-War Mind in Britain: An Historical Review*. London: George Allen & Unwin, 1928.

Pletcher, David M. *The Diplomacy of Annexation: Texas, Oregon, and the Mexican War*. Columbia, Mo.: University of Missouri Press, 1973.

Poliakov, Léon. *The Aryan Myth: A History of Racist and Nationalist Ideas in Europe*. New York: Basic Books, 1974.

Pratt, Julius W. *Expansionists of 1898: The Acquisition of Hawaii and the Spanish Islands*. Baltimore: Johns Hopkins Press, 1936.

Puleston, W. D. *Mahan: The Life and Work of Captain Alfred Thayer Mahan, U.S.N.* New Haven, Conn.: Yale University Press, 1939.

Reuter, Bertha Ann. *Anglo-American Relations during the Spanish-American War*. New York: Macmillan, 1924.

Russett, Cynthia Eagle. *Darwin in America: The Intellectual Response, 1865–1912*. San Francisco: W. H. Freeman and Co., 1976.

Samuels, Ernest. *Henry Adams: The Major Phase*. Cambridge, Mass.: Harvard University Press, 1964.

Saveth, Edward N. *American Historians and European Immigrants, 1875–1925*. New York: Columbia University Press, 1948.

Seager, Robert II. *Alfred Thayer Mahan: The Man and His Letters*. Annapolis, Md.: Naval Institute Press, 1977.

Semmel, Bernard. *Imperialism and Social Reform: English Social-Imperial Thought, 1895–1914*. London: George Allen & Unwin, 1960.

Shahane, Vasant A. *Rudyard Kipling: Activist and Artist*. Carbondale, Ill.: Southern Illinois University Press, 1973.

Sinclair, Andrew. *Jack: A Biography of Jack London*. New York: Harper & Row, 1977.

Snyder, Louis L. *The Idea of Racialism: Its Meaning and History*. New York: Van Nostrand Reinhold Co., 1962.

Solomon, Barbara Miller. *Ancestors and Immigrants: A Changing New England Tradition*. Cambridge, Mass.: Harvard University Press, 1956.

Stephens, W. R. W. *The Life and Letters of Edward A. Freeman*. 2 vols. London and New York: Macmillan, 1895.

Strauss, William L. *Joseph Chamberlain and the Theory of Imperialism*. Washington, D.C.: American Council on Public Affairs, 1942.

Tansill, Charles C. *Canadian-American Relations, 1875–1911*. New Haven, Conn.: Yale University Press, 1943.

Taylor, Charles C. *The Life of Admiral Mahan* . . . New York: George H. Doran Co., 1920.

Thayer, William R. *The Life and Letters of John Hay*. 2 vols. Boston and New York: Houghton Mifflin Co., 1915.

Thornton, Archibald P. *The Imperial Idea and Its Enemies: A Study in British Power*. London: Macmillan, 1959.

Trevelyan, George M. *Grey of Fallodon: The Life and Letters of Sir Edward Grey, afterwards Viscount Grey of Fallodon*. Boston: Houghton Mifflin Co., 1937.

Walcutt, Charles Child. *Jack London*. University of Minnesota Pamphlets on American Writers, no. 57. Minneapolis: University of Minnesota Press, 1966.

Walker, Franklin. *Frank Norris: A Biography*. New York: Russell & Russell, 1963.

Wall, Joseph F. *Andrew Carnegie*. New York: Oxford University Press, 1970.

Weinberg, Albert K. *Manifest Destiny: A Study of Nationalist Expansionism in American History*. Baltimore: Johns Hopkins Press, 1935.

Whyte, Frederic. *The Life of W. T. Stead*. 2 vols. New York and Boston: Houghton Mifflin Co., 1925.

Williams, Basil. *Cecil Rhodes*. New York: Henry Holt & Co., 1921.

Wilson, Angus. *The Strange Ride of Rudyard Kipling: His Life and Works*. New York: Viking Press, 1978.

Wisan, Joseph E. *The Cuban Crisis as Reflected in the New York Press (1895–1898)*. New York: Columbia University Press, 1934.

Young, Kenneth. *Arthur James Balfour: The Happy Life of the Politician, Prime Minister, Statesman and Philosopher, 1848–1930*. London: G. Bell and Sons, 1963.

Zabriskie, Edward H. *American-Russian Rivalry in the Far East: A Study in Diplomacy and Power Politics, 1895–1914*. Philadelphia: University of Pennsylvania Press, 1946.

Ziff, Larzer. *The American 1890s: Life and Times of a Lost Generation*. New York: Viking Press, 1966.

Articles

Blake, Nelson M. "The Olney-Pauncefote Treaty of 1897." *American Historical Review* 50 (January 1945): 228-43.

Campbell, Charles S. "Anglo-American Relations, 1897–1901." In *Threshold to American Internationalism: Essays on the Foreign Policies of William McKinley*. Edited by Paolo E. Coletta. New York: Exposition Press, 1970.

Dennett, Tyler. "The Open Door Policy as Intervention." *Annals of the American Academy of Political and Social Science* 168 (July 1933): 78–83.

Farwell, Byron. "Taking Sides in the Boer War." *American Heritage* 27 (April 1976): 21–25, 92–97.

Horsman, Reginald. "Origins of Racial Anglo-Saxonism in Great Britain before 1850." *Journal of the History of Ideas* 37 (July-September 1976): 387–410.

Muller, Dorothea. "Josiah Strong and American Nationalism: A Reevaluation." *Journal of American History* 53 (December 1966): 487–503.

Pratt, Julius W. "The Ideology of American Expansion." In *Essays in Honor of William E. Dodd by His Former Students at the University of Chicago*. Edited by Avery Craven. Chicago: University of Chicago Press, 1935.

Sears, Louis Martin. "French Opinion of the Spanish-American War." *Hispanic American Historical Review* 7 (February 1927): 25–44.

Seed, Geoffrey. "British Reactions to American Imperialism Reflected in Journals of Opinion, 1898–1900." *Political Science Quarterly* 73 (June 1958): 254–72.

———. "British Views of American Policy in the Philippines Reflected in Journals of Opinion, 1898–1907." *Journal of American Studies* 2 (1968): 48–64.
Sloan, Jennie A. "Anglo-American Relations and the Venezuelan Boundary Dispute." *Hispanic American Historical Review* 18 (November 1938): 486–506.
Wallace, Elisabeth. "Goldwin Smith on England and America." *American Historical Review* 59 (July 1954): 884–94.
Williams, William A. "Brooks Adams and American Expansion." *New England Quarterly* 25 (June 1952): 217–32.

Index

Abbott, Lyman, 25, 120, 123, 170, 171, 191 n. 1
Adams, Brooks, 64, 164, 165, 167, 170, 173, 191 n.1, 212 n. 32; and China, 158–61; and Lodge, 158; and racial Darwinism, 35–36, 158–59; and Roosevelt, 158, 161
Adams, George Burton, 42, 63, 104
Adams, Henry, 39, 71, 82, 92, 143, 158, 191 n. 1; and Hay, 160–61, 165, 212 n. 34; and Lodge, 79, 80; and race, 185 n. 55; and Teutonic origins theory, 42, 43, 185 n. 55
Adams, Herbert Baxter, 41–42, 43, 175
Aguinaldo, Emilio, 121
Alaska boundary question, 132, 168–70
Aldrich, Thomas Bailey, 56
Alverstone, Lord, 169
Anglo-American Committee, 119–20
Anglo-German understanding, proposed, 152, 154
Anglo-Japanese Alliance, 166, 176, 213 n. 50; Hay favors U.S. joining, 167
Anglo-Saxonism; and Anglo-American rapprochement, 12–14, 60–61, 73–74, 94, 174, 177; Anglo-Saxon characteristics, alleged, 12, 19, 20–21, 55–56, 59, 81, 104, 126, 138; Anglo-Saxon superiority, evidence of, 21–23; decline of, 164, 174–77; defined, 11–12; early versions of, 26–28; in literature, 57–60; pervasiveness, 60, 215 n. 1; and race, vague conception of, 18–19; and racial mission, 17–18, 23–25, 34–35, 44, 50–51, 53–54, 57, 58, 83, 124–25, 126–27, 128, 177. *See also* Darwinism, racial; Teutonic origins theory,
Armenian massacres, 101, 104
Armour, Philip D., 107
Arnold, William C., 115
Asquith, H. H., 107, 117
Atkinson, Edward, 104
Austin, Alfred, 98, 114

Bagehot, Walter, 29–30
Balfour, Arthur, 13, 52, 79, 82, 83, 86–87, 104, 110, 116, 152, 176; and Anglo-American friendship, 89–90, 94; Anglo-Saxonism of, 73, 89–91; calls for Anglo-Saxon alliance, 101, 111, 121, 195 n. 60; and Russia, 70; and Venezuela boundary dispute, 90, 100–101, 106
Bancroft, George, 37
Beard, Charles, A., 175
Becker, George F., 134
Benton, Thomas Hart, 27
Bérard, Victor, 58, 183 n. 33
Beresford, Lord Charles, 35, 117, 119, 123, 126, 140, 150, 173; and defense of open door, 154–55; mission to China, 154
Besant, Sir Walter, 20–21, 107, 119
Bethell, Sir Richard, 99
Beveridge, Albert, 25, 128; and Russia, 70–71, 211 n. 26
"Black Week," 135–36
Blaine, James G., 78
Boers, 99, 100; seen as backward race, 132, 135, 138–39. *See also* Boer War

232

INDEX 233

Boer War, 50, 153, 174; and Anglo-American relations, 130–47 passim, 177, 205 n. 6; and Continental powers, 130, 131, 204 n. 1; as a Darwinian struggle, 138–39; and election of 1900, 142–44; and U.S. public opinion, 130–31, 146, 147, 176

Boxer Rebellion, 67, 149, 160

Brassey, Lord, 119

Bryan, William Jennings, 142, 143, 144, 161

Bryce, James, 11, 77, 82, 107, 119, 123, 125; and Venezuela boundary dispute, 97, 99, 100.

Buller, Sir Redvers, 136

Burgess, John W., 42, 56, 75

Canada, 21, 46, 72, 78, 79, 90, 97, 99, 121, 185 n. 68; and Alaska boundary question, 168–69

Carnegie, Andrew, 82, 103–4, 200 n. 14, 206 n. 20; and race federation, 51–54

Chadwick, French E., 201 n. 23

Chamberlain, Joseph, 13, 77, 82, 87, 104, 110, 111, 127, 143, 151, 162, 176, 204 n. 4, 214 n. 60; and alliance sentiment in 1898, 114, 116, 122–23, 125; and Anglo-American friendship, 88–89, 94; Anglo-Saxonism of, 73, 88; and imperial federation, 49, 88; influence of, 88; proposes Anglo-American-German alliance (1899), 152–53; and Russia, 122, 152, 173, 210 n. 8; and Venezuela boundary dispute, 89, 99, 100, 101, 121

Chamberlain, Mary Endicott, 88, 140

China, 48, 67, 68, 90, 100, 121, 122; and Anglo-American economic interests, 149–50, 156; as scene of Anglo-Saxon contest with Slavs, 71, 93, 148–68 passim, 173

Choate, Joseph, 136

Churchill, Lady Randolph, 203 n. 54

Clarke, George Sydenham, 63, 123, 126

Clayton-Bulwer treaty, 79, 144

Cleveland, Grover, 82, 107; and Venezuela boundary dispute, 95, 96, 97, 102, 111, 197 n. 22

Colquhoun, Archibald, 155, 162, 173; proposes anti-Russian alliance, 153–54

Cramb, J. A., 24, 25

Cullom, Shelby M., 213 n. 42

Curzon, Lord, 82

Darwin, Charles, 28–29, 30, 32, 43, 76. *See also* Darwinism, racial

Darwinism, racial, 56, 150, 158, 161–62; and Boer War, 138–39; and international relations, 12–13, 29–37, 63; relationship to Anglo-Saxonism, 36–37, 45–46, 62–63, 72; and Spanish-American War, 119, 139; undermining of, 164, 174–75

Davis, Cushman K., 213 n. 42; and Anglo-American alliance, 202–3 n. 44, 210 n. 7

Day, William R., 165

Delcassé, Théophile, 204 n. 1

De Lôme letter, 113

Demolins, Edmond, 65–66, 201 n. 22

Dewey, George, 121, 200 n. 13

Dicey, Albert V., 123

Dicey, Edward, 24, 69, 100

Dilke, Charles W., 47–48, 49, 89, 123, 125

Dual Alliance, 65, 104, 124

Durand, Sir Mortimer, 92

Edmunds, George F., 56

Eliot, Charles W., 55

Entente Cordiale, 176

Expansion, U.S.: British support for, 125–28, 203 n. 50

Field, Marshall, 107

Fiske, John, 32, 76, 185 nn. 61, 62; and Immigration Restriction League, 56; recognition in England, 43; and Teutonic origins theory, 42–45

Flower, B. O., 123
Ford, Alexander Hume, 157
Foster, John W., 165
France, 37, 124, 151, 158, 171; and Boer War, 130, 204 n. 1; decadence of, 64, 65–66; and Great Britain, 100; and "Latin race," 63, 153, 162; race theories in, 17; and Spanish-American War, 116, 119, 124
Freeman, Edward Augustus, 38, 39, 43, 45, 175, 185 n. 62; visit to U.S., 39–40, 42
Froude, James Anthony, 38, 47, 48

Gatacre, Sir William, 136
German-Americans, 120, 134, 144
Germany, 22, 37, 40, 54, 64, 89, 124, 137, 150, 152, 158, 160, 171; and Boer War, 204 n. 1; and Great Britain, 66, 99, 100; race-thinking in, 17, 27, 41; as rival of Anglo-Saxon powers, 66–68, 124; and Spanish-American War, 124, 128; and the U.S., 66–67
Giddings, Franklin H., 20, 65; and Russia, 69, 71–72, 157
Gladden, Washington, 19, 117
Gladstone, William, 47, 87, 97, 107
Gobineau, Joseph Arthur de, 27
Godkin, E. L., 96, 135, 137, 197 n. 22
Goschen, Viscount, 77, 113
Green, John Richard, 38–39, 175
Grey, Earl, 114, 119
Grey, Sir Edward, 116–17, 153, 178

Haggard, Rider, 98
Hale, Edward Everett, 55
Hammond, John Hays, 206 n. 13
Harcourt, Sir William, 82; and Venezuela boundary dispute, 97, 196 n. 8
Hardy, Thomas, 98
Hart, Albert Bushnell, 42
Hay, Adelbert, 145, 209 n. 48
Hay, John, 13, 73, 88, 114, 116, 117, 122, 123, 155, 170, 176; and Brooks Adams, 158, 160–61, 165; and Henry Adams, 160–61, 212 n. 34; and Anglo-American relations, 83–84, 94, 118, 164–65, 210 n. 13, 213 n. 47; Anglophilia of, 82–83; his Anglo-Saxonism, 83, 165; and Boer War, 131, 132, 133–34, 136, 137, 140–41, 142, 143, 145–46, 205 n. 7, 208 n. 34; English acquaintances of, 82; and Germany, 67; and Japan, 171; and Lodge, 82; and open door policy, 156, 161, 164–65, 213 n. 47; and Roosevelt, 82; and Russia, 165, 166–67, 168, 173
Hay-Herbert treaty, 168
Hay-Pauncefote treaties, 79, 144–45
Hearst, William Randolph, 113
Herbert, Michael, 166, 168
Hewitt, Abram S., 120
Higginson, Thomas Wentworth, 55
Hoar, George F., 43, 139, 198 n. 40
Hollis, I. N., 134
Holmes, Oliver Wendell, 214 n. 60
Hopkins, Washburn, 139
Hosmer, James K., 42, 55–56, 123
Howells, William Dean, 137
Huxley, Thomas, 43, 76

Immigration: stimulating racism, 54–57
Immigration Restriction League, 56, 81
Imperial Federation League, 46–47, 51. *See also* Imperial federation movement
Imperial federation movement, 46–49, 53, 88; and Anglo-Saxonism, 46, 47, 49, 51
Imperialism: linked to racism, 17–18, 23–24, 25, 35–36, 62
Irish-Americans, 79, 108, 120, 122, 134

James, Henry, 82
James, William, 55, 120
Jameson raid, 99
Japan, 72, 90, 154, 160, 162, 164, 170, 176; as defender of Anglo-Saxon interests, 171–72, 214 n. 68; and Russia, 149, 150, 160, 166, 167,

171. *See also* Anglo-Japanese Alliance; Russo-Japanese War
Jefferson, Thomas, 26, 27
Jersey, Earl of, 119

Kemble, John Mitchell, 38, 43, 45
Kennan, George, 171
Kidd, Benjamin, 30–31, 32, 35, 58, 71, 88
Kipling, Rudyard, 59, 78, 83, 88, 126, 214 n. 63; as popularizer of Anglo-Saxonism, 57–58
Kitchener, Lord, 138
Kruger, Paul, 142, 145
Kruger telegram, 99–100

Lansdowne, Lord, 87, 166, 178
"Large policy," 118
Latins, 63, 67, 115, 176; decadence of, 64–65, 66; racial characteristics, alleged, 64; struggle with Anglo-Saxons, 119, 201 n. 23. *See also* France
Le Bon, Gustave, 81, 193 n. 29
Lee, Arthur, 78, 130
Lodge, Henry Cabot, 22, 73, 84, 88, 94, 117, 118, 127, 134, 158, 213 n. 42; and Alaska boundary question, 79, 168–69; and Boer War, 136, 137; and China, 150, 163, 213 n. 43, 214 n. 55; and Germany, 67; and Great Britain, 78–80; and immigration restriction, 80–82; and Roosevelt, 78, 82; and Spain, 115, 119; and Teutonic origins theory, 80; and Venezuela boundary dispute, 79, 101, 196 n. 17
London, Jack, 58–59, 60, 188 n. 101
London, Lord Mayor of, 83, 85, 113
Lorne, Marquis of, 140
Low, Sidney, 123
Lowell, Augustus, 75
Lyell, Sir Charles, 43

McCormick, Cyrus, 107
McKinley, William, 83, 108, 114, 116, 145, 151, 155, 163, 164; and Boer War, 131, 133, 141, 205–6 n. 12; and election of 1900, 142, 143, 144, 161
Mahan, Alfred Thayer, 19, 53, 73, 80, 88, 108, 113, 118, 158, 170, 183 n. 29; and Anglo-American friendship, 63, 85, 94, 103, 164; Anglo-Saxonism of, 84, 85, 86, 103, 128, 193 n. 42; and Boer War, 132, 134, 136, 137, 139, 146, 209 n. 29; and Far Eastern policy, 161–63, 173, 212–13 n. 41; influence in Great Britain, 84–85; and Lodge, 84; and the "one true policy," 85; opposes Anglo-American alliance, 86; his racial Darwinism, 85–86, 161–62; and Roosevelt, 84, 163–64, 176
Maine: British response to sinking of, 113
Maitland, Frederick, 38
Manchuria, 148, 149, 150, 160, 165–66, 167, 168, 170
Manila Bay, Battle of, 71, 117, 121, 173
Maxey, Edwin, 138
Meredith, George, 98
Mills, David, 63, 151
Monroe Doctrine, 67, 79, 207 n. 24
Moore, John Bassett, 197 n. 22
Morley, John, 77, 98
Motley, John Lothrop, 40
Muraviev, Mikhail, 204 n. 1
Murray, Steward L., 17

Nationalism: linked to racism, 17–18
New Englanders: and immigration restriction, 56; and Teutonic origins theory, 41
Norris, Frank, 59–60

Olney, Richard, 197 n. 29; and arbitration treaty, 105, 107, 109–10; and race patriotism, 104–5, 110, 121; and Venezuela boundary dispute, 95, 96, 104–5
Olney-Pauncefote treaty, 105, 107–11; significance, 105, 111
Open door policy, 124, 149, 155, 156, 164, 165, 170, 183 n. 29, 210 n. 8,

Open door policy (*continued*)
211 n. 22, 212 n. 32; and Anglo-American relations, 156, 213 n. 47

Paine, Robert Treat, 56
Pan-Slavism, 17, 70
Parkman, Francis, 40
Pauncefote, Sir Julian (later Lord), 97, 104, 105, 109, 117–18, 131, 141, 144–45, 151, 166
Pearson, Karl, 31–32
Peel, Viscount, 107
Philippines, 25, 80, 121, 125, 127, 132
Port Arthur, 149, 151, 168, 172, 173, 210 n. 8
Pulitzer, Joseph, 96, 108, 197 n. 22, 198 n. 47
Pullman, George M., 107

Quincy, Josiah, 211 n. 26

Reid, Whitelaw, 22, 56, 120, 191 n. 1, 197 n. 22, 202 n. 41, 203 n. 54; and Boer War, 134, 137
Reinsch, Paul S., 157
Rhodes, Cecil, 49, 50–51, 53, 88, 133
Rhodes, James Ford, 134
Roberts, Lord, 138, 142
Rockhill, W. W., 156
Roosevelt, Theodore, 13, 30, 73, 79, 81, 83, 88, 92, 99, 115, 118, 125, 127, 165, 178, 201 n. 22; and Brooks Adams, 158, 161, 167, 170; and Alaska boundary question, 168–69, 170; and Anglo-American friendship, 77, 78, 94, 128–29, 164; and Boer War, 132, 133, 135, 136–37, 141–42, 145, 146, 207 n. 24, 208 n. 36; his British acquaintances, 77–78; and France, 65; and Germany, 67, 76–77; and immigration restriction, 74; and Japan, 74, 164, 171–72; and Latins, 76; and Lodge, 78; and Mahan, 84, 163–64, 170, 176; and racial Darwinism, 76; and Russia, 71, 77, 163–64, 166, 167, 168, 170–72, 173, 213 n. 45, 215 n. 72; and Teutonic origins theory, 75–76; and Venezuela boundary dispute, 78, 96–97; his views on race, 74–76
Root, Elihu, 169
Rosebery, Lord, 19, 48–49, 84, 85, 98, 107, 125; and imperial federation, 46–47
Ross, Edward A., 56
Royce, Josiah, 55
Ruskin, John, 98
Russia, 17, 22, 64, 124, 137, 156, 174, 177; and Asiatic barbarism, 69, 93; and Boer War, 130, 204 n. 1; and China, 148–49, 165–66, 167, 168; expansion of, 68; and Great Britain, 68–69, 100, 122, 166, 171, 176; racial characteristics of Russians, alleged, 70; and "Slavic race," 63; and Spanish-American War, 124; as threat to Anglo-Saxons, 69, 70–72, 93, 150–51, 152, 153–54, 155, 157–67 passim, 173. *See also* Russo-Japanese War
Russo-Japanese War, 13, 17, 68, 92, 148, 160, 171, 172

Salisbury, Lord, 86, 89, 97, 109, 118, 120, 131; on international relations, 87; opinion of the U.S., 87; and Venezuela boundary dispute, 96, 100
Saltonstall, Leverett, 56
Sandars, John S., 90
Schurz, Carl, 11, 26–27, 181 n. 4
Seeley, J. R., 47, 48, 89
Selborne, Lord, 196 n. 13
Seven points, convention of the, 166, 167
Shaw, Albert, 170, 191 n. 1, 207 n. 28
Sherwood, Sidney, 104
Sion College conference, 106
Smith, Goldwin, 185–86 n. 68
Spanish-American War, 65, 72, 78, 83, 84, 158; and Anglo-Saxonist

feeling, 112–29 passim, 174, 177; and British actions favoring the U.S., 120–21; and discussion of Anglo-American alliance, 112, 113, 114, 116, 118, 121–25, 128, 202 n. 41, 203 n. 46; and racial view of Spanish, 114–15; as war of races, 117, 118–19, 139, 201 n. 23

Spencer, Herbert, 29, 31, 32, 43, 45, 76, 107

Spring Rice, Cecil, 73, 79, 82, 118, 127, 133, 158, 172; and Roosevelt, 77–78, 91–92, 93; and Russia, 69, 92, 93–94; and Spanish-American War, 115, 117

Stead, W. T., 53, 70, 119, 186 n. 70, 201 n. 26; and Anglo-American arbitration, 106, 107; and race union, 49–50; and Venezuela boundary dispute, 98–99, 100

Strachey, John St. Loe, 98, 116

Straus, Oscar S., 125, 203 n. 47

Strong, Josiah, 25, 71, 182–83 n. 26; and American imperialism, 183 n. 29; and racial Darwinism, 32–35; and Russia, 69, 70

Stubbs, William, 38, 43, 45, 175

Sutherland, Duke of, 119

Tattnall, Josiah, 148

Teutonic origins theory, 37–45, 48, 58, 75, 80; and Anglo-Saxonism, 45–46; links to Darwinism, 40–41, 43; popularity of, 37, 42, 45; summarized, 37–38; undermining of, 174–75

Thursfield, James R., 103, 136

Tracy, Benjamin, 120

Triple Entente, 176

Turner, Frederick Jackson, 175

Turner, Senator George, 169

Twain, Mark, 137

Tyler, Moses Coit, 42

Vanderbilt, Cornelius, 120

Venezuela boundary dispute, 78, 79, 91, 95–105, 110–11, 147, 197 n. 22; and Anglo-Saxonist sentiment, 13, 89, 90, 95, 97–99, 100–101, 103–5, 110–11, 174, 177

Vereeniging, Peace of, 145

Victoria, Queen, 21, 54, 85, 120

Wales, Prince of, 85, 97, 113

Walker, Francis A., 56

Washington, Booker T., 74

Wheeler, Benjamin Ide, 135

White, Andrew D., 42

White, Henry, 67, 83, 90, 109, 110, 117, 131, 133, 134, 140, 208 n. 34

Williams, Frederick Wells, 157

Wilson, Woodrow, 42

Wolcott, Senator Edward O., 103

Wolseley, Lord, 98

Woolsey, Theodore, 197 n. 22

York, Duke of, 85, 97, 113